Global Women's Entrepreneurship Research

Global Women's Entrepreneurship Research

Diverse Settings, Questions and Approaches

Edited by

Karen D. Hughes

University of Alberta, Canada

Jennifer E. Jennings

University of Alberta, Canada

JUL 19 2012

Edward Elgar

Cheltenham, UK • Northampton, MA, USA

Published by
Edward Elgar Publishing Limited
The Lypiatts
15 Lansdown Road
Cheltenham
Glos GL50 2JA
UK

Edward Elgar Publishing, Inc.
William Pratt House
9 Dewey Court
Northampton
Massachusetts 01060
USA

A catalogue record for this book
is available from the British Library

Library of Congress Control Number: 2011932894

MIX
Paper from
responsible sources
FSC® C018575

ISBN 978 1 84980 462 2

Typeset by Servis Filmsetting Ltd, Stockport, Cheshire
Printed and bound by MPG Books Group, UK

Contents

List of contributors   vii
Foreword by Candida G. Brush   xiii
Acknowledgements   xvii

Introduction: showcasing the diversity of women's
entrepreneurship research   1
Karen D. Hughes and Jennifer E. Jennings

PART I   DIVERSE SETTINGS

1   Turkish businesswomen in the UK and Netherlands: the
    effects of national context on female migrant entrepreneurs   15
    Anne Laure Humbert and Caroline Essers

2   Women-owned SMEs in Bangladesh: challenges in institutional
    financing   36
    Salma C. Zohir and Patricia G. Greene

3   Academic women's entrepreneurship in Spain and Scotland:
    a multilevel institutional approach   56
    M. Mar Fuentes-Fuentes, Sarah Y. Cooper and Ana M. Bojica

4   Gender-based firm performance differences in the United States:
    examining the roles of financial capital and motivations   75
    Susan Coleman and Alicia Robb

PART II   DIVERSE QUESTIONS

5   How do social welfare and support systems influence the
    attitudes of female entrepreneurs towards risk and options?   95
    Nicholas C. Fairclough

6   Should women go into business with their family partner?   114
    *Manely Sharifian, P. Devereaux Jennings and
    Jennifer E. Jennings*

 7   Are women more likely to pursue social and environmental
     entrepreneurship?   135
     *Diana M. Hechavarria, Amy Ingram, Rachida Justo and
     Siri Terjesen*

 8   Do highly accomplished female entrepreneurs tend to 'give
     away success'?   152
     Mary Riebe

PART III   DIVERSE APPROACHES

 9   More gender equality, less women's self-employment:
     a multi-country investigation   171
     *Kim Klyver, Suna Løwe Nielsen and
     Majbritt Rostgaard Evald*

10   Sectoral segregation or gendered practices? A case study of
     roles and identities in a copreneurial venture   189
     Maura McAdam and Susan Marlow

11   Gender and the multidimensional nature of entrepreneurial
     self-efficacy: factor-analytic findings   204
     Cristina Díaz García

12   Conceptualizing 'woman' as an entrepreneurial advantage:
     a reflexive approach   226
     Albert James

Conclusion: reflecting on the diversity of women's entrepreneurship
research   241
Karen D. Hughes and Jennifer E. Jennings

Index   245

Contributors

Ana M. Bojica, PhD, is Assistant Professor in the Department of Management at the University of Granada, Spain. Her research focuses on the relational capacities and processes that enable value creation in specific entrepreneurship domains such as women's entrepreneurship, social entrepreneurship and corporate entrepreneurship. She is co-author of several articles and book chapters on this topic.

Susan Coleman is a Professor of Finance at the University of Hartford located in West Hartford, Connecticut, USA. She teaches courses in entrepreneurial and corporate finance at both the undergraduate and graduate levels. Dr Coleman's research interests include entrepreneurial and small business finance. She has published extensively on the topic of financing women-owned firms and is frequently quoted in the business press. Dr Coleman is currently writing a book (with Alicia Robb) entitled *A Rising Tide: Financing Strategies for Women-owned Firms.*

Sarah Y. Cooper, PhD, is Senior Lecturer in Entrepreneurship in the University of Edinburgh Business School at the University of Edinburgh, UK. Her research examines technology commercialization, women's role in entrepreneurship and enterprise education. She is co-author of *The Management of Innovation in High Technology Small Firms* and *New Firms in the Biotechnology Industry: Their Contribution to Innovation and Growth.*

Cristina Díaz García, PhD, is Assistant Professor in the Department of Business Administration in the School of Economics and Business at the Albacete Campus of the University of Castilla-La Mancha in Spain. She is author of the book *Influencia del género en los recursos y resultados de las pequeñas empresas* and publications in scientific journals and international conferences' proceedings. Her research interests are in gender, entrepreneurship and, recently, innovation.

Caroline Essers, PhD, is an Assistant Professor at the Nijmegen School of Management, Radboud University of Nijmegen, and an Associate Professor at the VU Amsterdam, the Netherlands. She holds a master's degree in human geography. Her research focuses on the identity construction of female entrepreneurs of Moroccan and Turkish descent. She previously worked for the Department of the Middle East, Radboud University of Nijmegen. Caroline has published her work in various journals, such as *Organization Studies, Human Relations, Organization*, and *Gender, Work and Organization*.

Majbritt Rostgaard Evald received her PhD from the Faculty of Social Sciences, University of Southern Denmark (SDU). She is currently Associate Professor at the Department of Entrepreneurship and Relationship Management at SDU. Her research is mainly focused on corporate entrepreneurship, with a particular interest in sources of open innovation. She has published some articles and book chapters including a co-authored chapter in *International Research Handbook on Successful Women Entrepreneurs.* Currently she is co-editing an international textbook on entrepreneurship.

Nicholas C. Fairclough, LLB, MBA (University of Virginia), is a doctoral student in the Department of Strategic Management and Organization at the University of Alberta, Canada. Prior to his current studies he was an English-qualified lawyer for 15 years, working in the banking and private equity sectors in Europe and the Far East. Latterly, he worked as a consultant to Andersen Worldwide in Geneva. His research interests are institutional theory, networks and alliances, and the organization and management of professional service firms.

M. Mar Fuentes-Fuentes, PhD, is Full Professor at the Department of Management at the Faculty of Economics and Business, University of Granada, Spain. Her research interests include women entrepreneurs, academic entrepreneurship, social capital and quality management. She is co-editor of *Entrepreneurship: An Approach to the State of the Art.*

Patricia G. Greene, PhD, is the President's Distinguished Professor in Entrepreneurship at Babson College, USA. Her research specializes in the combination of opportunities, resources, and leadership to create value. Her most recent book is the edited volume *The Development of University-Based Entrepreneurship Ecosystems: Global Practices* (with Fetters, Rice and Butler).

Diana M. Hechavarria is a doctoral candidate in the Department of Management (College of Business) at the University of Cincinnati, USA. Her research and teaching interests address new venture planning, entrepreneurship, innovation and gender. Diana's research has been published in *Journal of Small Business and Entrepreneurship, Small Business Economics* and *The International Journal of Entrepreneurship and Management*.

Karen D. Hughes is a Professor in Strategic Management and Organization (Alberta School of Business) and Sociology (Faculty of Arts) at the University of Alberta in Canada. She holds a PhD from the University of Cambridge. Her research focuses on gender, diversity and organizations, with a special interest in women's entrepreneurship and professional work. She is the author of *Female Enterprise in the New Economy* and *Work, Industry, and Canadian Society* (with Harvey Krahn and Graham Lowe). She is co-editor (with Jennifer Jennings) of this volume, as well as a special issue on women's entrepreneurship for *Entrepreneurship Theory and Practice.*

Anne Laure Humbert, PhD, is a Senior Lecturer in the Department of Economics and Statistics and Senior Researcher in the Centre for Enterprise and Economic Development Research (CEEDR) at Middlesex University Business School, London, UK. Her main research interests focus on research design, (social) entrepreneurship and gender. Anne Laure has published her work in various journals, such as *Community, Work and Family*, *Equality, Diversity and Inclusion* and the *International Journal of Gender and Entrepreneurship*.

Amy Ingram is an Assistant Professor in the College of Business and Behavioral Science at Clemson University, USA. She received her PhD from the University of Cincinnati, College of Business. Her research focuses on organizational innovation, organizational paradox, strategic cognition, entrepreneurship, and family business.

Albert James, MBA, is a third-year PhD student in the Department of Strategic Management and Organization (School of Business) at the University of Alberta, Canada. Prior to entering the PhD programme he worked extensively with various small entrepreneurial firms. His research interest is in entrepreneurism and non-family members of family businesses.

Jennifer E. Jennings, PhD, is an Associate Professor in the Department of Strategic Management and Organization at the Alberta School of Business, Canada. Her research interests include women entrepreneurs, family enterprise, entrepreneurial passion and storytelling, and work–family issues. In addition to being a co-editor of this volume, she is a field editor at the *Journal of Business Venturing* and a guest co-editor of an *Entrepreneurship Theory and Practice* special issue on women's entrepreneurship research.

P. Devereaux Jennings, PhD, is the Winspear Professor of Business at the Alberta School of Business, Canada, where he teaches strategy and organization theory. Dev is currently pursuing research in three areas:

environmental strategy and regulation, clean and nanotech start-ups, and family business dynamics. He is currently Co-Editor of *Strategic Organization* and field editor for the *Journal of Business Venturing*. Dev received his PhD and MA at Stanford University and his BA at Dartmouth College.

Rachida Justo is an Assistant Professor of Entrepreneurship and Social Entrepreneurship at the IE Business School, Spain. Her research focuses on female entrepreneurs and social entrepreneurship and has been published in academic outlets such as the *Journal of Business Venturing* as well as in several edited books. Rachida Holds a PhD from the Universidad Autónoma de Madrid, for which she received the 'Outstanding Award for Best Doctoral Dissertation' in 2008.

Kim Klyver, PhD, is a Professor in the Department of Entrepreneurship and Relationship Management at the University of Southern Denmark. Kim has previously held positions at Swinburne University of Technology and Stanford University. His research mainly examines nascent entrepreneurship, entrepreneurial networks, female entrepreneurship, and entrepreneurship policy. He has published a long list of peer-review journal articles and his research has won several awards. Recently, he co-edited and published *Handbook of Research on New Venture Creation*.

Susan Marlow, PhD, is Professor of Entrepreneurship at the University of Birmingham, and Visiting Professor at Manchester Metropolitan University and the University of Leeds, UK. Her research interests centre upon the influence of gender upon entrepreneuring; she is Editor of the *International Small Business Journal*, Vice President for Research of the UK Institute of Small Business and Entrepreneurship, an invited Fellow of the Royal Society of Arts and holder of the Queens Award for Enterprise Promotion.

Maura McAdam, PhD, is a Lecturer of Management in Queen's Management School, at Queen's University Belfast, UK. Her research explores three complementary themes: female entrepreneurship, high-technology based enterprises and support mechanisms, such as incubators and science parks. She is an invited Fellow of the Royal Society of Arts (FRSA) as well as an Elected Board Member of the ISBE (Institute for Small Business and Entrepreneurship).

Suna Løwe Nielsen received her PhD from Aalborg University, Denmark. She is currently an Assistant Professor at the Department of Entrepreneurship and Relationship Management, University of Southern Denmark. During her PhD studies she worked as a research fellow at the Arthur M. Spiro Center for Entrepreneurial Leadership, Clemson University (USA). Her main research area is the entrepreneurial process from the point of view of women, students and creative designers. She has published several articles, and at present, she is co-editing an international textbook in entrepreneurship.

Mary Riebe, PhD, leads a dual career as a business owner and university professor. Her doctorate research pertains to women growing their businesses in the USA, Finland and Ireland. She is founder of two centres for women entrepreneurs at two American universities. She maintains a strategic consulting practice created in 1987. Passionate about advancing women entrepreneurs, she is a frequent motivational speaker and published author on personal and professional challenges facing women globally in business growth.

Alicia Robb is Senior Research Fellow at the Ewing Marion Kauffman Foundation, USA and is the principal investigator on the Kauffman Firm Survey. Previously she was an economist at the Division of Research and Statistics, Board of Governors of the Federal Reserve System and an economist at the Office of Economic Research at the US Small Business Administration. The author of *Race, Families and Business Success: African-American, Asian-, and White-Owned Businesses* published by MIT Press, Dr Robb has authored more than a dozen journal articles. She is currently working on her second book (with Susan Coleman) on financing strategies for women-owned businesses.

Manely Sharifian is a PhD student in the Department of Strategic Management and Organization (School of Business) at the University of Alberta, Canada. Her research interests include natural environment, clean technologies and entrepreneurship. She received her MSc in management and the economics of innovation at Chalmers University in Sweden, and her BSc in industrial engineering at Amirkabir University in Iran.

Siri Terjesen is an Assistant Professor in the Kelley School of Business at Indiana University, USA. Siri's research has been published in leading journals such as *Strategic Management Journal, Strategic Entrepreneurship Journal, Entrepreneurship Theory and Practice, Small Business Economics* and *Journal of Operations Management*. It has been profiled in outlets such as *US News & World Report, Christian Science Monitor, Voice of America, The Times* (UK) and CNBC Europe. She holds a Master's degree from Norges Handelhøyskole and a PhD from Cranfield University.

Salma C. Zohir, PhD, is a Research Fellow at the Bangladesh Institute of Development Studies. She has worked extensively in the areas of employment, gender and development, and industry, as well as on economic and social issues in Bangladesh. Her most recent work includes co-authored publications *SME Development in Bangladesh with Emphasis on Policy Constraints and Financing* and *An Inventory and Statistics on Violence against Women in Bangladesh: Who Is Doing What and Where.*

Foreword

It is a given that entrepreneurship is a legitimate field of study, with more than 50 journals, 2200 members of the Academy of Management Entrepreneurship Division, and the Babson College Entrepreneurship Research Conference (BCERC) drawing more than 600 abstracts every year. Yet, studies focusing on or including women entrepreneurs are few, even though we know from the Global Entrepreneurship Monitor (GEM) that women entrepreneurs are developing businesses, creating jobs, innovating and solving social problems in most countries around the world (Kelley et al. 2010).

Since the mid-1980s, most research on women's entrepreneurship focused on factors influencing the start-up of ventures (Gatewood et al., 2003). Notably absent was an understanding of factors affecting growth. In 1999, I and my colleagues Nancy Carter, Elizabeth Gatewood, Patricia Greene and Myra Hart launched the DIANA project to study the phenomenon of women's entrepreneurship in the United States. At the time, women-led ventures were smaller than those of their male counterparts, whether measured by size of revenues generated or the number of people employed. We asked, *'Why do women owned businesses remain smaller than those of their male counterparts?'* A multi-method research effort was undertaken to examine supply of and demand for growth capital relative to women entrepreneurs. Our US research showed that women entrepreneurs seldom acquire sufficient funds to grow their businesses aggressively and to reach their full potential. This raised a new question, 'Do women face *unique* challenges in acquiring growth capital?' While the collective research showed demand by women entrepreneurs for equity capital (Brush et al., 2001), there was and still is a mismatch between the women, their ventures and sources of growth funding (Brush et al., 2004). The DIANA project findings prompted great interest among policy-makers, practitioners and educators wanting to learn more about ways to increase women entrepreneurs' receipt of growth capital by providing a better infrastructure of programmes and curricula for women who wished to grow larger business (Gatewood et al., 2009).

Simultaneous to the DIANA project research, interest in women entrepreneurs and growth of their ventures was rising in most countries around the world. To capture and leverage that interest, the DIANA project team, in partnership with ESBRI (Entrepreneurship and Small Business Research Institute, Sweden), convened an international gathering of scholars in 2003 to develop a shared research agenda. The goal was to exchange ideas and learn from each other about the current state of research on creation and support for new women-led businesses, and particularly, support and development of growth oriented businesses. Our purpose in creating the DIANA International collaborative was twofold:

- To provide a platform from which to develop, conduct and share a global research agenda.
- To create an international community of scholars dedicated to answering the questions about women entrepreneurs and growth oriented businesses.

Following our first DIANA International Conference, in 2003, we produced a report discussing the importance of growth oriented women-led businesses and summarizing the state of knowledge about these businesses in the initial countries involved. This report was released in spring 2005 and provides a summary of the presentations about the state of women's entrepreneurship by country.

In 2004, the second DIANA international conference was held where participants presented working papers, which were peer reviewed, revised and finally submitted for consideration for an edited book. In 2005, we produced an edited volume, *The DIANA Project International: Research on Growth of Women-owned Businesses* that included a series of country reports highlighting an overview of the state of women's entrepreneurship in eight different countries, noting the extent and nature of women's participation in entrepreneurship, growth orientation and access to resources for growth. A second series of chapters covering six countries delved more deeply in to the relationship between social and human capital, financing, risk, motivations and skills of women entrepreneurs as these affect growth.

In 2007, following a conference in Belfast, Ireland, Collette Henry, Elizabeth Gatewood, Anne de Bruin and I co-edited a second volume, *Women's Entrepreneurship and Growth Influences: An International Perspective*. This volume built on the 2005 book, examining women's entrepreneurship across a variety of developed and less developed countries using a multi-level framework (individual, venture, environment). The first set of chapters explored how contextual factors, and especially the social and family embeddedness of entrepreneurs, have a differential impact on men and women, while the second set of chapters examined strategies, constraints and enablers of growth and performance, considering a wide variety of topics, including self-efficacy, mentors, networks, socio-political and technology sector factors.

This book marks the third edited volume examining women's entrepreneurship around the world. It emerges from the 2010 DIANA International Conference in Banff, Canada, which attracted more than 80 scholars who presented scholarly work. It moves well beyond the 'state' of women's entrepreneurship and access to resources for growth studied the first book, and builds on the theme of 'context', the constraints and enablers across multiple levels that were explored in the second book. This book focuses on diversity among women entrepreneurs. For too many years, women entrepreneurs have often been studied as a single group, where differences in circumstances and perspectives have been homogenized. Understanding the heterogeneity of women's entrepreneurship is not only crucial to developing theory, identifying policies, practices and educational initiatives for women, but to our understanding of entrepreneurship generally.

In addition to the evolution in scholarship on women's entrepreneurship reflected in this volume, this book also represents a step forward in creating that legacy of growth for the next generation of DIANA International scholars. Karen Hughes and Jennifer Jennings have embraced the leadership mantle for Diana International in making this book a reality. Their passion, rigorous attention to detail and their care in working with the authors of these chapters takes research on women's entrepreneurship to a new level. Transgenerational entrepreneurship is a concept that reflects the way that families create an ongoing legacy of entrepreneurial growth by developing the mind-set and methods for creating new streams of wealth across generations. Karen, Jennifer and all the contributors to this volume are the next generation, creating transgenerational entrepreneurial wealth for women's entrepreneurship.

Candida G. Brush
Franklin W. Olin Chair in Entrepreneurship
Chair, Entrepreneurship Division
Director, Arthur M. Blank Center for Entrepreneurship Babson College,
Wellesley, MA, USA

REFERENCES

Brush, C.G., N.M. Carter, E.J. Gatewood, P.G. Greene and M.M. Hart (2001), 'The Diana Project: women business owners and equity capital: the myths dispelled', report prepared for the Kauffman Foundation, Kansas City, MO.

Brush, C.G., N.M. Carter, E.J. Gatewood, P.G. Greene and M.M. Hart (2004), *Clearing the Hurdles: Women Building High Growth Businesses*, Englewood Cliffs, NJ: Prentice Hall-Financial Times.

Gatewood, E.J., C.G. Brush, N.M. Carter, P.G. Greene and M.M. Hart (2009), 'Diana: a symbol of women entrepreneurs' hunt for knowledge, money and the rewards of entrepreneurship', *Small Business Economics*, **32** (2), 129–44.

Gatewood, E.J., N.M. Carter, C.G. Brush, P.G. Greene and M.M. Hart (2003), *Women Entrepreneurs, Their Ventures, and the Venture Capital Industry: An Annotated Bibliography*, Stockholm: ESBRI.

Kelley, D., N. Bosma and J.E. Amoros (2010), *The Global Entrepreneurship Monitor 2010 Global Report*, Wellesley, MA: Babson College and the Global Entrepreneurship Research Association (GERA).

Acknowledgements

This volume emerges from the 2010 DIANA International Conference on Women's Entrepreneurship Research held in Banff, Canada. It continues the very lively 'global conversation' sparked by the original founders of the DIANA project: Candida Brush, Nancy Carter, Elizabeth Gatewood, Patricia Greene and Myra Hart. Since its inception, the DIANA project has been a rich source of scholarly inspiration. We want to thank the DIANA founders for their leadership in encouraging research and collaboration on women-led business, and for providing us with the memorable experience of hosting the 2010 DIANA conference in Canada. Sincere thanks also to the conference delegates from 20 countries around the globe whose participation, enthusiasm and innovative research did so much to make the 2010 DIANA conference a success.

We are deeply grateful to the contributors to this volume for responding to our call for new research and thinking about the 'diversity' of women's entrepreneurship. The 12 chapters presented here showcase the work of 26 researchers hailing from seven different countries. Each contribution offers a unique perspective on the field, broadening existing horizons of knowledge and providing fresh glimpses of women's enterprise around the globe. It has been a pleasure to work with this talented group of scholars and we thank each of them for sharing research that contributes to a richer, more robust understanding of the field.

Fruitful research collaboration relies not only on good ideas and dedicated colleagues, but also on strong institutional support. We are very grateful to the original sponsors of the 2010 DIANA conference whose generous support has made this collaborative book project possible: the Alberta School of Business at the University of Alberta; Babson College; the Department of Strategic Management and Organization within the Alberta School of Business; and the Social Sciences and Humanities Research Council of Canada (SSHRC). Special thanks to Mike Percy and Yoni Reshef at the Alberta School of Business for their enthusiastic support of the DIANA conference from start to finish, and to Kerri Calvert at the University of Alberta for help in securing SSHRC funding.

As we put the finishing touches on this manuscript, we are keenly aware of the 'many hands' that have lightened the work. We especially want to thank Jacqueline Solc for lending her superb organizational talents to the 2010 DIANA conference, and William Silver for his stellar editorial assistance in the final stages of this project. At Edward Elgar, we have been fortunate to work with Alan Sturmer and Caroline Cornish, whose helpful advice and encouragement have been greatly appreciated at so many points along the way. We also want to thank the editors of the previous DIANA books for providing such helpful advice and excellent templates for us to emulate: Candida Brush, Nancy Carter, Anne de Bruin, Patricia Greene, Elizabeth Gatewood, Myra Hart and Colette Henry.

Finally, in an age where global collaboration is more and more the norm, it has been a pleasure to work with a colleague who is 'just down the hall'. We thank one another for an enjoyable collaboration, and also extend heartfelt thanks to our families for their enthusiastic support and encouragement of our work.

Introduction: showcasing the diversity of women's entrepreneurship research

Karen D. Hughes and Jennifer E. Jennings

RESPONDING TO THE CALL FOR DIVERSITY

Just as it is difficult to deny the impact that female entrepreneurs are having on the world economy, so too is it hard to overlook their diversity. Data from the Global Entrepreneurship Monitor (GEM), for example, reveal striking differences in the proportion of women engaged in entrepreneurial activity around the world, with rates lower than 4 per cent in countries such as Belgium and France yet higher than 38 per cent in countries such as Thailand and Peru (Allen et al., 2007). The GEM data also reveal considerable variability in the motivations, backgrounds and perceptions of women who pursue entrepreneurship – even among those in the same geographic region. Indeed, out of all the possible themes to emphasize within the conclusion of their report, Allen and her colleagues chose to highlight the 'diversity of circumstances and perspectives' that characterize female entrepreneurs the world over (2007: 40; see also Minniti, et al., 2005).

Other researchers have not only remarked upon the heterogeneity of women entrepreneurs but also called for greater appreciation of their diversity by scholars and policy-makers alike. Each of us, for instance, has highlighted this theme in previous, independently conducted research on self-employed and business-owning women in Canada. Noting that 'it is diversity that most characterizes the female face of enterprise', Hughes argued that academic scholars and public policy analysts must work towards a richer, more nuanced, understanding of women's entrepreneurial endeavours (2005: 194). Similarly, Jennings and Provorny Cash remarked:

> To date, much of our knowledge derives from comparisons between the 'average' male and female entrepreneur. In order to best help female entrepreneurs, we need to identify and understand any systematic differences *between* them. Otherwise, we risk the danger that our policy initiatives will be based upon a theoretical 'prototypical' female entrepreneur that, in reality, does not capture the essence of many women business owners at all. (2006: 83; emphasis in original)

We are not the only ones to articulate such a call. In their introduction to the *Entrepreneurship Theory and Practice* special issues, de Bruin et al. challenged researchers to 'capture the heterogeneity of what constitutes women's entrepreneurship' (2006: 590), arguing that 'comparisons between groups of women will allow us to fully understand gendered processes and gendered attributes in new ventures' (2007: 329). Similarly, scholars of gender and organizations more broadly have noted the value of an 'intersectional' approach that can illuminate the diversity among women (Browne and Misra, 2003; Holvino, 2010; McCall, 2005). Encouragingly, there are signs that this theme is being heard, understood and appreciated within the policy realm. An analyst with Industry Canada, for example, concluded his recent report with the remark that 'investigating female business owners as a homogeneous group will likely mask' their varying challenges, needs and concerns (Jung, 2010: 19).

In keeping with the spirit of such calls, this book celebrates the variety of women's entrepreneurship research being conducted by scholars affiliated with the DIANA International Research Network. Founded in 1999 by Professors Candida Brush, Nancy Carter, Elizabeth Gatewood, Patricia Greene and Myra Hart, this open and collaborative network comprises researchers around the world who are committed to advancing knowledge about female entrepreneurs. Since its inception, the number of countries represented by participants in the network's bi-annual conference has steadily increased. So, too, has the number of regions in which their studies are situated. At the most recent conference that was held in Banff, Canada, in August 2010, researchers from over 20 countries exchanged knowledge about women engaged in entrepreneurship within almost every continent. This edited volume – the third in the Diana International series – represents just a sample of the eclectic, informative and thought-provoking work being produced by those affiliated with this global research network.

PORTRAYING THE HETEROGENEITY IN CURRENT RESEARCH

Overarching Tripartite Structure

To help structure the diverse studies included in this collection, and lend coherence to the overall volume, our organizing framework draws upon three currents salient within recent discourse about how to incorporate heterogeneity within future research. One such current calls for greater attention to contextual factors – a theme emphasized not only by women's entrepreneurship scholars such as Ahl (2006) but also by general entrepreneurship scholars such as Zahra (2007) and broader organizational scholars such as Bamberger (2008; see also Bamberger and Pratt, 2010). Consistent with this call, the first component of our overarching tripartite framework focuses upon the *diverse settings* in which research on women entrepreneurs is currently being conducted, whether those settings represent entire socio-economic regions, specific national contexts, or certain industrial, institutional or familial contexts.

Another prominent theme emphasizes the importance of adopting different perspectives and asking new questions – especially those that have been silenced within mainstream research on a focal topic to date. In her critique of the women's entrepreneurship literature, for example, Ahl noted that 'the growth argument', in particular, 'is a strong discursive practice [that] allows research to consider certain questions and ignore others' (2006: 602). Extending this argument, Calás et al. (2009) demonstrated the variety of unasked questions worthy of investigation when entrepreneurship, more generally, is viewed from a critical and reflexive standpoint. Within the broader organizational literature, the call for different perspectives is perhaps most evident in a recent *Academy of Management Review* special issue entitled, 'Where are the new theories of organization?' Consistent with this theme, the second component of our overarching tripartite framework focuses upon the *diverse questions* currently addressed by women's entrepreneurship scholars around the world.

A final theme commonly emphasized within treatises on advancing scholarship in a focal field focuses upon the importance of utilizing multiple methodologies. Such a theme is evident within recent reviews of the women's entrepreneurship literature, especially with respect to the need for embracing less orthodox methods (for example, Ahl, 2006; de Bruin et al., 2007). Similarly, Neergaard and Ulhøi critiqued the entrepreneurship literature more generally as 'lacking in methodological diversity' even though, rather ironically, 'the entrepreneurial phenomenon itself, in all its complexity and dynamics, invite[s] a methodological toolbox of broad variety' (2007: 1). Intriguingly, within the broader field of organizational studies there is a trend towards greater methodological diversity as well. For instance, Buchanan and Bryman's recent handbook on organizational research methods showcases a wide array of innovative work (2009). As such, the third component of our overarching framework showcases the *diverse approaches* that the scholars in this volume have collectively adopted within their work on women entrepreneurs.

Table I.1   *Framework for capturing the variety of studies included in the collection*

	Diverse settings	Diverse questions	Diverse approaches
Macro	Chapter 1: The effects of national culture on female migrant entrepreneurs in the UK and the Netherlands	Chapter 5: How do welfare regimes influence women's entrepreneurship around the world?	Chapter 9: A multi-country analysis of the effects of gender equality on rates of female self-employment
	Chapter 2: The impact of policy initiatives on women-owned SMEs in Bangladesh	Chapter 6: Should women go into business with their family partner?	Chapter 10: A single case study of copreneurial roles and identities within a gendered industry
Meso	Chapter 3: The influence of institutions on academic women entrepreneurs in Spain and Scotland	Chapter 7: Are women more likely to pursue social and environmental entrepreneurship?	Chapter 11: A factor analysis examining the nature of women's entrepreneurial self-efficacy
	Chapter 4: The effects of money vs motivations on the performance of female-owned firms in the US	Chapter 8: Do even highly accomplished female entrepreneurs tend to 'give away success'?	Chapter 12: A reflexive approach on the potential advantages inherent in being a female entrepreneur
Micro			

Underlying Multi-level Substructure

As illustrated in the visual representation of our organizing framework presented in Table I.1, we have further structured the chapters comprising the above-noted major parts according to a *macro-to-micro logic*. Each of the lead chapters focuses upon a macro-environmental factor relevant to women's entrepreneurship, such as the effects of policies or culture at the national level. The middle chapters draw attention to meso-level influences, such as the intermediaries who provide support to female entrepreneurs or the sectoral, institutional or familial contexts in which they are embedded.

The final chapter within each part highlights micro-level considerations, such as the resources, motivations and attitudes held by these women.

Structuring the chapters within each section in this manner not only further illustrates the diversity of women's entrepreneurship research currently being conducted by DIANA International scholars, but is also consistent with the multi-level approach advocated within recent overview articles and books on the topic (for example, Brush et al., 2009; 2010; Elam, 2008) as well as within entrepreneurship research in general (for example, Davidsson and Wiklund, 2001; Rindova et al., 2009). Moreover, by starting each part with a macro-oriented chapter, we offer a small step towards addressing the critique that prior work on female entrepreneurs has tended to adopt the individualist focus that permeates the entrepreneurship literature more broadly (Ahl, 2006). Synopses of the individual chapters appear below.

PREVIEWING THE VARIOUS CHAPTERS

Part I Diverse Settings

Precisely how different national and industrial contexts shape the nature and trajectory of women's entrepreneurial venturing are questions ripe for exploration, especially given the dramatic expansion of women-led enterprise around the globe (Brush et al., 2010). In our first part we explore a diverse range of settings – from those rarely examined, to those representing more familiar terrain.

In Chapter 1, Anne Humbert and Caroline Essers offer insights into Turkish business women operating in two distinct national contexts: the UK and the Netherlands. Drawing on life history narratives and structuration theory, Humbert and Essers explore how the intersections of gender, ethnicity, citizenship and national context shape women's entrepreneurial identities and daily business practices. Their qualitative study reveals distinct approaches to networking, financing, coaching and entrepreneurial identity work. Speaking to the influence of national context, Humbert and Essers conclude that Turkish women in the Netherlands experience more tensions between their identities as women, migrants and entrepreneurs than those in UK, who are more included within mainstream and Turkish business circles.

In Chapter 2, Salma Zohir and Patricia Greene examine a context where women's entrepreneurial activity has been less frequently studied: Bangladesh. Focusing on small and medium-sized enterprise (SME) financing, they offer a valuable assessment of women-led business, integrating existing survey data and primary interview and focus group research with female entrepreneurs and institutional lenders. Despite macro-level policies that have sparked growth and diversity in women's enterprise in the country, significant barriers to financing remain. Zohir and Greene's study suggests intriguing parallels to other national contexts with respect to demand- and supply-side barriers to financing, while also showing how unique aspects of Bangladeshi culture (for example, gender attitudes) carry special ramifications for women seeking financial capital. They conclude their chapter with specific recommendation for policy change.

Broadening the reach of 'diverse settings', Chapter 3 by Mar Fuentes-Fuentes, Sarah Cooper and Ana Bojica consider the intersections between national and industrial contexts, focusing on academic women and female-led 'spin offs' in the university sectors of Scotland (University of Edinburgh) and Spain (University of Granada). Guided by institutional theory, and drawing on in-depth interviews with female academic entrepreneurs and technology transfer officers, the authors trace the competing influence of macro-, meso- and individual factors. Their study highlights the importance of meso-level factors, showing that few women academics engage in commercialization and spin-offs, and that universities need to adopt gender-aware policies and practices that can counteract bias and negative influences from the macro-environment. These insights are critical given the growing role of science, engineering and technology (SET) fields in knowledge-based economies, and the need for female entrepreneurs to flourish there.

Our first section concludes with Chapter 4 by Susan Coleman and Alicia Robb, who examine the links between financial capital, motivations and expectations, and firm performance for male- and female-led firms in the USA. Although the USA is certainly one of most studied settings for women entrepreneurs, this also makes it an ideal setting to explore critical debates about the gender gap in financing and firm performance. Drawing on longitudinal data, and testing hypothesis derived from resource-based theory and motivational theory, Coleman and Robb offer several new insights. In particular, while finding few differences in the performance of male- and female-owned firms after controlling for standard factors, their analysis suggests that gender differences in motivation, start-up capital and a desire for controlled growth may all play a central role in understanding the performance gap.

Part II Diverse Questions

Writing about research on women, Sandra Harding (1987) famously noted that the questions we ask are as determinative of our knowledge as any answers we might discover. Echoing this perspective, recent commentators on the field of women's entrepreneurship research have also noted how certain questions have been amplified, muted or unheard in scholarship to date (Ahl, 2006; Calás et al., 2009). Our second part is therefore dedicated to taking up diverse questions, showcasing both *new questions* that have not been asked before, as well as *familiar questions* that are re-framed in fresh, innovative ways.

Beginning at the macro-level of analysis, Chapter 5 by Nicholas Fairclough raises questions about the linkages between institutional and individual levels of analysis, focusing on the specific role that social welfare provision and policy play in shaping women's entrepreneurial activity across nations. Drawing on the 'welfare regimes' framework of political scientist Esping-Andersen, as well as a 'real options' perspective, Fairclough draws on existing research to develop propositions as to how distinct social welfare policy provisions and approaches might shape patterns of women's entrepreneurship with respect to start-up and success; the negotiation of work–family conflict; and the navigation of necessity and opportunity entrepreneurship.

In Chapter 6, Manely Sharifian, Devereaux Jennings and Jennifer Jennings consider an important, but largely unexamined, question: whether women (and men) benefit from going into business with their spouse or significant other. Working from a family embeddedness perspective, and drawing on survey data from small business owners in Western Canada, the authors compare copreneurial and non-copreneurial firms with respect to their satisfaction and performance in both work and family spheres. While their analysis finds no difference in business performance, copreneurs do experience higher family satisfaction. Moreover, intersections between work and family spheres reveals that experiencing greater equity at home (for example, sharing of household tasks) positively influences family satisfaction for copreneurs, but with adverse effects on business performance and satisfaction. The authors conclude by suggesting several new avenues for future research.

New questions are also posed in Chapter 7, which examines interconnections between the rise of women's entrepreneurship and alternative strands of entrepreneurship; in particular, 'social entrepreneurship' and 'ecopreneurship'. Noting that few studies have explored these links, Diana Hechavarria, Amy Ingram, Rachida Justo and Siri Terjesen examine whether female entrepreneurs are more likely than their male peers to emphasize social and environmental value creation as part of their entrepreneurial goals. Drawing on theories of hegemonic masculinity, and utilizing data from the 2009 Global Entrepreneurship Monitor survey of 52 countries, the authors find that male entrepreneurs do indeed give greater priority to traditional economic outcomes (for example, profit), while women place more emphasis on social and environmental concerns. Notably this is the case both for *actual* business practices as well as for *desired goals*.

Part II concludes with a critical revisiting of familiar questions about women's relationship to achievement and success. In Chapter 8, Mary Riebe utilizes data from online questionnaires with a small group of highly successful women in the USA who have been operating a business for more than five years. Surveying the wide body of psychologically oriented literature from the North American context, Riebe argues that the women in her study do not conform to earlier research findings concerning attributions of success, silencing and recognition, relational approaches and conflict management. Such findings raise questions, Riebe concludes, not only about established scholarship but also about the changing nature, and sophistication, of women's entrepreneurial endeavours.

Part III   Diverse Approaches

In light of the growing methodological plurality of social science research generally, it is not surprising that entrepreneurship research is embracing a much broader array of research approaches. As noted earlier, there is growing awareness that the dynamic and complex nature of entrepreneurial endeavours requires a 'methodological toolbox' that is up to the task (Neergaard and Ulhøi, 2007: 1).

In Chapter 9, Kim Klyver, Suna Løwe Nielsen and Majbritt Rostgaard Evald utilize hierarchical logistic regression to test findings from previous qualitiative studies on the relationship between gender equality at the *institutional level* and employment choice at the *individual level*. Building on the observation that existing studies fail to capture the economic, cultural and political contexts in which individual choices occur, the authors merge two comprehensive datasets – the Global Entrepreneurship Monitor and the World Economic Forum's Global Gender Gap index – in order to examine the links between institutional contexts and individual employment patterns in 50 different countries. Results confirm that countries with high levels of institutionalized gender equality have much *lower* rates of female entrepreneurial activity. Moreover, split-age comparisons suggest that 'family friendly' policies (for example, generous maternity and childcare provisions) have a dampening effect on self-employment for women of child-bearing age.

The value of an interpretist approach is illustrated in Chapter 10, where Maura McAdam and Susan Marlow explore how gender is collectively constructed and performed in entrepreneurship. Focusing on a female-dominant sector, and utilizing an in-depth, interview-based case study of a copreneurial *au pair* business in New Zealand, they explore the reversal of normative gender relations – where a female partner is positioned as the 'publicly visible' leader, while the male partner provides 'behind-the-scenes' support. While on the surface, McAdam and Marlow argue, this business seems to disrupt established gender binaries, a closer reading reveals a reinscription of traditional gender norms, with the male partner controlling influential decisions on financing, growth and strategic management, while his partner offers a reassuring 'feminine face' that meshes with deeply held normative assumptions conflating femininity and care.

Utilizing a factor-analytic approach and adopting a gendered perspective, Chapter 11 by Cristina Díaz García explores the issue of entrepreneurial self-efficacy (ESE); that is, the subjective assessment of one's skills, ability, and knowledge related to business start-up and management. Questioning prior research with respect to gender differences as well as the typical unidimensional conceptualization of ESE, Díaz García draws on Spanish survey data to show that ESE is in fact multidimensional, encompassing *decisional, financial* and *relational* components. Equally important, she shows that gender differences in ESE are not as pronounced, or constant, as past research suggests. Contrary to findings of lower ESE for women, Díaz García shows that ESE is context specific, with gender differences in specific facets (for example, decisional, financial and relational) varying by education, business experience, age, growth intentions, as well as location in traditional versus non-traditional sectors.

We conclude our final part with Chapter 12, by Albert James, who offers a reflexive critical essay on the dominant approaches that have been used to frame research on women's entrepreneurial activity. Echoing Ahl's (2006) observations about the 'problem-based' nature of research on women entrepreneurs, James contends that such approaches eclipse questions about the success of women entrepreneurs. His case study of a successful female entrepreneur operating in a male-dominated industry identifies ways in which female identity, experiences and competencies may operate as an 'advantage'. Resonating with current strands of debate within positive psychology (Cameron et al., 2003), James outlines an alternative model of female entrepreneurship – one he contends scholars might use productively to capture and understand the factors and conditions that allow women entrepreneurs to flourish.

ADVANCING OUR UNDERSTANDING OF THE DIVERSITY OF WOMEN ENTREPRENEURS

In the same way that the DIANA International Research Network and affiliated conferences have done so much to broaden and enrich knowledge about women's entrepreneurship, it is our hope that this third volume by Elgar contributes empirically, theoretically and methodologically towards a richer, more complete, picture of the diversity embraced within women's entrepreneurial activity around the world. Moreover, in keeping with a 'virtuous cycle' of research (Brush et al., 2010), we hope this volume also offers insights to policies and programmes that seek to support the rich and varied nature of women's entrepreneurial ambitions.

REFERENCES

Ahl, H. (2006), 'Why research on women entrepreneurs needs new directions', *Entrepreneurship Theory and Practice*, **30** (5), 595–621.

Allen, I.E., A. Elam, N. Langowitz and M. Dean (2007), '2007 report on women and Entrepreneurship', *Global Entrepreneurship Monitor.*

Bamberger, P. (2008), 'From the editors: beyond contextualization – using context theories to narrow the micro-macro gap in management research', *Academy of Management Journal*, **51** (5), 839–46.

Bamberger, P.A. and M.G. Pratt (2010), 'From the editors – moving forward by looking back: reclaiming unconventional research contexts and samples in organizational scholarship', *Academy of Management Journal*, **53** (4), 665–72.

Browne, I. and J. Misra (2003), 'The intersection of gender and race in the labour market', *Annual Review of Sociology*, **29**, 487–513.

Brush, C.G., A. de Bruin, and F. Welter (2009), 'A gender-aware framework for women's entrepreneurship', *International Journal of Gender and Entrepreneurship*, **1** (1), 8–24.

Brush, C.G., A. de Bruin, E.J. Gatewood, and C. Henry (2010), 'Introduction: women entrepreneurs and growth', in C.G. Brush, A. de Bruin, E.J. Gatewood, and C. Henry (eds), *Women Entrepreneurs and the Global Environment for Growth*, Cheltenham, UK and Northampton, MA, USA: Edward Elgar Publishing, pp. 1–18.

Buchanan, D.A. and A. Bryman (2009), 'The organizational research context: properties and implications', in D. Buchanan and A. Bryman (eds), *The Sage Handbook of Organizational Research Methods*, Thousand Oaks, CA: Sage Publications, pp. 1–18.

Calás, M.B., L. Smircich and K.A. Bourne (2009), 'Extending the boundaries: reframing "Entrepreneurship as Social Change" through feminist perspectives', *Academy of Management Review*, **34** (3), 552–69.

Cameron, K.S., J.E. Dutton and R.E. Quinn (2003), 'Foundations of positive organizational Scholarship', in K.S. Cameron, J.E. Dutton, and R.E. Quinn (eds), *Positive Organizational Scholarship: Foundations of a New Discipline*, San Francisco, CA. Berrett-Koehler, pp. 3–13.

Davidsson, P. and J. Wiklund (2001), 'Levels of analysis in entrepreneurship research: current research practice and suggestions for the future', *Entrepreneurship Theory and Practice*, **25** (4), 81–100.

De Bruin, A., C.G. Brush and F. Welter (2006), 'Introduction to the special issue: towards building cumulative knowledge on women's entrepreneurship', *Entrepreneurship Theory and Practice*, **30** (5), 585–93.

De Bruin, A., C.G. Brush and F. Welter (2007), 'Advancing a framework for coherent research on women's entrepreneurship', *Entrepreneurship Theory and Practice*, **31** (3), 323–39.

Elam, A.B. (2008), *Gender and Entrepreneurship: A Multilevel Theory and Analysis*, Cheltenham, UK and Northampton, MA, USA: Edward Elgar Publishing.

Harding, S. (1987), 'Is there a feminist method?', in S. Harding (ed.), *Feminism and Methodology*, Bloomington, IN: Indiana University Press, pp. 1–14.

Holvino, E. (2010), 'Intersections: the Simultaneity of race, gender, and class in organization studies', *Gender, Work and Organization*, **17** (3), 248–77.

Hughes, K.D. (2005), *Risky Business? Women, Self-Employment and Small Business in Canada*, Toronto, ON: University of Toronto Press.

Jennings, J.E. and M. Provorny Cash (2006), 'Women's entrepreneurship in Canada: progress, puzzles and priorities; in C.G. Brush, N.M. Carter, E.J. Gatewood, P.G. Greene and M.M. Hart (eds) *Growth Oriented Women Entrepreneurs and Their Businesses: A Global Research Perspective*, Cheltenham, UK and Northampton, MA, USA: Edward Elgar Publishing, pp. 53–87.

Jung, O. (2010), 'Small business financing profiles: women entrepreneurs', *SME Financing Data Initiative*, Small Business and Tourism Branch, Industry Canada.

McCall, L. (2005), 'The complexity of intersectionality', *Signs: Journal of Women in Culture and Society*, **30** (3), 1772–801.

Minniti, M., I.E. Allen and N. Langowitz (2005), '2005 report on women and entrepreneurship', *Global Entrepreneurship Monitor*.

Neergaard, H. and J. Parl Ulhøi (2007), 'Introduction', in H. Neergaard and J. Parl Ulhoi (eds), *Handbook of Qualitative Research Methods in Entrepreneurship Research*, Cheltenham, UK and Northampton, MA, USA: Edward Elgar Publishing, pp. 1–14.

Rindova, V., D. Barry and D.J Ketchen Jr (2009), 'Entrepreneuring as emancipation', *Academy of Management Review*, **34** (3), 477–91.

Zahra, S.A. (2007), 'Contextualizing theory building in entrepreneurship research', *Journal of Business Venturing*, **22**, 443–52.

PART I

Diverse Settings

1. Turkish businesswomen in the UK and Netherlands: the effects of national context on female migrant entrepreneurs

Anne Laure Humbert and Caroline Essers

INTRODUCTION

Labour market participation is considered as key to the socio-economic integration of migrants in Western countries. The importance of ethnic minority entrepreneurship[1] as a source of employment opportunities for migrant populations is considerable. However, most studies on ethnic minority entrepreneurship, implicitly or not, concentrate on male entrepreneurs or ignore the roles women play in these businesses (Westwood and Bhachu, 1987; Essers and Benschop, 2007). Moreover, the discourse on womanhood seems to be in conflict with the discourse on entrepreneurship; being a woman and an entrepreneur at the same time seems hardly possible (Ahl, 2004). Accordingly, the mainstream entrepreneurial discourse sketches an image of the 'other' other, the female migrant entrepreneur as different per se (Strüder, 2003). This chapter explores this discourse by looking more closely at Turkish[2] businesswomen and examining how this discourse, as captured by national structures, affects these female migrant entrepreneurs within two different national contexts: the Netherlands and the UK. The contrast between the UK and the Netherlands is particularly valuable because of the variation in uptake of entrepreneurship among Turkish female migrants. The variation is possibly linked to differences in national policies, particularly those that aim to stimulate (female) migrant entrepreneurship, differences in migratory regimes and policies, and differences in national cultures. Theoretically, this comparison is important because of the contingent nature of gender. By this we mean that both actors and contexts affect the meaning of gender, and how it is seen and interpreted.

Entrepreneurial rates among Turkish migrants in Europe are lower than those of the general population. The majority of Turkish businesses operate within Germany, while the remainder is concentrated in the Netherlands, France and Austria (Panayiotopoulos, 2008). There are also some very active pockets of entrepreneurial activities in some areas of London. Evidence shows that the number of economically independent Turkish businesswomen is growing. According to data from the European Labour Force Survey, the proportion of self-employed women of Turkish origin in the UK leapt from 6 to 21 per cent between 2000 and 2010, although these numbers are based on very small samples. In the Netherlands only 4 per cent of the population of Turkish origin are entrepreneurs, 18 per cent of which are women (CBS, 2009). In the UK the self-employment rate is estimated to be 20 per cent for Turks (Basu and Altinay, 2002; Altan, 2007), 20 per cent of which is estimated to be women (Basu and Altinay, 2002; Strüder, 2003).

This chapter uses six life-story narratives conducted with Turkish businesswomen in both countries to illustrate how these Turkish migrant businesswomen practice entrepreneurship within these two national contexts. The project analyses the experiences of the participants from the perspective of four main themes, which are derived from the empirical analysis and include: financing, networking, coaching and ethnicizing. By contrasting the UK and the Netherlands, we show how diverse structures may affect processes of entrepreneurial agency. The institutional contexts are highly relevant to the analysis undertaken in this chapter; they are crucial in determining some of the thresholds in markets by regulating the start of a business (Kloosterman and Rath, 2001: 195). Certain institutions can help start up a business by providing material support. However, they can also increase or decrease the entrepreneurial culture. Equally, the societal perception of these women is paramount. In this case, there are Muslim women who are trying to make a career within a highly polarized Dutch society in which Turks are often discriminated against. In British society, Turks can be seen as more European. Their otherness might be visible through the veil, which is considered to be incompatible with the Dutch self-image as an emancipated society (Nieuwkerk, 2003). Alternately, in the UK the association of Turkish women with migration and/or Islam is somewhat weaker and combined with a different perception of the veil. In the UK the meaning of the veil ranges from a form of empowerment for the women choosing to wear it, to a means of seclusion and containment by others (Bodman and Tohidi, 1998). Demonstrating the perceived opportunities and legitimacy of less traditional entrepreneurs, this chapter contributes to the growing body of work on female ethnic, migrant entrepreneurs.

THEORY

Theoretically, this chapter draws upon insights from debates related to structure and agency in the context of migrant entrepreneurship. We aim to demonstrate how two different national contexts may differently influence entrepreneurs with a comparable background and migrant trajectories, leading to different forms of agency. In previous research, two main approaches have been used to study entrepreneurial behavior: the opportunity structure approach and the agency approach. Linking both approaches generates insight into the entrepreneurial possibilities, experiences and actions of Turkish businesswomen.

The opportunity structure approach has been described as the classical approach, and focuses on the 'individual-opportunity nexus' in entrepreneurship. The entrepreneurial performance of entrepreneurs depends on the fit between what they can supply and what the market demands (Light and Rosenstein, 1995; Kloosterman and Rath, 2001). The second school is the agency approach and maintains an anthropological, narrative perspective. This theory centralizes the entrepreneur's viewpoint and carries a more agency-centered approach. The American tradition of studies on migrant entrepreneurship that emphasizes the role of culture and ethnicity in explaining the process of business creation among migrants (Light and Gold, 2000) can also be associated with this school.

Some authors departing from the opportunity structure approach claim that opportunities exist independently of the entrepreneur (Chabaud and Ngijol, 2005). However, this has been criticized since opportunity structures are social phenomena, embedded in social contexts, and may differ according to time and place. The agency approach believes that entrepreneurs' actions are the essential source of opportunities. In line with this, we argue that opportunities cannot be assumed to be objective phenomena created by different actors, like the government or institutions (Alvarez and Barney, 2006). The agency approach takes a much more narrative understanding; life-stories of migrant entrepreneurs reflect their agency (the capacity of individuals to act independently) and are an articulation of their voices (Essers and Benschop, 2007).

Informed by both perspectives, this chapter considers the agency of Turkish women as a process of interaction and allows participants to reflect on various opportunity structures, within the remit of the four themes identified above: financing, networking, coaching and ethnicizing. The idea of the interaction between structure and agency is related to Gidden's structuration theory (1984), in which social science is neither the experience of the subject, nor the existence of any form of societal totality. The point where these two realms are incorporated and, ultimately, synthesized can be described as the duality of structure. At this point social structures make social action possible; at the same time social actions create those very structures (Giddens, 1984: 144). Since migrant entrepreneurship has not been examined from this perspective before, or through using cross-country comparison, this study aims to fill a gap in the existing literature.

For this purpose, we draw on female and migrant entrepreneurship literature. Research into female entrepreneurship has been criticized for taking an essentialist (biological) and individualist stance, and ignoring the effect of the environment and external factors (Ahl, 2006). Several more traditional entrepreneurship studies have provided insights into the motives, activity and success rates of female entrepreneurs; however, literature that links gender and entrepreneurship show that many studies tend to centre on 'the woman entrepreneur' (Buttner, 2001), distinguishing her from the normal (read: male) entrepreneur. Ogbor (2000) notes that women who construct their entrepreneurial identities are often inclined to go through processes of masculinization. Discursive analyses of literature on female entrepreneurship note the gender subtext of the hegemonic entrepreneurial discourse that traditionally displays masculinity (Ahl, 2004; Bruni et al., 2004).

Although these studies contribute to the 'deconstruction' of masculinity within entrepreneurship, they mostly address the positions of white women, remaining unreflective of ethnicity and excluding migrant women. The dominant representation of entrepreneurship is criticized for its ethnocentric subtext as well as its stereotyping and othering, which can force ethnic minority businesspeople to assimilate or 'Westernize' in order to succeed in business (Ogbor, 2000). This may weaken their position as, for instance, the literature on ethnic minority businesses has stressed the importance of family networks for migrant entrepreneurs (Portes, 1995; Kloosterman and Rath, 2001). Therefore, in this chapter, the concept of 'female ethnicity,' which refers to the various meanings of femininity within ethnic contexts (Essers et al., 2010), is used as an intersectional notion that helps to relate women entrepreneurs' agency to the structures surrounding them in their experience and adjustment to opportunity structures.

MIGRATION CONTEXT AND OPPORTUNITY STRUCTURE IN BOTH COUNTRIES

The UK and the Netherlands present similar contexts in many respects, with similar economic measures (for example as measured by gross

Table 1.1   National contexts

	Netherlands	UK
Ease of Doing Business Index	30	5
Migratory regime	Hybrid	Colonial
Labour force (2008) in millions	9	31
GDP per person employed in $ (2008) in thousands	47	52
Female labour force participation age 15+ (2008) as %	59	55
Net migration (2008) in thousands	110	948
Female vulnerable employment (2008) as %	8	7
Migrant stocks, % of population (2005)	11	10
Population born in Turkey or Cyprus (2009) in thousands	158 (76 ♀)	122 (58 ♀)

Sources: World Bank and World Development Indicators, OECD International Migration.

domestic product – GDP), female labour market participation and female vulnerable employment, net migration and actual stock of migrants (see Table 1.1). However, based on the Ease of Doing Business Index it appears to be easier to establish a business in the UK than in the Netherlands, as the UK had a score of one while the Netherlands had a score of 30 (where one denotes the most friendly business regulatory framework).

With regards to migration histories, the UK can be classified as a colonial regime (Kofman et al., 2000), as it occupied many colonies all over the world for a long period of time, including Cyprus (although Turkey itself is not a former British colony). Today, most migrants still originate from former colonies of the British Empire. The UK is home to the second largest Turkish diaspora behind Germany. Due to the English colonial heritage in Cyprus, many Turkish Cypriots fled to the UK because of the political conflict in Cyprus. Turks from the mainland migrated between 1950 and 1970, and are, just like in the Netherlands, 'guest workers'[3] who stayed longer than intended. Turkish Cypriots migrated as a direct result of political instability in Cyprus and, in the case of UK, they also migrated through migratory channels opened up by their Greek Cypriot neighbours.

The Netherlands can be classified as a hybrid model (Kofman et al., 2000): a mixture of a colonial regime and guest worker regime. Because it attracted many guest workers, the Netherlands has a big Turkish community that mostly originates from mainland Turkey. Turks comprise the largest migrant group in the Netherlands. They migrated in the 1960s and 1970s to work in the Netherlands. These 'guest workers' were supposed to be temporary (Lutz, 1996). However, their stay was prolonged, and the Dutch government ended up supporting family reunification (Lutz, 1996; Odé, 1996); these migrants contributed to the contested, so-called 'multicultural society.'

In both countries nationalism has been increasingly framed against the dangers of Muslim fundamentalism and the incompatibility of Western norms and values, and those of the migrant (often Muslim) other. Racialized debates about the incommensurability of Muslim and non-Muslim values have had an enormous impact on public opinion, adding to the disquiet following 9/11. An 'us versus them' dichotomy has resulted in negative images of people of Turkish descent, mostly Muslim. Muslimas' (female Muslims) femininity is used symbolically to represent the other. An important symbolic marker of Muslimas' otherness is the head-scarf. The dichotomy of Muslims versus non-Muslims in Holland is not as present in the UK, possibly due to the fact that the UK has historically been constructed as a nation-state that works to 'meld together a culturally and linguistically diverse population' (Panayiotopoulos, 2008: 398).

METHODOLOGY

Life-story interviews were conducted as means to gather rich qualitative data, explore these phenomena and provide some first impressions. Besides using the biographical method focusing on 'life-chapters' (MacAdams, 1993), an interview guide was produced to study participant experiences within the four identified themes (financing, networking, coaching and ethnicizing). These included open-ended questions and allowed new themes to be introduced by participants. Stories referring to various sub-themes were discursively analysed in order to interpret why and how they emerged in a particular context. In this way, the ambiguities within and among the narratives were sought (Lieblich et al., 1998).

Interviews were conducted in London in the UK, and in the six largest cities (including Amsterdam) within the Netherlands. The sample is thus heavily biased towards mid-sized to large urban areas. Participants were identified using professional networks, personal contacts and community agents. Although the total number of interviews for the overall project was 24, and all interviews were used in the framework of analysis, this chapter focuses on the six most illustrative ones. For this chapter, the three most illustrative life-stories of both countries were chosen to represent how the women interviewed experience and react to their national context. We chose to present in total six stories here, as we want to provide more holistic insights into these women's lived practices and the way they experience their entrepreneurship (Alvesson and Sköldberg, 2000). These were not only the most illustrative and contrasting cases, but they also allowed us to show the variety of ways that Turkish businesswomen experience their national context. The selected life-stories concern those women who informatively articulated their reflections on their agency and the structures around them. To provide a contextual background to the women portrayed in this chapter, the main characteristics of the participants are outlined in Table 1.2.

Interviews typically lasted between one and two hours, and were recorded and fully transcribed. Transcripts have furthermore been transferred onto a software program that facilitates complex management and analysis of qualitative data (NVivo). The researchers read and coded all the transcripts independently (translated into English where appropriate) and communicated regularly to examine, discuss and seek consensus on the direction and interpretation of the data. They then interrogated the data to identify and code detectable differences and themes across the interviews. Additionally, some background information on the national contexts was acquired through desk-research, and some thematic interviews were conducted with officials in order to better contextualize the interviews.

FINDINGS

Financing

None of the women in the UK relied on formal sources of finance, with all trading in areas where a low level of start-up capital was required. Generally, the UK participants were reluctant to approach banks for capital and linked it to not wanting to be in a position where they could not make their repayments. This reluctance seems to be related to an aspect of Turkish culture, where official borrowing is seen as too risky and therefore not desirable. This is also in accordance with migrant entrepreneurship literature (Kloosterman and Rath, 2001; Portes, 1995). However, Dünya (UK) states she would rather not borrow money from family and instead raise money to start up her company by relying on bootstrapping, which contrasts the migrant entrepreneurship literature:

> Borrowing money from the bank, loans, I think that it is going to put me under pressure, you know, paying them back for 5, 10 years, so I'm not that person . . . All the money I got with the business I put it in the business again to make it bigger and in this case I never had loans or anything involving my family.

Table 1.2 Key participant characteristics

	Name	Age	Marital status	Children	First generation?	Business partner?	Business venture
NL	Mechan	33	Single	None	No	Yes, sister	Nail studio
	Selene	32	Married	1	Yes, arrived in NL at 6 months	No	Lawyer
	Ceylan	45	Married	2	Yes, arrived at 15	No	Consultancy agency for societal issues
UK	Arzu	39	Single	None	No	No	PR consultant
	Dünya	32	Single	None	Yes, arrived at 25	Yes, originally with her partner, now on her own	Souvenir shop
	Neslihan	49	Married	2	Yes, arrived at 23	Yes, originally with her husband, now on her own	Network marketing cosmetics

Neslihan (UK) also speaks of how issues such as finance are closely linked to the Turkish culture by describing how she and her husband had financed their first business: 'Well, if you know the Turkish community, we have money at our weddings; they don't give you presents, they give you money.' If needed, the Turkish community itself may function as an important source of finance. The extent to which individuals can rely on this mechanism, however, depends on their circle of family and friends. This practice is also highly related to the concept of trust.

Mechan (NL) and Dünya (UK) both stress the 'pressure' and 'pigeon-holing' of loans. Yet, the Turkish businesswomen in the Netherlands seemed to be less reluctant to apply for an official loan, but did stress the importance of having good contacts and networking to succeed in this task. Ceylan (NL) states: 'So I needed additional capital. That's what the ABN Amro did. But networking, that's so important isn't it; I had good contacts at the ABN Amro.'

Selene (NL) is particularly positive about the Rabobank: 'This is really a bank for Turkish entrepreneurs, they just love Turks! That was the entrance, through my husband. He had contacts with the Rabo.' An official from Rabobank reinforced Selene's statement and claimed that Rabobank targets Turkish entrepreneurs since it has always focused on the local community. Although in the Netherlands not many participants experienced overt discrimination, one female Turkish real-estate agent felt discriminated against by, interestingly, the very same Rabobank. She experienced discrimination when she applied for an extra buffer to finance a new project, despite being a member of the board at that bank. The official reason the bank gave her was that they found it strange that she was young, had a nice car and a big house. However, she felt they suspected her of handling 'black money', as she was Turkish. This is in line with Essers and Benschop's earlier findings on 'subtle discrimination' among such businesswomen (2007) and supported by Marlow and Patton (2005). Selene (NL) identified different treatment for Turkish entrepreneurs: 'They are of course a lot more critical with a "Mohammed" than with a "Van Vliet"'.

Selene's statement demonstrates these women's awareness of their otherness when seeking a loan. Expectations of failure, based on perceived discrimination on the basis of a combination of sex and ethnic identity, may be a reason why Mechan (NL) and Dünya (UK) were reluctant to apply for a loan in the first place, although this might be a self-fulfilling prophecy. Arzu (UK) confirms this problem and discusses how the likelihood of obtaining funding does not solely rest on competence: 'I think sometimes women can be their own most enemy; just go out and be yourself and be confident . . . especially if you're preaching to a guy.'

Similarly, women entrepreneurship literature discusses the 'problematics' of female entrepreneurs presenting themselves less confidentially to bank and other officials (Buttner and Rosen, 1988; Bruni et al., 2004), although Brush et al. (2009) recently gave statistical evidence that this is often a myth.

Finally, hardly anyone was aware of the possibility of micro-financing, which some regretted as they could have borrowed money without building a high debt. This is remarkable, as many local and national organizations advertise this possibility. Yet, a policy-maker explained this might be because such organizations do not use the right channels to target these migrant communities.

Networking

The social environment appeared to be a very important stimulating or constraining factor. Some businesswomen recognize how families can provide stimulation despite community resistance. Selene (NL) says:

> 13 years ago it was, being a girl: 'gosh, does she really have to study?' There was some resistance. Honor and shame still play a big role. Women cannot be better than men. But my parents stimulated me and my sister tremendously to do this. My parents wanted me to finish school and to be independent. Yes, and then they see lawyer practice [name], that is real nice. That is my maiden name.

Obviously, Selene's (NL) parents really supported her to be independent; they seem to be proud about her having her own practice, which carries their own name. However, the family can also be restricting, as Arzu (UK) suggests, particularly in some sub-communities:

> Cypriot Turkish women generally get pushed now to spend more time educating themselves . . . But if you're from the Turkish community or Kurdish community, particularly the Turkish-Kurdish community, they're probably not as empowered, have to live in a much more confined way . . . One of the things that are limiting women from becoming more successful, it is because their family want them to have kids and there's this kind of pressure, you have to be at home for your kids.

Hence, although family environments can be supportive, because these entrepreneurs are both women and of Turkish origin, it may be difficult to get community support for their entrepreneurial behavior as this might imply shame or go against family and gender role expectations. Yet, being known in the Turkish community can be a real unique selling point, as Selene (NL) says:

> You need to have a name to get your clients; they need to find you. In that sense I take advantage of my Turkish background. Certainly with Turkish clients, no interpreter necessary . . . They think you understand, so that's an advantage. On the other hand, that's a disadvantage, they look at a woman. And at the beginning, this was difficult. If you have a man in front of you around his 50s . . . and then here I am, 24, 25, very young and Turkish. Three things together: Turkish, young and woman, and then you have to tell someone like that we are going to do it like this.

Having the same ethnic background might be advantageous, although the intersectionality of gender, ethnicity and entrepreneurship (as also illustrated by Essers et al., 2010) may become a problem when talking with someone positioned at the intersection of opposite identities. Women in the UK also spoke about a degree of interaction within the Turkish community, possibly for pragmatic reasons such as a common language. This was particularly true for recent migrant clients who do not have a very good level of spoken English.

Not only was being known in the Turkish community an asset for migrants, it was also a source of support to draw upon, particularly at the start up phase of the business. Dünya (UK) felt that there was a great amount of support from the community:

> There is a positive effect because there is a community, a Turkish community and if you need anything so you can ask. Being Turkish in this country makes you in that case different and you know, they're more helpful . . . I don't describe them as family, I mean they're relationships, kind of friendly relationships . . . They have this sort of moral; they're still living in this.

These arrangements were not without drawbacks. The informality of some arrangements proved to be problematic for Arzu (UK):

> So people who have an alternative outlook, people who get concerned when you put a contract in front of them, like you are trying to do something wrong . . . So I think perhaps, there's an evolution that needs to happen within my community, and it is happening, but [with] the older generation . . . When you're younger, saying you want to do business differently, they take you as disrespectful for challenging [the way it has always been done].

Many of the businesswomen in the UK belonged to networks, including Turkish specific networks. The experience was usually seen as beneficial, which is also confirmed by insights on businesswomen in general (see for instance Brush et al., 2009). Neslihan (UK) and Arzu (UK) explain how these networks are useful by drawing on social contacts and the community. Moreover, Arzu (UK) is a member of a professional organization linked to her area of trading and sees it as very valuable to her (although it is not tied to her community): 'The organization gives me lots of professional support . . . I don't want to be purely stocked in the Turkish world, it's too narrow and not always very fulfilling.'

In the Netherlands, however, Turkish businesswomen narrated some tensions with networking in general. Selene (NL), for example, sees the intersection of her gender and ethnicity negatively in some networks: 'It would be good though to start a network for Turkish businesswomen only, because Dutch businesswomen don't have to network that much; they don't need to prove a lot. And, [she laughs], the Turkish entrepreneurial association Hogiaf, that's a real men's world.'

On the contrary, Ceylan (NL) show how together gender and ethnicity can be played to her advantage:

> I was member of the board of a women's entrepreneurial association . . . That was to give them a signal like, 'Hey boys, we are there as well!' . . . In Holland a lot of things happen behind the scenes. When I notice this I put this on the agenda . . . When they don't allow me, I just make sure I come in. I am a woman and an ethnic minority, but I am an entrepreneur. So I experience to have an advantage as a woman. When I go sell something to a male bureaucrat, I am less threatening, I can make more jokes, and so I am in.

These quotes demonstrate how Turkish businesswomen often feel networks are too masculine or white to enter, leading them to build networks of their own. Yet, being 'three things together: Turkish, young and woman' can also be experienced as an advantage in trying to attract clients from the same ethnic community. However, active networking often seems superfluous, and is not undertaken because of a lack of time and feelings of exclusion linked to either ethnicity or gender (or perhaps even age). It is important to note here that the issue of being excluded in male-dominated networks has frequently been reported before (Ibarra, 1993; Timberlake, 2005).

Coaching

Like many other Turkish businesswomen, Mechan (NL) is not that enthusiastic about governmental support:

> We need to pay a lot of taxes in the Netherlands, and we hardly see anything back from this . . . And the local government invents all these multi-culti projects; you get a project like drinking coffee together. Then I really feel like, what is this, get real! If I want to drink coffee with my neighbour, I will do this myself.

Alternatively, Ceylan (NL) feels she can 'fight' for minority people and contribute socially through her entrepreneurial practice. Her entrepreneurial identity collides with her Kurdish background, as well as with her Turkish identity:

> I was a teenager of 15, and I was against injustice, then I already fought for minorities [in Kurdistan]. I learned the language, started doing voluntary work, after a year I started teaching minority women. We moved to a real 'African' neighbourhood, nice and dynamic . . . Perhaps unconsciously I therefore started my company in this social area. I started it as an ideal, to really contribute . . . I like enterprising, taking risks, could be part of my Turkish root.

Hence, Ceylan's experience with diverse ethnic communities seems to have added to her entrepreneurship and entrepreneurial identity.

In the UK, few women relied on official forms of coaching but many stressed the importance of having more female role models in the Turkish community, particularly given the perceived success of Turkish men. Arzu (UK) says: 'Many [Cypriots] are throwing themselves into various businesses, supermarkets or kebab-shops or whatever it is, and there's a lot of male success stories. But I think there isn't a similar story with women.'

Generally, the women found coaching to be a positive initiative, although most of them did not benefit from it. They often found their own help informally and identified that seeing more female role models could stimulate entrepreneurship among Turkish women. Essers (2009) and Mirchandani (1999) also discuss the importance of having more female migrant models in entrepreneurship. Additionally, some women seem to feel they owe something to the society in which they found possibilities. Therefore, these businesswomen appear to be 'idealistically' attracted to actively coach others with their participation in Western society; at the same time, these women favour a more proactive stance by the Chambers of Commerce and schools in promoting entrepreneurship.

Ethnicizing

On the question of how they experienced the debate about Muslims and Islam in politics Mechan (NL) answered:

> They abuse religion, by getting attention like this and then link it to Turkish people. Because of that, discrimination grows. While all these years, it was less, less, less. But because they keep bringing up the Muslim in the media in a negative way . . . I think both, men and women, are troubled with this negative perception.

Mechan (NL) feels that Islam is being abused to discriminate against Turkish people. The increasing media attention that shows a negative perception of Muslims, primarily Turks in both countries, is one of the reasons that discrimination in these countries grows. The political climate regarding Muslims makes them more aware that they are different, and further polarizes them. This negative experience might be the reason why Mechan does not want to be attached to any Dutch institution (see also Essers and Benschop, 2007). Selene (NL) also had a negative experience when she registered at the Chamber of Commerce:

> The male officer asked if I knew what an advokaat [advocaat is the Dutch word for lawyer] with a 'k' was [k = an alcoholic drink]. A real offence, as he probably hinted at the expectation that being a Muslima I wouldn't drink, which I do. I could also only hire a car when I finally showed my business card.

Selene's (NL) words show the prejudices she encountered. Individuals that these women entrepreneurs have to professionally interact with may suspect that being Muslim, a woman and an entrepreneur cannot go well together. Therefore women like Selene explicitly have to prove that this is actually a misunderstanding. Essers et al. (2010) frame this simultaneity of identities (religion, gender and entrepreneurship), or intersectionality, in terms 'female ethnicity': the way others make sense of their gender because of their ethnicity often inhibits their entrepreneurial legitimacy. However, the political context within the UK is experienced differently and the existing tension between natives and non-natives is regarded as less visible than in the Netherlands. This affects perceptions greatly, as seen in the interviews conducted for this project, and these perceptions vary depending on the background of the women. The visibility of other-ness for Turkish Cypriot women in the UK is, for example, usually quite low. As Neslihan (UK) explains: 'We are from Cyprus . . . we have the English cultural events . . . we are really like English women, we can be anything we want to be.' Dünya (UK) echoes this feeling of not being very different from native women: 'No, I don't think being a Turkish woman has an impact on my business. I mean being a woman is a question that we need to answer, but being a Turkish woman, I don't see any problem. I don't think being Turkish or English . . . There's no difference, in this country.'

Participants described the experience of being a Turkish woman entrepreneur in the UK in rather positive terms. Although being a woman might affect their position as an entrepreneur, being Turkish does not, in their opinion, negatively affect their enterprising. On the contrary, Dünya (UK) seems to imply that being a Turkish business-woman gives her a better position in the UK society. Arzu (UK) agrees with this:

The nice thing is when you're with a certain type of person, it doesn't matter about my ethnic background, my gender, none of these things matters because part of being a Londoner is you're a human being first . . . I think the media certainly try to reinforce the stereotypes, but I find London great for that because there's a creative entrepreneurial spirit that makes all that irrelevant. So as a Londoner, I don't have . . . within my community I think you're definitely more conscious of being a woman; I don't try to live up to any expectations. So if you can find a happy balance where you can define yourself in your own way, and I think running your own business can help you do that, you are setting the rules, the boundaries.

Accordingly, businesswomen in the UK may find it a little bit easier to describe themselves using multiple layers of identities and drawing on the ones they see as positive. In Arzu's (UK) case, this entails drawing on her identity as a Londoner and an autonomous, agentic entrepreneur, while reflecting on her sex and age status within her community and the gender and ethnic stereotypes as enforced by the media. Overall, Arzu (UK) sees entrepreneurship as a positive outcome for women in the Turkish community and a strategic way to find one's place within the Turkish and UK community. Entrepreneurship may give these women an opportunity to create their own identity.

The statements from the Dutch-Turkish businesswomen demonstrate that they feel offended to be connected with, and othered through, their (assumed) Muslim faith, instead of their professional identity as entrepreneurs. Selene (NL) appears to be very upset about such prejudices, but uses her accomplished position as a lawyer to acquire the respect she deserves. In her interview she moreover seems to 'warn' Dutch society that if the Dutch keep applying this attitude of treating Turkish people unequally (legally and such), they will lose much young Turkish potential. On the contrary, Ceylan (NL) rejects the victim role and refuses to be 'sent away'. She even uses her otherness in her business to show the positive side of minorities.

SUMMARY

Networking is seen as difficult, time-consuming and exclusionary on the grounds of gender and ethnicity. In the UK, we note a greater usage of business Turkish networks and sense of inclusion within mainstream networks. Participants mostly do not feel the need to be coached formally. Moreover, although entrepreneurialism is picked up 'naturally', paying more attention to this profession at school and actively approaching potential entrepreneurs is regarded positively.

Overall, Turkish businesswomen in our study relied more on informal sources of finance, such as friends, family or the community, particularly in the UK. For those that approached the bank, having the right contacts to obtain a loan, as well as the right name or appearance, seemed essential. There were no perceptions of discrimination at the structural level, although the question was posed at the agentic level.

We observe that the Dutch context is experienced with more ethnic tension than in the UK. The businesswomen feel their position as women, of Turkish origin (that is, their female ethnicity) and entrepreneurs is problematic. This combination of identities is perceived as incompatible or shameful. Familial support may compensate and strengthen entrepreneurial attitudes and identities, and women entrepreneurs' position as Turks may be advantageous.

Finally, the societal context appears to be experienced more negatively in the Netherlands, as opposed to experiences of the Turkish businesswomen in the UK. It is clear that the political climate in the Netherlands has changed in a rather hostile manner against ethnic minorities, particularly those of Muslim faith. Islam is being used in societal discourses to exclude this group and the need for these allegedly non-adjusted citizens to integrate is constantly being stressed. This atmosphere makes it difficult for these businesswomen to deal with their identity as entrepreneurs, women and Turkish. In the UK, our participants do not feel as different, and seem to be able to distance themselves from negative pigeonholing in the media.

DISCUSSION

The differences in these experiences might be explained by the fact that the political climate towards Turks/Muslims in the UK is less polarized than in the Netherlands, or because of different migration histories. The interviewed Turks in the UK might feel less cultural difference between their community and the English. Moreover, their experiences can also be contextualized within different economies, the UK being a liberal market economy and the Netherlands being a coordinated market economy. Although one might expect that the Dutch coordinated market economy would provide much more institutionalized support leading to (proportionally) much more entrepreneurship among this group than the UK's liberal market economy, this coordinated market economy might entail too many obstructing rules. Finally, the differences might also be explained from the fact that the interviewed English-Turkish businesswomen were all situated in London, a highly cosmopolitan world-city where the (native) population may be more adjusted to the presence of Turkish people than in smaller towns. Further, in London, Turkish women may have more agency to distance themselves from 'traditional' communities. Indeed, the experiences of Turkish businesswomen outside of very cosmopolitan areas such as London may be very different.

It is important to note that these are only indications, and we cannot or do not aim to generalize to the whole population of Turkish migrant businesswomen in either of the two countries. However, we may also detect different forms of agency among these women when connecting them with opportunity structures. They adjust to, deploy and alter various opportunity structures in order to enhance their entrepreneurial possibilities in various ways. Mechan's (NL) reaction is to figuratively or literally distance herself from the negative opinions regarding (Muslim) Turks within Western society, since this atmosphere along with institutional interference from the institutional opportunity structure impedes her entrepreneurial activity. In doing so, she sustains the hegemonic discourse on the 'different, other Muslim'. However, although seemingly adjusting to various opportunity structures, Mechan's reaction eventually offers her more room to do entrepreneurship in her desired way. In a way Dünya in the UK also appears to be taking some distance from various opportunity structures, as she refuses to engage with any formal institutions. This may of course be detrimental to her business due to her reliance on bootstrapping. Dünya exploits opportunity structures by conforming to a 'Western' way of doing business, and renders her own otherness invisible.

Selene's (NL) reaction to these opportunity structures is to find strength from within and alter her approach. While building on her growing experience, knowledge and professionalism, she subtly tries to change the system from within. Casually showing her business card to enforce respect as a Turkish female entrepreneur and talking about her profession with disadvantaged youth are a few examples of this kind of reaction. We see some similarity with Neslihan's (UK) reactions, as she is also quite pragmatic in not letting her ethnic identity affect her business practices, while at the same time capitalizing on the Turkish community where possible.

Ceylan (NL) reacts more aggressively to alter these opportunity structures. She was a member of the board of a women's entrepreneurial association and set up a network for Turkish businesswomen. Moreover, she explicitly makes use of her gender and ethnic identity as a unique selling point, helping society through her business and by initiating projects on entrepreneurship at schools. Ceylan actively fights to change the various opportunity structures that surround her. Arzu (UK) seems to be doing this, as she is energetically involved in several networking and professional organizations and uses them to actively change the way things are done in business inside and outside of the Turkish community.

CONCLUSION

In conclusion, we feel that the political opportunity structure was experienced with more tension in the Netherlands, and less polarizing in the UK. The institutional opportunity structure was experienced neutrally in both countries, however the societal opportunity structure was experienced more negatively in the Netherlands. In response to the intersection of being Turkish, female, possibly Muslim and an entrepreneur, we found that our participants employed one or more strategies in turn, as outlined in Table 1.3. It seems that a fundamental question arising from this research project is to reflect on which of these employed strategies led to either agentic or structural (or both) change.

The contributions of our research entail that we have demonstrated these Turkish businesswomen are no 'structural dopes'; to some extent they are determined by their contexts yet they have a say in how this affects their entrepreneurship and entrepreneurial identity. They discursively claim their entrepreneurial identity and thus legitimacy, by actually deploying their sometimes-detrimental contexts. This is in line with Alvesson and Billing's (2009: 98) conceptualization of identity work which refers to 'aiming at achieving a feeling of a reasonably coherent and positive sense of self, necessary for coping with the ambiguities of existence, work tasks and social relations'. Our study has provided new insights into such forms of identity work by female entrepreneurs. As authors such as Watson (2009) have stated, little has been done to link conceptually the structural

Table 1.3   Summary of strategies adopted

	Agency	Structure
Compliance	Not reflecting on identity	Not engaging with institutional structures
Blending in	Make 'otherness' invisible	Engaging with structures on an 'equal' basis
Reclaiming and adapting	Reclaim identity	Capitalize on community
		Engage with structures as an 'ethnic' member
		Create and alter structures to represent standpoint
	−> Agentic change?	−> Structural change?

level of entrepreneurship with the individual level (entrepreneurial identities). Through our interviews we have shown how different national contexts may have a different impact on such entrepreneurial identity work. Future research involves focusing on the conceptual relationship between gender, ethnicity, religion and entrepreneurial identity work of Turkish businesswomen, while including more Turkish businesswomen from other, smaller cities in the UK in order to grasp a better insight into how diversity in context may affect entrepreneurial identity work.

NOTES

1. Entrepreneurship is seen as covering a wide range of activities, including undeclared or unregulated economic activity related to self-employment and enterprise. Enterprises associated with goods and services which themselves are illegal are excluded from this definition.
2. By Turkish, we mean women whose parents were born in Turkey or Turkish Cyprus, or who were born in these original home countries themselves. This includes women from the mainland, Turkish Cypriots and Kurdish refugees from Turkey (Turkish passport holders but ethnically Kurdish). Turkish therefore also includes women of Cypriot or Kurdish origins and includes those with or without Dutch/UK nationality. Distinctions between these groups will be taken into account within the analysis.
3. In theory, the guest worker system relies on the rotation of largely male workers with no family responsibilities in the host country working for a set period of time before returning to their homeland.

REFERENCES

Ahl, H. (2004), *The Scientific Reproduction of Gender Inequality: A Discourse Analysis of Research Texts on Women's Entrepreneurship*, Malmö: Liber AB.

Ahl, H. (2006), 'Why research on women entrepreneurs needs new directions', *Entrepreneurship Theory and Practice*, **30** (5), 595–621.

Altan, C. (2007), 'Turkish immigrants are among "biggest benefit claimants"', *Londra Gazete*, **4**, (October).

Alvarez, S. and J.B. Barney (2006), 'Discovery and creation: alternative theories of entrepreneurial action', *Strategic Entrepreneurship Journal*, **1** (1–2), 11–26.

Alvesson, M. and Y.D. Billing (2009), *Understanding Gender and Organizations*, London: Sage.

Alvesson, M. and K. Sköldberg (2000), *Reflexive Methodology*, London: Sage.

Basu, A. and E. Altinay (2002), 'The interaction between culture and entrepreneurship in London's immigrant businesses', *International Small Business Journal*, **20** (4), 371–93.

Bodman, H.L. and N. Tohidi (1998), *Women in Muslim Societies: Diversity within Unity*, Boulder, CO: Lynne Rienner.

Bruni, A., S. Gherardi and B. Poggio (2004), 'Doing gender, doing entrepreneurship: an ethnographic account of intertwined practices', *Gender, Work and Organization*, **11** (4), 406–29.

Brush, C., N. Carter, E. Gatewood, P. Greene and M. Hart (2009), *The Diana Project: Women Business Owner and Equity Capital: The Myths Dispelled*, Babson College Research Paper, no 2009/11.

Buttner, E. (2001), 'Examining female entrepreneurs' management style: an application of a relational frame', *Journal of Business Ethics*, **29** (3), 253–69.

Buttner, H. and B. Rosen (1988), 'Bank loan officers' perceptions of the characteristics of men, women, and successful entrepreneurs', *Journal of Business Venturing*, **3** (3), 249–58.

CBS (2009), *Allochtonen in Nederland*, Voorburg/Heerlen: CBS.

Chabaud, D. and J. Ngijol (2005), 'The recognition of market opportunities by entrepreneurs: towards a constructivist perspective', paper written at the Ecole de Management de Normandie, France.

Essers, C. (2009), *New Directions in Postheroic Entrepreneurship: Narratives of Gender and Ethnicity*, Malmö: Liber AB.

Essers, C. and Y. Benschop (2007), 'Enterprising identities: female entrepreneurs of Moroccan and Turkish origin in the Netherlands', *Organization Studies*, **28** (1), 49–69.

Essers, C., Y. Benschop and H. Doorewaard (2010), 'Female ethnicity: understanding Muslim immigrant businesswomen in the Netherlands', *Gender, Work and Organization*, **17** (3), 320–39.

Giddens, A. (1984), *The Constitution of Society*, Cambridge: Polity Press.

Ibarra, H. (1993), 'Personal networks of women and minorities in management: a conceptual framework', *Academy of Management Review*, **18** (1), 56–87.

Kloosterman, R. and J. Rath (2001), 'Immigrant entrepreneurs in advanced economies: mixed embeddedness further explored', *Journal of Ethnic and Migration Studies*, **27** (2), 189–201.

Kofman, E., A. Phizacklea, P. Raghura and R. Sales (2000), *Gender and International Migration in Europe: Employment, Welfare and Politics*, London: Routledge.

Lieblich, A., R. Tuval-Mashiach and T. Zilber (1998), *Narrative Research: Reading, Analysis and Interpretation*, London: Sage.

Light, I. and S. Gold (2000), *Ethnic Economies*, San Diego, CA: Academic Press.

Light, I. and C. Rosenstein (1995), 'Expanding the interaction theory of entrepreneurship', in A. Portes (ed.), *The Economic Sociology of Immigration: Essays on Networks, Ethnicity and Entrepreneurship*, New York: Sage, pp. 166–212.

Lutz, H. (1996), 'De grenzen van een Europese identiteit: Vrouwelijke immigranten in Fort Europa', *Tijdschrift voor Vrouwenstudies*, **17** (2), 165–79.

MacAdams, D. (1993), *The Stories We Live By: Personal Myths and the Making of the Self*, New York: William Morrow.

Marlow, S. and D. Patton (2005), 'All credit to men? Entrepreneurship, finance, and gender', *Entrepreneurship Theory and Practice*, **29** (6), 717–35.

Mirchandani, K. (1999), 'Feminist insight on gendered work: new directions in research on women and entrepreneurship', *Gender, Work & Organization*, **6** (4), 224–35.

Nieuwkerk, K. (2003), 'Multiculturaliteit, islam en gender', *Visies van Nederlandse nieuwe moslima's Gender Tijdschrift voor Genderstudies*, **6** (3), 6–20.

Odé, A. (1996), *Migrant Workers in the Dutch Labour Market Today*, Amsterdam: Thesis Publishers.

Ogbor, J. (2000), 'Mythicizing and reification in entrepreneurial discourse:

ideology-critique of entrepreneurial studies', *The Journal of Management Studies*, **37** (5), 605–35.

Panayiotopoulos, P.I. (2008), 'Turkish immigrant entrepreneurs in the European Union: a political-institutional approach', *International Journal of Entrepreneurial Behaviour & Research*, **14** (6), 395–413.

Portes, A. (1995), *The Economic Sociology of Immigration: Essays on Networks, Ethnicity, and Entrepreneurship*, New York: Russell Sage Foundation.

Strüder, I. (2003), 'Migrant self-employment in a European global city – the importance of gendered power relations and performances of belonging for Turkish women in London', *International Small Business Journal*, **21** (4), 485–87.

Timberlake, S. (2005), 'Social capital and gender in the workplace', *Journal of Management Development*, **24** (1), 34–44.

Watson, T. (2009), 'Entrepreneurial action, identity work and the use of multiple discursive resources: the case of a rapidly changing family business', *International Small Business Journal*, **27** (3), 251–74.

Westwood, S. and P. Bhachu (1987*)*, *Enterprising Women; Ethnicity, Economy, and Gender Relations*, London: Routledge.

2. Women-owned SMEs in Bangladesh: challenges in institutional financing

Salma C. Zohir and Patricia G. Greene

INTRODUCTION

The role of women in building the small business economy and driving economic growth in countries around the world is increasingly being recognized (Kelly et al., 2010; Allen et al., 2008; Brush et al., 2006; Minnitti, 2006). However, the most recent Global Entrepreneurship Monitor (GEM) report, drawing on annual national assessments of entrepreneurial activity, shows that women's participation in entrepreneurship varies greatly according to country (Kelly et al., 2010). These differences are generally attributed to factors such as culture, access to resources, industrial bases and governmental policies (Brush, et al., 2006; Acs et al., 2005; Minnitti et al., 2005). Many questions remain about how these factors (and potentially others) impact entrepreneurial behaviours and outcomes.

Access to capital is reported as a challenge for most entrepreneurs around the world (Allen et al., 2008). Capital is considered as one of the primary fuels to support business growth, and yet consistently questions arise around women's ability to access necessary capital (Carter et al., 2003; Greene et al., 2006). While the role of small and medium enterprises (SMEs) is seen as vital for the growth and development of Bangladesh (Ahmed, 2008), little is known about the role of women in this environment. This chapter adds to the body of knowledge regarding women entrepreneurship by providing a profile of female-run SMEs in Bangladesh. In focusing on Bangladesh, we summarize the degree and type of institutional (governmental) support for female-run SMEs, present the results of primary research into the barriers women entrepreneurs face with respect to financing, and conclude with recommendations for change.

WOMEN IN SMES IN BANGLADESH

The existing repositories of information, such as the Bangladesh Small and Cottage Industries Corporation (BSCIC) and the Board of Investment (BOI) (for medium and large industries), do not generate or maintain gender-disaggregated data. However, while statistics on the number of women entrepreneurs are scarce, several surveys have been undertaken that address gender. Their findings show that while the formal labour force participation of women has doubled since 1995–96, it is still quite low at only 29 per cent by 2005–06 (BBS, 2008). At that time most of the increase was due to a growth in self-employment. While about 16 per cent of the women in the labour force in 2005–06 were self-employed, there were significant geographical differences. Approximately 30 per cent of urban females in the labour force were self-employed, in contrast to only 12 per cent of rural females (BBS, 2008).

A slightly earlier study offers a different perspective. According to data generated by the Economic Census, conducted by the Bangladesh Bureau of Statistics (BBS) in 2001–03 (Chowdhury, 2006), women owned only 3 per cent of all enterprises. The study showed that while most SMEs are micro and small enterprises, the percentage of those businesses owned by women is just over half of 1 per cent. The share of women-owned enterprises increased with the size of the enterprise. These results may have emerged because this study underestimated the clusters of manufacturing enterprises in cities and towns where male owners of enterprises outnumber female owners of enterprises.

Yet another study, the 2003 Private Sector Survey of Enterprises, reveals that micro, small and medium enterprises (MSMEs) employed more than 31 million people and contributed 25 per cent to the gross domestic product (GDP). This study found that women owned 6 per cent of MSMEs. In contrast, studies by the Ministry of Industries (MOI) and the Power and Participation Research Center (PPRC) (2006) reported that women owned 5 per cent and 1 per cent of MSMEs. Additionally, another source found that while women entrepreneurs make up less than 10 per cent of the total number of entrepreneurs in South Asia, in Bangladesh the proportion is estimated to be at 6 to 7 per cent (Ahmed, 2008). Despite the range of results, these surveys indicate a low level of participation by women entrepreneurs in formal business. However, the Labour Force Survey gives a much higher figure. This survey suggests that women-owned micro enterprises have been under-sampled in the enterprise surveys, especially in urban areas. One reason for this could be that many women are engaged in business in the informal sector and therefore do not have trade licenses. Informal businesses could account for about

Table 2.1   Distribution of ownership by gender

Sector	Female	Male	Mixed
Agriculture	18	25	29
Fishing	1	4	6
Manufacturing (boutique, handicrafts)	47	14	23
Construction	–	1	3
Wholesale and retail, trade	23	42	25
Hotels and restaurant	7	5	11
Transport, storage and communication	1	1	–
Real estate, renting and business activities	1	3	4
Health and social work	–	1	–
Other service activities	1	3	–
Total	100	100	100

Source: Daniels (2003).

half of women-owned enterprises (BWCCI, 2008). These enterprises were likely to be excluded from enterprise surveys.

Based on a review of existing surveys (the 2003 Private Sector Study (Daniels, 2003), the 2006 South Asia Enterprise Development Facility (SEDF) study and the Bangladesh Women Chamber of Commerce and Industries (BWCCI) study (BWCCI, 2008)), Islam et al. (2010) noted that women-owned SMEs in Bangladesh are described in terms of: (1) characteristics of the enterprises; (2) demographic characteristics of women entrepreneurs; (3) training in SMEs; and (4) women entrepreneurs' access to financing.

Characteristics of the Enterprises

The 2003 Private Sector Survey (Daniels, 2003) found that 18 per cent of woman-owned businesses were in agriculture, compared with 25 per cent for men. This figure of 25 per cent might actually reflect problems with category definitions. If agriculture includes rice processing, then women's business ownership could be 18 per cent. But if rice processing is considered a manufacturing activity, it would be counted under manufacturing. Because it is very unlikely that 47 per cent of women-owned enterprises are in manufacturing, compared with 14 per cent of male-owned enterprises (see Table 2.1), the survey probably over-sampled rural and micro enterprises and underestimated the clusters of manufacturing enterprises in cities and towns where male owners of enterprises outnumber female owners of enterprises. Table 2.1 also shows that while women tend to be more heavily concentrated in manufacturing (boutique, handicrafts) industries, men tend to be more concentrated in trade and retail areas. The BWCCI study (BWCCI, 2008) reinforced that women entrepreneurs were mostly involved in manufacturing (62 per cent), mainly in boutiques, handicrafts and food processing, followed by service and trade.

Like most studies from developed and developing countries, the SEDF (2006) study found that female-owned businesses have smaller employment and sales figures than male-owned businesses; most women were also sole proprietors. Moreover, women entrepreneurs preferred to start their businesses in sectors where female employment was already concentrated, since they would have ready role models. Raihan (2007) argues that women's choice of food processing, clothing and textile sectors reflects resource constraints, as well as an aversion to risk-taking and a preference for low entry barriers and low financial risks.

Demographic Characteristics of Women Entrepreneurs

The 2003 Private Sector Survey (Daniels, 2003) demonstrated that women entrepreneurs are younger than their male counterparts. The average age was 33 for women and 36 for men. Another study revealed that about 58 per cent of women entrepreneurs belonged to the 15–30 year age group; another 27 per cent belonged to the 31–40 year age group (BWCCI, 2008). The SEDF study (2006), in contrast, reported the average age of women entrepreneurs as 45 years old. The SEDF study also reported that women had an average of nine years' experience. This again raises questions about the sample frame, in this case suggesting that older women were over-sampled.

The 2003 Private Sector Survey noted that, in general, more women entrepreneurs had higher levels of education than their male counterparts. The percentage of women entrepreneurs with at least 10 years of formal education varied between 65 (SEDF, 2006) and 85 per cent (BWCCI, 2008). The higher education level in the BWCCI study (BWCCI, 2008) correlates with the higher number of younger women entrepreneurs in that study. That study suggests that as younger women receive an education they are more likely to engage in entrepreneurship. This is particularly true for those women between the ages of 15 and 30 who have at least 10 years of formal schooling. Like the earlier Labour Force Survey 2005–06, this study highlighted that enterprises owned by women are mostly in urban areas. The study further noted that more than two-thirds of the women entrepreneurs' fathers or husbands had received at least 10 years of schooling (Secondary School Certificate), and in most cases their fathers or husbands were also involved in the business. About half the women business owners were married women, one-third were unmarried and the rest were divorced or widowed (BWCCI, 2008).

Training on SME

According to the 2007 BWCCI, more than 70 per cent of women entrepreneurs had received training from a range of organizations, including non-governmental organizations (NGOs), the BSCIC, the Ministry of Youth, the Ministry of Women's and Children's Affairs, and other women's associations. However, most of the training was not based on a prior assessment of needs and thus it was often not relevant to women-led enterprises. Furthermore, those who did not receive training were more likely to be from rural areas.

Access to Financing

Studies have shown that access to finance is one of the most critical issues for women entrepreneurs (Ahmed, 2008; BWCCI, 2008; Raihan, 2007; MOI, 2004; Daniels, 2003). Access to finance was cited in the 2003 Private Sector Study as the key problem during startup and operation. This finding recurred again in the 2004 National Task Force Report on SMEs (MOI, 2004).

In Bangladesh, micro enterprises have access to institutional finance from microfinance institutions while medium-size enterprises have access to commercial loans. The small enterprises are the 'missing middle' in terms of institutional finance because they are too large to qualify for micro credit assistance programs but too small to quality for bank loans. The situation is even more challenging for women. The BWCCI (BWCCI, 2008) study noted that about 79 per cent of women entrepreneurs had no access to formal financial institutions and only 19 per cent had ever received institutional finance (including from NGOs). Furthermore, studies have noted that women contribute around 26 per cent of the total amount deposited in banks, but they receive only 2 per cent of the total amount of outstanding loans (Choudhury and Raihan, 2000). In 2003, only 6 per cent of women entrepreneurs had received loans from commercial banks, compared with 14 per cent for male entrepreneurs. On the other hand, a greater proportion of women entrepreneurs received loans from NGO microfinance institutions, with 22 per cent of women receiving funding from these organizations versus 16 per cent of men (Daniels, 2003). Overall, as in most countries, money from women's personal savings and their family's savings represent the main source of capital for starting a business for women in Bangladesh.

Institutional factors have an important impact on the nature and extent of female entrepreneurship. Raihan (2007) notes that while the lack of institutional financing is a problem for most new and small firms, it has a greater impact on women entrepreneurs because they lack other sources of financing. The financing needs of men and women depend not only on socio-economic and sociocultural factors, such as where an entrepreneur lives (rural, semi-urban, urban) and the entrepreneur's educational background, but also on the size and type of the enterprise. A study focusing on tailoring shops (Zohir, 1994) found that women-owned boutiques require short-term loans, with the peak demand during festivals.

The SEDF study (2006) reported that the average size of a loan to a woman-owned enterprise was tk300000.[1] Also, these loans were more likely to be of short-term duration. The average interest rate was 13 per cent. The average time required to process an SME loan was 57 days for male-owned enterprises, in contrast to 145 days for women-owned enterprises. Moreover, the study suggested that women enterprises increase their debt level as the businesses mature. About 46 per cent of women entrepreneurs in the study had approached a financial institution for a loan in the last three years, yet the credit penetration rate was only 5 per cent. However, women-led enterprises were identified in the survey as more likely to borrow money in the next three years (85 per cent of women entrepreneurs reported an intention to borrow).

Chowdhury (2006) notes that the heterogeneity of women entrepreneurs in Bangladesh must be taken into account when addressing their access to financing. The participation of educated women in small business ownership by choice, rather than necessity, is a relatively new phenomenon. In earmarking resources for women-owned SMEs, government policies need to be different for each group.

NATIONAL COMMITMENTS FOR WOMEN'S ENTREPRENEURSHIP

Several national commitments have been made in support of women business owners and their ability to access finance. An analysis of the National Action Plan, Five-Year Plans, the Poverty Reduction Strategy Paper, Industrial Policy and SME Development Policy uncovers several governmental policies that address these issues. These policies provide insights into gaps in macro policies that need to be addressed.

National Action Plan (NAP)

The NAP for Women's Advancement was developed in 1997. Its main objectives to develop women's entrepreneurship were to: (1) adopt a comprehensive and sustainable industrial policy that promotes equity for men and women; (2) increase the number of women entrepreneurs; (3) further develop women's entrepreneurial skills; (4) ensure women's access to markets; (5) provide infrastructure facilities for women entrepreneurs; (6) upgrade women's technical expertise and develop technology suitable for women; and (7) provide linkages with bankers and establish contact with the Ministry of Finance to allocate credit quota for women in the commercial banks (MWCA, 2002).

Five-Year Plans

The importance of women entrepreneurs in Bangladesh was first highlighted in the second Five-Year Plan (1980–85). It recommended the creation of an environment that would foster women's increased participation in the economy by expanding opportunities, training, credit and entrepreneurship development. This policy was carried forward in the third Five-Year Plan (1985–90). With the fourth (1990–95) and fifth (1995–2000) Five-Year Plans, women became eligible for micro credit programs and placed within the context of a macro framework with a multi-sectoral thrust. The fifth Five-Year Plan emphasizes women's legal rights in property inheritance, as well as equal rights to training and credit facilities (MWCA, 2002).

Poverty Reduction Strategy Paper (PRSP)

The PRSP of the Ministry of Planning emphasized entrepreneurship as an important means to women's advancement. It proposed changes to family and inheritance laws to ensure women's equal access to the right to own and inherit property. It also recommended measures to provide access to credit for SMEs. The recommendations related to women entrepreneurs included: (1) to offer one-stop business development services for SMEs; (2) to target women in credit and skill-building programs and projects; (3) to distribute government-owned land (*khas*) in the name of female member of the households; (4) to give women access to local and international markets; (5) to make the banking system more women friendly by introducing innovative collateral provisions for women who do not own land; (6) to provide effective mechanisms for obtaining collateral-free loans from local banks and other sources; (7) to allocate budgetary funds for making small-scale loans to women; and (8) to create a computer portal for women entrepreneurs.

Industrial Policy

Although the NAP, the Five-Year Plans and the PRSP addressed women entrepreneurs, it was not until 2005 that the issue finally received attention in the industrial policies (IPs) of the Ministry of Industries (*IP 2005* and *IP 2009* (draft) – GOB, 2005b, 2008). At that time the Ministry devoted a separate chapter to women entrepreneurs. The IPs considered SMEs a priority sector and a major driving force for industrialization; consequently, assisting women entrepreneurs was given a special priority. Generating productive employment, mainstreaming women into the industrial process and poverty alleviation were underlying objectives of *IP 2005* and *IP 2009* (draft). To improve access to capital for women entrepreneurs in SMEs, both *IP 2005* and *IP 2009* (draft) noted that steps would be taken to offer women entrepreneurs pre-investment advice and assistance in creating and implementing projects. The SME Foundation would provide the necessary assistance and services (such as one-stop service centers for information about product opportunities, credit, market data, legal services and technology). *Industrial Policy 2005* and *IP 2009* (draft) also proposed that: (1) incentives and financial support be considered for women entrepreneurs to establish themselves in small and cottage industries as well as medium enterprises; (2) the government would assess the feasibility of a separate industrial zone for women entrepreneurs, and enforce preferential treatment and quotas for women in new zones and marketplaces; and (3) access to financing for women by financial institutions as well as by government and private banks would be improved. This would entail evaluating and strengthening existing bank programs for women entrepreneurs, arranging collateral-free or group collateral loans, and offering special guarantees for women entrepreneurs. The government would also need to formulate special policy documents pertaining to financing for women entrepreneurs. Public sector technical institutions would create training programs that enhance the efficiency of women entrepreneurs. Finally, the government would remove legal barriers to women's economic and business empowerment, particularly in relation to their participation in enterprises (GOB, 2005a, 2008).

SME Development Policy

SME Policy Strategies 2005 (GOB, 2005a) recommended that women entrepreneurs be accorded preferential treatment wherever appropriate through support to accelerate the retention and promotion of women entrepreneurs. The government identified 11 booster sectors (see Table 2.2). Studies have shown that women entrepreneurs are mainly engaged in

Table 2.2   Booster sector for SMEs

1	Electronics and electrical
2	Software development
3	Light engineering and metal-working
4	Agro-based industry
5	Leather-making and leather goods
6	Knitwear and ready-made garment
7	Plastics and other synthetics
8	Healthcare and diagnostics
9	Educational services
10	Pharmaceuticals/cosmetics/toiletries
11	Fashion-rich personal effects, wear and consumption goods

Source: MOI (2004).

boutiques carrying women's and children's clothing, handicrafts, beauty services, processed food and baked goods. Yet the categories of handicrafts, beauty services and processed food and baked goods remain outside designated booster sectors. In emphasizing financing for small enterprises, the SME Policy Strategy noted that 80 per cent of the total resources available for SMEs would be allocated specifically to small enterprises. Government owned Bangladesh Small Industries and Commerce Bank Limited (BASIC) and privately owned BRAC Bank would work together as lead banks and be responsible for the distribution of credit and venture capital funding in the short run (GOB, 2005b).

Although mainstreaming women entrepreneurs was recognized as a national priority, important policy guidelines like the Prudential Regulations for SME financing of Bangladesh Bank (2004) and the Micro Credit Regulatory Act (2006) of Bangladesh Bank do not have specific regulations concerning women's entrepreneurial development. *Industrial Policy* 2009 (draft) also recommended a one-stop service center and collateral-free loans for women entrepreneurs as strategies to overcome significant barriers to women's economic and business empowerment.

Access to credit, entrepreneurial skills training and markets, in addition to equal legal rights to own property, were the key areas addressed in macro policies. The NAP and PRSP went so far as proposing a quota to measure women's access to credit from commercial banks. A major change in focus in the Five-Year Plans and the PRSP was the introduction of innovative, collateral-free loans for women entrepreneurs. Although the PRSP mentioned one-stop business development services and fiscal incentives, it does not elaborate on these issues.

FINDINGS: BARRIERS IN ACCESS TO FINANCE FOR WOMEN ENTREPRENEURS

A qualitative methodology was used for this study. Data was collected in three ways: a series of in-depth interviews with 10 women entrepreneurs and 10 officials of financial institutions, three focus group discussions consisting of seven or eight women entrepreneurs affiliated with three well-established women's associations, and final validation discussions were held with officials of the SME Foundation, the Bangladesh Bank, and the research division of Dhaka Chamber of Commerce and Industry (DCCI).

Each of the discussions started with a focus on the importance of access to finance for women in SME enterprises. This was followed by a discussion of the barriers faced by women entrepreneurs. Finally, participants were asked about the role of public policy in overcoming barriers women face. The personal and professional backgrounds of each of the women entrepreneurs were also collected, as well as selected characteristics regarding their businesses. Responses led to the identification of two broad themes: demand-side and supply-side constraints in access to institutional finance. Within these themes we developed subcategories of social perceptions and practices, personal and business characteristics, and banking requirements to analyse the responses we received.

Demand-side Barriers

Social perceptions and practices

The concept of women's entrepreneurship is still not well accepted by families or by society in general in Bangladesh. Business is considered a male domain. Very few women enter business with the support of their family; moreover, those who do usually have other family members engaged in the business (BWCCI, 2008). Several of the women entrepreneurs suggested that there is a need to bring about positive attitudinal changes in society regarding women's mobility and work.

The current set of expectations around family obligations also leads to an additional challenge. Women often need to interrupt their careers owing to their family obligations. Business interruption means that the track record of women entrepreneurs often lacks continuity, something that financial capital providers look for while assessing loan applications. The lack of a track record with a bank was reported as a critical problem in pursuing start-up capital.

Culture and society also play into the decisions women make about funding their businesses. The women entrepreneurs we spoke with confirmed a reluctance to take out large loans because of a fear of defaulting.

One female entrepreneur stated, 'Debt is bad and it should be avoided. Business should be expanded from your business earnings'. The representatives from the financial institutions recognized this aversion to debt and reinforced the perception that woman are less bankable than men. One stated:

> When women apply for loan, they often ask for as little as possible. The sectors where women mainly set up their business are not in the SME loan programmes. Women often are not serious about the growth of their business. But women are considered to be creditworthy as their repayment rate is high.

Personal and business characteristics

About 84 per cent of women-owned enterprises in Bangladesh are based at home, compared to 48 per cent of male-owned enterprises (Daniels, 2003). Many women entrepreneurs work from rented property or at home to conserve capital; few women entrepreneurs own land or buildings. This situation was reported as causing several challenges. First, it means that few women can meet the traditional 'collateral requirement' for institutional finance. The women entrepreneurs report being asked to give security for collateral-free loans. This includes post-dated cheques for each payment and one undated cheque for the full value of the loan, including the entire interest payment.

Many of the women entrepreneurs also lack information about credit facilities, financial instruments, business networks and the lending terms of financial institutions. While the system above gives the creditor assurance that claims for repayment could be realized quickly, it also requires six months of bank statements. However, women-owned enterprises usually lack bank accounts in the name of the enterprise and therefore cannot provide cheques in place of collateral.

There is an additional challenge for women entrepreneurs who do receive loans and find it difficult to repay them before their project generates cash flow. Often due to the nature of their business, women report needing a grace period of at least three months to repay the loan. Consequently, women entrepreneurs in Bangladesh often prefer services such as the Micro Industries Development Services (MIDAS) because they offer a two-month grace period.

Restricted networking opportunities is another limitation women experience, women with home-based businesses. Networking by women entrepreneurs can represent an important resource for information about institutional financing. There are about 12 associations of women entrepreneurs recognized by the Dhaka Chamber of Commerce and Industry (DCCI, 2009). The main associations, mostly operating in urban areas, are the National Association of Small Industries of Bangladesh, the Bangladesh Women's Chamber of Commerce and Industries, the Women Entrepreneurs' Association of Bangladesh, the Women Entrepreneurs' Association, the Bangladesh Federation of Entrepreneurs, the Chittagong Women's Chamber of Commerce and Industries, and the Bangladesh Home Workers Women's Association. However, to become a member, women entrepreneurs must have a trade license and tax identification number. Although membership could potentially provide a basis for institutional financing, many urban and rural women business owners are not members of these associations. Furthermore, these women's associations do not have a strong link with industry associations and chambers of commerce. There is also no client database, so it is difficult for loan officers to identify and communicate with women entrepreneurs who might be eligible for loans.

Another networking challenge exists around the building and maintaining of important relationships that support borrowing activities. Women entrepreneurs reported that it takes time to build relationships with the bank manager. Therefore, when new bank managers were hired, the women were apprehensive about delays to the loan approval process.

Supply-side Barriers

The perception of women-owned businesses as being less bankable was confirmed when the respondents from the financial institutions further characterized many women-owned businesses as operating without a trade license, tax identification number or bank account in the name of the enterprise. This situation challenges their traditional business model, given that banks cannot lend to businesses that have no banking history. The one exception was the BRAC Bank, which did not require a banking history and therefore was more accessible for women entrepreneurs.

High administrative costs
Bankers reported that they face higher administration costs with loans to women-owned businesses. This arises as bankers have to spend more time with women entrepreneurs to complete the application forms and gather the relevant information. Financial institutions need reliable information about a firm's cash flow in order to assess its ability to repay loans, particularly collateral-free loans. However, financial transactions and books of accounts are often not well documented in women-owned enterprises in Bangladesh. Financial institutions must therefore undertake extra time and expenditure to assess the track record of the enterprise and its credit

worthiness. The higher cost of loans is also connected to the fact that women-owned businesses are generally small, and the business owners are generally pursuing small loans. The bankers we spoke with also indicated a reluctance to lend to women entrepreneurs because of a slow and costly legal process that results in the case of a loan default. The combination of small loans at a high administration cost was seen as a major challenge to a capital provider.

Our banker participants further considered women entrepreneurs as high-risk borrowers because they lack collateral. Women entrepreneurs represent (or are viewed as representing) activities in the informal sector, which means they deal with cash transactions, may lack bookkeeping skills, and engage in businesses with little growth potential. These factors combine to make them risky to bankers. In addition, most women entrepreneurs in SMEs do not have a credit history, so there is no Credit Information Bureau (CIB) report on them. Although the Bangladesh Bank circular has set tk100000 as the lower limit for collateral-free loans, none of the financial institutions surveyed provided such loans. For loans of tk100000, the Bangladesh Bank would find it burdensome to provide CIB reports; thus, it discourages financial institutions from providing such small loans.

Largely due to reasons such as the perception of risk and the cost of administration, women-owned businesses often face a high interest rate. Most women consider the rate of interest to be unaffordable at 15 to 18 per cent. Bangladesh Bank reports testing other models, including collateral-free loans, under a refinancing scheme with an interest rate for women entrepreneurs set at 10 per cent. However, very few women entrepreneurs had received such loans and, notably, the bankers opined that this rate does not allow them to cover the cost of administering and monitoring the loans. It was further suggested that if the development partners could provide grants for financing women entrepreneurs, then Bangladesh Bank could charge a 2 per cent bank rate from financial institutions.

Complex loan process
Women entrepreneurs also report a long and complicated loan process, largely due to the many documents required for the loan application (see Table 2.3). A survey of SMEs in Bangladesh noted that entrepreneurs have to make approximately 15 visits for one bank loan, as compared to three visits for loans from informal money lenders and 2.25 visits for loans from relatives and friends (Choudhury and Raihan, 2000). Studies on boutiques show that their owners turn to moneylenders during festivals due to complexity of the loan process (Zohir, 1994).

Table 2.3   List of documents required for collateral free loans

1	Two years valid Trade License/Certificate of incorporation
2	Tax Identification Number (TIN)
3	For limited Company, copy of the Memorandum and Article of Association of the Company and Incorporation.
4	For partnership, copy of partnership agreement.
5	Income statement from bank where the entrepreneur maintains a current account
6	One year bank statement of the enterprise
7	Statement of sales, purchases, inventory, and balance sheet
8	Statement of loans if any
9	For rented premise, then copy of two years agreement for rental.
10	Four copies of loan applications
11	Project profile/business plan
12	Credit Information Bureau (CIB) report from Bangladesh Bank
13	Clearance certificate from the electricity office
14	Nationality certificate/voter ID card

Source: Information obtained from financial institutions.

Guarantors as security

One of the most significant barriers women entrepreneurs face, as reported by the women we spoke with, concerns the practice of financial institutions needing two personal guarantors as securities. These individuals must have a substantial savings account; one must be the woman's spouse and the other must be another family member. In an ongoing study by MIDAS, it was noted that in Rajshahi, one husband refused to be a guarantor for a loan for his spouse. The women entrepreneurs considered this to be the most significant barrier in their access to institutional finance.

Finally, a common problem reported by the financial institutions is that after a loan is sanctioned to a woman-owned enterprise, it is often later discovered that men managed the enterprise. While this challenges the nature of the 'special' programs for women business owners, it also creates challenges for the banks' relationship managers – who face difficulties in collecting loan repayment installments from these enterprises.

Overall, the primary demand side obstacles are based on societal perception, gender roles, the home-based nature of the businesses, restricted information and networks. The supply side barriers result from high administrative costs and high risk, owing to a lack of collateral. It is also time-consuming to deal with women entrepreneurs; there is a complex loan process and an extensive list of requirements that banks demand, including a banking history, long-term relationships with bank managers and the need to have a spouse guarantee a loan.

RECOMMENDATIONS FOR CHANGE

Solutions focused on social perceptions and practices, the characteristics of women business owners and their enterprises, and banking practices can be identified from both the demand perspective (stemming from women entrepreneurs) and the supply-side perspective (from those providing institutional financing). A comprehensive and forward-looking policy package is needed to promote the growth of a vibrant women-owned SME sector in Bangladesh. It should lay the groundwork for changing how women entrepreneurs are perceived – not only by their families and financial institutions, but also by themselves. Interviews with women entrepreneurs and representatives of financial institutions highlighted the need for two broad strategies for the sixth Five-Year Plan. The first is to improve financial procedures; the second is to enhance the capabilities and expertise of women entrepreneurs. The specific interventions we suggest are discussed below.

Improve Financial Procedure

A fundamental policy weakness is the lack of an official definition of women entrepreneurs in SMEs. Financial institutions have interpreted a Bangladesh Bank document as defining women business owners as women who are sole proprietors, or own more than half of a partnership or private company. Although most women entrepreneurs are sole proprietors of their companies, in Bangladesh it is common for partnerships and private companies to list wives, mothers or daughters as partners or directors (in order to avoid taxes). This means that financial institutions assume that women are not actually the entrepreneurs themselves. Since it is difficult for financial institutions to determine the exact share of ownership held by women, businesses are often considered 'women fronted enterprises.'

It would be more helpful to combine 'micro' and 'small' enterprises together and reclassify the SMEs as 'MSMEs'. This new category would make the SME growth strategy more favorable to poor women on the outer margins of the business world. These new definitions could be used to anchor a new and necessary national database that provides profiles of women entrepreneurs. Further, as part of its monitoring, the Bangladesh Bank should ensure that financial institutions provide gender-based statistics.

Clarifying the definition of women entrepreneurs and organizing data collection is an important start. The *Industrial Policy 2005* and *Industrial Policy 2009* (draft) also presented a need to integrate women into all SME financing instruments. Proposals addressed the bank level as well as the level of the individual woman-owned business. To counter the bias held by many bankers that women-owned SMEs are high risk, often due to their small size and home-based situation, the government could provide credit guarantee schemes for women-owned SMEs that would compensate lenders against the risk of borrower default and ensure repayment. Other proposals included collateral-free loans, lower rates of interest, smaller loan sizes, three-month grace periods for the start of repayment and spouse guarantor-free loans.

It was also suggested that the Bangladesh Bank should oversee loan refinancing to ensure that these requirements are being met. It should ensure that if at least 10 per cent of the funds are not disbursed to women entrepreneurs, financial institutions would not be eligible for refinancing. Additionally, the Bangladesh Bank should promulgate guidelines for financial institutions and training programs for lending officers. The Bangladesh Bank should also ensure that the directive regarding recruitment of women in the NCBs is enforced, so as to increase the number of women in banking.

To further support lending, the government could offer grants to subsidize SMEs. The Bangladesh Bank has already established several directives, including collateral-free loans of tk2 500 000 at an interest rate of 10 per cent, a special 15 per cent fund for women entrepreneurs and 100 per cent refinancing. Further, the Bangladesh Bank could lower its interest rate, provide loans to the financial institutions at a rate of two per cent and establish an 80 per cent target for women-owned businesses in the manufacturing cluster.

Moreover, the Bangladesh Bank could support the development of other means of funding for women-owned enterprises. For instance, the government could provide loan guarantees or lines of credit to support lending to women-owned businesses. Other government measures like the Entrepreneurship Equity Fund could be enlarged and the private sector could be encouraged to develop venture capital funds to support women-owned businesses with a high growth potential. Other financial products such as domestic factoring and credit wholesaling could also be advanced.

Women need to be educated about these programs in order to make informed decisions about how to use them. Overall, financial products need to be customized by the SME department to meet the needs of women entrepreneurs and their SMEs, with the goal being to bring the bank to the doorsteps of the women entrepreneurs. One way to approach this is through the development of an office to support women-owned businesses and locate it within local government agencies. These offices could be particularly helpful in granting women trade licenses more cheaply and efficiently.

Finally, the Ministry of Finance needs to allocate special funding to facilitate linkages between women entrepreneurs and financial institutions. The Women Entrepreneurs' Forum in the SME Foundation could be a platform for creating an environment that encourages entrepreneurship. The SME Foundation could provide a one-stop service and complementary website that offers information about credit, markets, legal services and technology for women entrepreneurs.

Enhancing Capabilities

Change in societal practices is critical to ensuring women's legal rights regarding business ownership. Macro policies should ensure equal rights in property and inheritance by amending family and inheritance laws. They should also ensure access to information and skills, managerial training, financing, markets, technology and government owned land (*khas*).

Networking with women entrepreneurs' organizations and the Women's Entrepreneurship Forum at the SME Foundation would improve women's access to information about financing. The Women Entrepreneurship Forum, in collaboration with the SME Foundation, has tried to facilitate access to business resources, services and information for existing and potential entrepreneurs. One goal of the Women's Entrepreneurship Forum is to ensure that the Gender Action Plan is actually implemented.

Role models are critical to the advancement of women's business ownership. Associations of women entrepreneurs and the SME Foundation have begun to recognize successful women entrepreneurs. Also, DHL Express, the *Daily Star*, and the DCCI have recognized women's entrepreneurship through the Bangladesh Business Award. Financial institutions acknowledge the importance of these awards by giving loans to the winners on a priority basis. This kind of recognition needs to be taken more seriously by women's organizations as a strategic way to facilitate access to institutional finance. The inclusion of women in relevant business organizations also needs to increase, including organizations such as the Business Forum, the board of directors of the SME Foundation and various committees that focus upon SMEs.

Awareness of the resources available to women needs to be built into other areas as well. Women entrepreneurs should increase public awareness about the availability of loans for SMEs. They should publicize the problems of access to financing in the media, and organize workshops for improving women's access to finance. In the field of education, an entrepreneurial component could be included at all levels of training programs and in the secondary education system. Further training on entrepreneurial and business skills could be delivered at the district levels through business development centers. These educational strategies should include technology and design centers, as well as training on international business basics. Finally, women entrepreneurs need to undertake advocacy programs with banks and policy-makers.

CONCLUSION

This chapter considers how public policy can address the barriers faced by women entrepreneurs in gaining access to institutional financing in Bangladesh. Policy-makers and researchers in Bangladesh have noted that access to finance is the most critical factor for women entrepreneurs in SMEs. Despite several commitments made by the government to advance gender equality, women entrepreneurs in SMEs face barriers in obtaining institutional financing. Challenges can be seen on both the demand side and the supply side, as issues relating to social perceptions and practices, personal and business characteristics, and banking requirements. Interviews with women entrepreneurs and bank representatives offered two broad strategies for the sixth Five-Year Plan: the first is to improve financial procedures; the second is to enhance the capabilities and expertise of women entrepreneurs. A comprehensive and proactive policy package addressing these issues needs to be developed to support a vibrant women-owned SME sector in Bangladesh.

NOTE

1.   In 2010, US$1 = tk70 approx.

REFERENCES

Acs, Z., P. Arenius, M. Hay and M. Minniti (2005), *2004 Global Entrepreneurship Monitor Executive Report*, Babson Park, MA, and London: Babson College and London Business School.

Ahmed, M.U. (2008), 'The women SME entrepreneurs and business leaders of Bangladesh speaks for themselves', paper presented at the second national SME Women entrepreneurs conference, SME Foundation, Dhaka, Bangladesh, February.

Allen I.E., A. Elam, N. Langowitz and M. Dean (2008), *Global Entrepreneurship Monitor: 2007 Report on Women and Entrepreneurship*, available at: www.gem-consortium.org (accessed 15 January 2011). Bangladesh Bureau of Statistics (BBS) (2008), *Report on Labour Force Survey 2005–06*, BBS, April.

Bangladesh Women Chamber of Commerce (BWCCI) (2008), 'Building women in business: a situation analysis of women entrepreneurs in Bangladesh', paper released by Bangladesh Women Chamber of Commerce and Industry in cooperation with The Center for International Private Enterprise, February.

Brush, C.G., N.M. Carter, E. Gatewood, P.G. Greene and M. Hart (eds) (2006), *Growth Oriented Women Entrepreneurs and Their Businesses: A Global Research Perspective*, Cheltenham, UK and Northampton, MA: Edward Elgar Publishing.

Carter, N.M., C.B. Brush, E.J. Gatewood, P.G. Greene and M.M. Hart (2003), 'Financing entrepreneurship: is gender an issue?', in The Center for Economic Progress (ed.), *Critical Junctures in Women's Economic Lives: A Collection of Symposium Papers*, Minneapolis, MN: The Center for Economic Progress, pp. 45–51.

Chowdhury, N (2006), 'Creating a gender action plan for women entrepreneurship: stanching financing, marketing, technology and mindset gaps', paper presented at The First National SME Women Entrepreneurs Conference, Dhaka, Bangladesh, 2 August.

Choudhury, T.A and A. Raihan (2000), 'Structural adjustment participatory review initiative Bangladesh, study theme 2(C): implications of financial sector reforms', The World Bank, Government of Bangladesh and Civil Society, Dhaka, Bangladesh.

Daniels, L. (2003), *National Private-Sector Survey of Enterprises in Bangladesh*, conducted by International Consulting Group in association with MIDAS and HB Consultants Ltd, available at: www.jobstrust.org/. . ./Sl%2033.%20Natinal%20Private%20Sector%20Survey.pdf (accessed 11 August 2011).

Dhaka Chamber of Commerce and Industry (DCCI) (2009), *Women Entrepreneurs' Directory 2009*, Dhaka: Dhaka Chamber of Commerce and Industry.

Government of the People's Republic of Bangladesh (GOB) (2005a), *Policy Strategies for Development of Small and Medium Enterprises (SME)*, Dhaka: SME Cell, Ministry of Industries, Government of the People's Republic of Bangladesh.

Government of the People's Republic of Bangladesh (GOB) (2005b) *Industrial Policy 2005*, Dhaka: Ministry of Industries, Government of the People's Republic of Bangladesh.

Government of the People's Republic of Bangladesh (GOB) (2008), *Industrial Policy 2009* (draft), Dhaka: Ministry of Industries, Government of the People's Republic of Bangladesh.

Greene, P.G., C.G. Brush and E.J. Gatewood (2006), 'Perspectives on women entrepreneurs: past findings and new directions', in M. Minnitti (ed.), *Praeger Perspectives on Entrepreneurship*, Westport, CT: Praeger, pp. 181–204.

Islam, K.M. Nabiul, S.C. Zohir and M. Hossain (2010), 'Institutional financing for women entrepreneurs in SME', in *SME Development in Bangladesh with Emphasis on Policy Constraints and Financing*, Background Studies for the Sixth Five Year Plan (2011–2015), no. 03, Bangladesh Institute of Development Studies, June.

Kelley, D., N. Bosma, N. and J.E. Amoró (2010), *Global Entrepreneurship Monitor*

2010 Global Report, available at: www.gemconsortium.org (accessed 15 January 2011).

Minnitti, M., P. Arenius and N. Langowitz (2005), *Global Entrepreneurship Monitor: 2004 Report on Women and Entrepreneurship*, Babson Park, MA and London: Babson College and London Business School.

Minnitti, M. (ed.) (2006), *Praeger Perspectives on Entrepreneurship*, Westport, CT: Praeger.

Ministry of Industries (MOI) (2004), 'Small and medium enterprises (SME) development in Bangladesh: a reasoned approach to letting SMEs count', The Taskforce on Small and Medium Enterprises, Ministry of Industries, Government of the People's Republic of Bangladesh.

Ministry of Women and Children's Affairs (MWCA) (2002), *Assessment of the Implications of Policies and Measures for Women Entrepreneurship Development in Bangladesh*, Dhaka: Ministry of Women and Children Affairs, Government of the People's Republic of Bangladesh.

Power and Participation Research Center (PPRC) (2006), *Local Business Dynamics: Ground Realities and Policies Challenges*, Dhaka: PPRC.

Raihan, A. (2007), 'Improving access to finance for women-owned SMEs', in F. Welter (ed.), *Handbook on Women-owned SMEs, Challenges and Opportunities in Policies and Programmes*, Malmö, Sweden: IKED-GKP, pp. 19–46.

South Asia Enterprise Development Facility (SEDF) (2006), *Results of the Banking Survey of the SME Market in Bangladesh: Final Report*, Dhaka, Bangladesh: South Asia Enterprise Development Facility.

Zohir, S. (1994), 'Financing of tailoring shops owned by women in Dhaka', *Small Firms Informally Financed – Studies from Bangladesh*, World Bank Discussion papers 153.

3. Academic women's entrepreneurship in Spain and Scotland: a multilevel institutional approach

M. Mar Fuentes-Fuentes, Sarah Y. Cooper and Ana M. Bojica*

INTRODUCTION

Despite the increasing research on female entrepreneurs, a more substantial comprehension of women's entrepreneurship in specific environments such as universities is still needed. In today's knowledge-based economy, universities and research institutes are seen as important actors in regional growth. Academic entrepreneurship, which involves the creation of new spin-off ventures to commercialize the results of academic research, has become an important objective for many universities (Wright et al., 2007). University spin-offs are a significant class of firms because they represent an economically powerful subset of high-technology start-ups (Shane, 2004).

Several studies have shown that although the number of women academics has significantly grown in recent decades, their involvement in the creation of spin-offs seems to be quite limited (Alcalá et al., 2007; Landry et al., 2006; Lowe and González-Brambila, 2007; Murray and Graham, 2007; Rosa and Dawson, 2006). Previous studies that explore the extent to which women are represented in the commercialization of science through disclosures and patents, as well as research into factors that influence the initialization of university start-ups, highlight three main inhibiting factors. First, structural factors, such as a lower presence of women academics in scientific areas closer to applied research (Bunker-Whittington and Smith-Doerr, 2005) and apparent barriers to the advancement of women into senior positions, have an impact (Bailyn, 2003; Rosser and Lane, 2002). Second, there are factors related to accessing resources, including financial, human or social capital (Mosey and Wright, 2008;

Rosa and Dawson, 2006; Stephan and El-Ganainy, 2007). Third, factors related to the social construction of gender and the stereotypes that surround it play a role; these include the traditional gender roles which assign more household chores to women (Etezkowitz et al., 2000; Ledin et al., 2007), the conflict between family life and work (Shaw and Cassell, 2007), gender profiles that present women as having greater risk aversion, a lower level of interest in money and financial transactions, and different attitudes towards competition (Niederle and Vesterlund, 2005; Stephan and El-Ganainy, 2007).

As spin-offs represent an important mechanism for technology and knowledge transfer (Steffensen et al., 1999), understanding the elements that favour or inhibit spin-off creation for academic women becomes fundamental for universities and can assist universities in utilizing all of their available human potential. On the other hand, compared with other commercialization options, such as patents and the licensing of patents, spin-off creation entails additional difficulties. As Vanaelst et al. (2006: 249) affirm: 'the decision to create a spinout challenges the researchers since they have to enter a business community that is different from the scientific one in which they have been active'. Therefore, if women have traditionally encountered obstacles to becoming entrepreneurs, it is important to understand the extent to which existing university policies and actions provide women with the necessary support to face typical business challenges.

Adopting an institutional theory approach, this study seeks to offer a more holistic understanding of the participation of academic women in the commercialization of science through spin-off creation. Academic women are embedded in the meso-environment of university structures, norms and policies. Furthermore, this meso-environment and the micro-institutional processes it encloses are also embedded within a wider macro-institutional environment (Brush et al., 2009; Emirbayer and Mische, 1998). By drawing on this framework, we seek to identify the factors that affect academic women's decisions to become involved in spin-off creation.

The desire to explore these factors in depth has led us to use an inductive empirical research approach at the University of Edinburgh (Scotland) and the University of Granada (Spain). A multiple-case design, including in-depth interviews with female academic entrepreneurs and the people responsible for Technology Transfer Offices (TTOs) and incubators in both universities, was used in an attempt to provide a more accurate account. We have focused specifically on academic women, and avoided comparisons with men, in our approach to the phenomenon.

THEORETICAL BACKGROUND: INSTITUTIONAL THEORY AND ACADEMIC WOMEN ENTREPRENEURS

Institutional theory asserts that individual behaviour is framed within established structures of meaning. These structures entail a web of socially constructed, taken-for-granted prescriptions of appropriate conduct, named 'institutions' (Greenwood and Suddaby, 2006; Scott, 2001). Institutions are 'constraints that shape human interaction' (North, 1990: 3), consisting of symbolic elements, social activities and material resources which create legal, moral and cultural boundaries (Scott, 2001). They offer the means to explain social conformity and reduce uncertainty, by establishing a stable structure for human interaction (Delbridge and Edwards, 2007). Institutions can be both formal (laws, political and economic rules) and informal (such as the culture of a given society, values and norms). Following the framework for women entrepreneurs developed by Brush et al. (2009), we identify two institutional levels that surround and mediate the entrepreneurial activity of academic women: the macro- and meso-environments.

The *macro-environment* refers to policies and social, cultural and institutional arrangements at the national level (Brush et al., 2009). It includes the macro-structures that frame gender roles and responsibilities within a society (Kantor, 2002). These structures not only shape how women perceive entrepreneurial opportunities, but also how the rest of the society perceives women entrepreneurs. Bruni et al. (2004) suggest that the way that women are viewed in society presents a major barrier for female entrepreneurs. Almost all cultures attribute domestic and family responsibilities to women. Household composition, gendered power relations and inequalities within the household account for differences in the entrepreneurial activity of men and women (Aldrich and Cliff, 2003). Owing to a lack of adequate professional and social support for raising children, maternity is a choice that harms women's professional aspirations. It imposes a dead-stop on a professional career that encounters obstacles from the very beginning (Alcalá et al., 2007), as women, and specifically women entrepreneurs, have to work hard to convince people that they are as competent as men (Bates, 2002). Furthermore, the gendered stereotyping of professions often leads women to choose specific careers that fit with their socially constructed roles and responsibilities (Blau et al., 2002). To successfully manage both career and household, women must demonstrate particular skills and achieve an appropriate work–life balance, for which they also need the support of their families and closest friends (Lituchy et al., 2003).

Specific research on female academics has emphasized that despite significant advances over the past 20 years, women usually have more domestic responsibilities than men. This equates to slower professional progress or an end to their careers (Forster, 2000). Shaw and Cassell (2007) suggest that women academics still experience a conflict between family life and work. Additionally, Rosa and Dawson (2006) observe inhibiting factors for women that relate to reconciling their family and professional lives.

In turning to the second institutional level, we define the *meso-environment* as the closer context in which women are embedded. This intermediate institution between the individual and the macro-environment includes university structures, norms and policies, and also the professional and social networks or formal academic associations that women take part in.

Prior research emphasizes structural elements of the academic environment as inhibitors to women's academic entrepreneurship. Although the proportion of academic women has increased significantly in recent decades, women continue to occupy less visible positions within academia (Alcalá et al., 2007; Rosa & Dawson, 2006). With regards to social capital and the establishment of entrepreneurial networks, some studies have identified gender differences in the development and management of networks (Aldrich, 1989; Olm et al., 1988). Forster (2000) indicates that a lack of mentors and the greater institutional power that men possess are two key factors that hinder the career progress of women academics. Alternatively, Stephan and El-Ganainy (2007) affirm that although there is little data to examine the hypothesis that women are excluded from academic social networks, their minimal presence as advisers on scientific committees for public companies and the fact that women rarely start companies are indicators of such exclusion. Noordenbos (2002) suggests there are very few women in scientific academies and argues this is partly due to the existence of closed social networks of men. Papers by Morley (1994) and Rhodes (1994) identify other difficulties for women academics that are less visible to the academy. For instance, women are excluded from groups and clubs, are required to adopt a 'masculine style' to ensure promotion, and are stereotyped in certain kinds of roles.

Regarding our last level of analysis, the *individual level,* prior research on the entrepreneurial activities of female academics emphasizes several factors that can impact their decision to create a spin-off: motivations, human capital (training and previous experience) and social capital (personal social networks).

In considering the motivations of female academics for creating spin-offs, studies by Cunningham and Lischeron (1991) and Birley (1989) demonstrate that, in general, there do not seem to be differences in men's and women's motivation to undertake entrepreneurial tasks. This includes both the process they follow when setting up businesses and the structure businesses take. Most research shows that individuals undertake entrepreneurial work in order to find satisfaction in their work, personal achievement, and greater autonomy and independence. Rosa and Dawson (2006) do not find significant differences between men and women in either their level of satisfaction as founders of spin-offs or in their perceptions of the difficulty of doing so (even though women find it more stressful and more difficult to combine their multiple obligations and responsibilities). On the other hand, academic women have been found to have greater risk aversion, possibly a lower level of interest in profit and financial transactions, and different attitudes towards competition (Niederle and Vesterlund, 2005). Studies also indicate that women have a lower predisposition to sell scientific achievements and a lower likelihood to seek business opportunities; women are also less likely to focus on research that offers opportunities for commercialization (Babcock and Laschever, 2003).

Concerning the role of human capital in academic women's decisions to create spin-offs, previous research suggests that a lack of experience in business, administration and management may influence women's confidence in starting a business, even when they possess high levels of scientific training (Rosa and Dawson, 2006). Moreover, academic entrepreneurs with less experience find structural gaps between their scientific research networks and those of industry; this restricts these women's capacity to recognize opportunities (Mosey and Wright, 2008). Further, women have traditionally had less exposure to commercial activity. However, the quality and impact of the commercial studies by women are the same as or better than those of male scientists (Allen et al., 2007).

Finally, human and social capital are related factors that impact women's ability to successfully recognize opportunities for exploiting university knowledge. For instance, Mosey and Wright's (2008) study of academics involved in technology-based firms in the UK found that academic entrepreneurs who have prior experience as owners of businesses also have larger social networks, and are therefore more effective in developing networks with experienced managers and potential investors.

METHODOLOGY

Research Design

While above we have presented a review of the research that has been conducted on female academic entrepreneurship, there is nonetheless a strong need for further work in this area. Consequently, our choice of inductive multiple-case design is an appropriate method of analysis (Yin, 2003), as it enables us to obtain a rich understanding of the factors that influence the participation of academic women in spin-offs or start-ups. The level of analysis for this study is the university; the unit of analysis is academic female entrepreneurs. This group is understood as those women, whether professors or researchers at a university, who are involved in the creation and development of a university spin-off or start-up. We define a university spin-off as a venture created by at least one professor or researcher around a core innovation or research result, which is initially developed at the university (Vohora et al., 2004).

Case Selection

Our research consists of a detailed field study that involves the participation of female academic entrepreneurs who were involved in initiating a university start-up or spin-off at the University of Granada, Spain and the University of Edinburgh, Scotland. We also consider the related institutional conditions prevailing within these two universities, as well as their wider macro-environments. Both cases were selected according to the criteria of literal replication (Yin, 2003); consequently, we expected similar results from both universities. Literal replication logic within the theoretical framework of institutional analysis refers to the similarities or differences between different factors belonging to the macro-institutional environment. These factors include gender policies, job segregation, gender pay gap, maternity leave, paternity leave and women's participation in the economy.

At the macro-level, Scotland and Spain represent environments with similar socio-economic conditions. The position of women in Spanish society is similar to the position of women in Scotland, as there have been significant changes in Spain during the past decade that have resulted from numerous reforms and new programmes (including positive discrimination by the Spanish government).[1] Despite the advances in legislation and the increasing participation of women in the economy,[2] women are still perceived in both countries in stereotypical terms (as primarily responsible for the home and family). Spain and Scotland experience significant occupational segregation, both horizontally and vertically.[3] According to the Spanish National Institute of Statistics, women represent only 27.7 per cent of doctoral students in engineering and technology and 26.5 per cent of PhDs in these fields. The Scottish government also acknowledges that women's participation in technology-based sectors is significantly low, as only one fourth of the women trained in the areas of science, engineering and technology are presently employed in these occupations (including academia). With regard to the politics of childcare, maternity leave in Scotland is double the length of that in Spain, yet paternity leave is essentially the same in the two countries (14 days in Scotland and 13 days in Spain). These data lead us to conclude that the macro-structures that surround the construction of gender in these two societies are similar. Therefore we can apply replication logic in these two cases.

At the meso-level, both universities were founded nearly 500 years ago and have a long tradition of academic and research excellence. Both are ranked in the top ten universities domestically. Employment rights for university staff are similar within each institution; promotion is heavily influenced by research quality, measured using traditional standards such as publications in leading journals and research income secured, rather than alternative measures, such as research impact or engagement in technology transfer. Moreover, the two universities have very similar structures for knowledge commercialization activities (TTOs, pre-incubators and incubators).

Data Collection

Data was collected using in-depth, face-to-face, semi-structured interviews with academic female entrepreneurs, the directors of the technology transfer offices, the managers of the business incubators, and other employees who develop and administer programmes and systems to support entrepreneurial academics. The interviews were held between July 2009 and April 2010. Interviews are a highly efficient way to collect rich empirical data, especially when the phenomenon of interest is episodic and infrequent, as with female academic entrepreneurship. Using different informants limits bias and gathers diverse perspectives on the phenomenon (Eisenhardt and Graebner, 2007). Following Eisenhardt (1989), we first collected background data for both universities. We also gathered information prepared by the respective universities and published in the media and on websites.

In the first phase of the research, we asked those in charge of firm creation at each university for a list of firms that they defined as spin-offs or start-ups founded by women, whether alone or in teams. There were six firms provided by the University of Edinburgh and 12 provided by the University of Granada that were created either partially or entirely by women. Second, we collected background information about these companies and their founders from their websites. We then checked this information with staff in charge of commercialization activities at the universities. The information obtained permitted us to determine the different kinds of connections that existed between the women founders and the universities, as well as the kind of business activity developed. In accordance with our focus on female academics and university researchers, we selected only those firms in which the female entrepreneurs were academics or researchers supported by the university (see Table 3.1).

We also conducted several interviews with individuals responsible for knowledge commercialization and business creation at the two universities and the entities involved. Four people were interviewed at the University of Edinburgh: the director of Launch.ed, the director and manager of the Edinburgh Pre-Incubator Scheme (EPIS) programme, and the director of Company Formation and Incubation. At the University of Granada, we held separate interviews with the director of Technology Transfer Office (OTRI) and the person responsible for the area of business creation. Since the University of Granada had a collaboration agreement with the incubator – Business Innovation Centre (BIC) – we interviewed the director and the managers there together.

FINDINGS

Following the theoretical framework adopted, we analysed the factors that affect academic women's involvement in spin-off creation at three different levels: the macro-institutional level, the meso-institutional level and the individual level.

Macro Level

The macro structures that frame gender roles and women's responsibilities within society can affect the decision of academic women to become entrepreneurs. Our findings affirm this. The prevailing cultural roles regarding women's responsibility in caring for family and children also seem to impact the career paths women choose. Some of our interview data gathered on this issue suggests that women academics perceive university teaching and research as a comfortable choice that enables them to reconcile family and professional life. This may also explain the low entrepreneurial orientation of women in the university environment. As Entrepreneur 3 from Granada states:

> I think that this is what makes women less decided to face something that we don't know how much will require of our time [creating a business]. You always keep part of your time for something that you consider important, because it is something that has been instilled into your head as important since you were a child: your children, your husband. While they [men] don't take this aspect into account. They don't have the consciousness to keep time for their wife and children.

Table 3.1   Summary of the academic women's and spin-off companies' characteristics from the universities of Edinburgh and Granada

Academic women entrepreneurs	Marital status	Children	Age	Academic background	Years of experience	Start-up year	Main activity of spin-off	Number of initial founders and gender profile	CEO
Entrepreneur 1 (Edinburgh)	Single	0	40–49	PhD in Zoology	15	2004	Disease and pest control	1	Yes
Entrepreneur 2 (Edinburgh)	Married	3	30–39	PhD in Artificial Intelligence	15	2006	Artificial intelligence	1	Yes
Entrepreneur 3 (Granada)	Married	3	50–59	PhD in Pharmacy	25	2007	Biotechnology	3 (1 woman and 2 men)	No
Entrepreneur 4 (Granada)	Married	0	20–29	PhD in Business Administration	4	2009	Social consultancy	4 (2 women and 2 men)	No

Moreover, adherence to traditional roles that assign household and child-care to the woman frequently leads to situations where the woman is the one to give up her career ambitions (which may include the creation of a spin-off). Entrepreneur 2 from Edinburgh says:

I've seen women at my age or even younger that have to make a decision, which normally is one or the other [be an academic within the university or create and manage a spin-off], and they generally take the safe route that is their work within the university; yes, a colleague from Aberdeen didn't create her own business because of this . . . My husband was the completely opposite, he quit his job in London to come and follow me with my firm, because it had more potential . . . And this is rare.

Maternity itself seems to be an obstacle for both the creation and management of spin-offs. The need to be able to obtain financial resources in moments of economic difficulty for the firm, and to be seen as credible by investors and clients, led Entrepreneur 2 from Edinburgh to conceal her last pregnancy. Furthermore, being the one who gives birth, which requires at least a temporary pause in the professional career, can lead women to decide to give up professional ambitions. Entrepreneur 2 (Edinburgh) notes, 'It is very hard for a woman to say, "I take the responsibility of you quitting your job and of both maternity and my career" . . . Because if it doesn't work [then] neither of them has a job.'

Finally, these social constructions around the gender roles women carry can lead women to see the business world, and the option of becoming an entrepreneur, as a domain for men. Entrepreneur 1 (Edinburgh) observes:

I know very few women that have. I think I would say definitely in Scotland, and I think probably anywhere, the business community is still very much dominated by men and always will be. I suppose women want to go off and have families and get stuck at home, etc. It's just not seen to be the kind of women's world, and the women you do get in it tend to be quite . . . kind of thrusting . . . kind of, 'I've got to make a point because I'm not a man' type thing, which I don't really like.

Meso Level

The university's institutional environment plays a decisive role in firm creation by academic entrepreneurs, due to the policies, support programmes, and resources made available to them. Further, the archival data we collected shows that the University of Edinburgh has a much better infrastructure as well as technical and human resources to support entrepreneurial activities than does the University of Granada. The University of Edinburgh also has a history of focused commercialization activity that spans more than 40 years. Consequently, the number of patents, contracts for licences and spin-offs or start-ups created is higher at the University of Edinburgh. Contrary to what we would expect, however, 12 (20 per cent) of the total number of the spin-off or start-up firms created at the University of Granada were founded by women; this is true for only 6 (4 per cent) at the University of Edinburgh (see Table 3.2).

These results cannot be explained by the specific actions of either of the two universities. Neither university has established special policies or programmes for women to provide incentives for either knowledge commercialization activities, in general, or the creation of spin-offs, in particular. Both universities do seem, however, to be aware of the lower number of women entrepreneurs. As one of the staff members responsible for the company formation and incubation area at the University of Edinburgh indicated, 'There hasn't been, to be honest. It's interesting, because most of my staff is female'. A discussion regarding the breakdown of the patents by gender at the OTRI of the University of Granada generated the following comment: 'To tell the truth, we have never done such a study, so I can't give you any data [regarding a gender analysis].'

When we consider other factors that might influence the number of firms established by women academics, we do not find differences between the two universities with regards to the proportion of academic women by area, as representation is similarly low in the areas of engineering, science and technology. Moreover, we do not find differences in the higher ranks of academia, where the probability of creating a spin-off is greater.

We may be able to attribute the greater number of firms created by women at the University of Granada to two factors. First, the University of Edinburgh has more experience in knowledge transfer activities and a narrower focus, as it only considers firms related to the areas of science and technology. This is not the case at the University of Granada, where 11 of the 12 firms created by women identified in this study are associated with activities related to the social sciences or consulting. Second, at the University of Granada, collaboration with the regional government provides an additional source of support that leads to greater heterogeneity in the firms created.

Individual Level

Previous literature has highlighted several key 'pull' and 'push' factors that impact academic spin-off behaviour, including: the desire to bring research into practice, the desire for wealth and the desire for independence (Shane, 2004). Almost all of the entrepreneurs expressed these motivations, either directly or indirectly. We wish to emphasize, however, that

Table 3.2   Summary of commercialization activities of universities of Granada and Edinburgh

	University of Granada	University of Edinburgh
Year of foundation	1531	1583
Students	63 106	27 618
Academic staff (faculty)	3761	3751
Women academic staff (faculty)	1343	1565
Degrees	Undergraduate:75; Postgraduate: 116 research, 181 taught	Undergraduate: 600; Postgraduate: 250 research, 300 taught
Start of commer-cialization activities	OTRI opened in 1989	1969. One of first UK commercialization offices
Infrastructure (physical resources)	Does not have own pre-incubator or incubator. Agreement to use the pre-incubator and incubator of the regional govern-ment, which are located in the Science Park.	Pre-incubator Incubator
Support programmes and resources to set up spin-offs	Programmes for doctoral students in science and technology. Business consultancy through an agreement with the regional government. Financial support for legal setting-up and website expenses	Programmes for students in science and technological areas. EPIS programme (mentoring, financial support, consultancy to set up the company). Company training and consolidation programmes (consultancy, investors, training and financial support).
Policies in equity participation	Yes, in spin-out Not in start-ups	Yes, in spin-out Not in start-ups
Disclosures*+	90 (last 5 calendar years)	580 (last 5 academic years)
Patents (filed)*+	86 (last 5 calendar years)	323 (last 5 academic years)
Licence agreements+	21 (last calendar 5 years)	200 (last 5 academic years)
Spin-out/start-up companies – total	56	154
Spin-offs/star-ups involving women – total	12	6
Domestic ranking (QS World University Rankings)	8 in Spain	5 in the UK
World ranking (QS World University Rankings)	401–500 (N/A)	20 (A1)

Note: * Information for 5 years to 2008.
+ Calendar year = January to December; academic year = September to August.

Source: University of Edinburgh and Granada website and interviews with TTO officers.

setting up a spin-off was not deliberate in three of the four cases analysed (push factors), and only one woman (Entrepreneur 2, Edinburgh) actively sought to create her own business (pull factors).

For Entrepreneur 1 (Edinburgh), the challenge of multiple short-term contracts essentially forced her to leave academia. One of the most convenient and immediate ways of continuing her professional career proved to be the commercialization of knowledge she gathered within the academic environment. Entrepreneur 2 (Edinburgh) is the only person in the sample who deliberately decided to create her own business. She says, 'I wanted to run this idea commercially; I didn't want more journal publications that are going to be filed in somebody's office' (Entrepreneur 2, Edinburgh). In this case, she points to the existence of economic drivers: 'Yes, but the economic [motivation] is also very strong . . . this business is a business that in the next three, five years may generate benefits.'

Entrepreneur 3 (Granada) is driven by commercialization and emphasizes the importance of undertaking activities with a practical application in the business environment. Entrepreneur 3's partner notes: 'In our department, we are a group that has many relationships with the business environment; our research looks for practical implications; 60 per cent of our research is done with firms, and it influences a lot.' Entrepreneur 4 from Granada admits that she had no previous intention of creating a firm. Alternatively, circumstances led to her choice: 'I did it because of the inertia, because I met those people [her future partners]. Really I had no previous intention of creating a firm before meeting them.'

Regarding human capital, three of the four entrepreneurs interviewed have specific business training: one entrepreneur from the University of Granada has a Bachelor's degree in Business Administration, while the two women from the University of Edinburgh received business training through support programmes they attended. However, only the entrepreneurs from the University of Edinburgh had specific business experience. Entrepreneur 1 had gained previous work experience as an employee and director of a spin-out company before the foundation of her own firm, while Entrepreneur 2's experience came from working different jobs and also from the family environment.

The social and work relationships developed by the entrepreneurs represent important resources that can stimulate and support spin-off creation and development. With regard to these types of relationships, previous literature stresses the existence of role models as an important factor that can positively influence the decision to create a firm. The data collected from our interviews with academic entrepreneurs demonstrates that role models can come from the family environment. The family is not only an important resource for emotional support, but can also provide financial support at key moments in the development of a spin-off. Whereas in the case of Entrepreneur 2 (Edinburgh) the spin-off was a joint venture between wife and husband, Entrepreneur 2's husband was primarily an equity investor who could help the firm in a moment of crisis. Similarly, Entrepreneur 4 (Granada) also counts on the support of her husband, but admits that he is reluctant to sign guarantees.

DISCUSSION AND CONCLUSIONS

This study explores the phenomenon of women's entrepreneurship in the academic context to determine how institutional and individual factors influence women academics' decision to set up a spin-off. Based on previous studies from the fields of institutional theory and women's entrepreneurship, we identify three institutional levels that can affect academic women's decisions to create spin-offs.

Our findings at the macro level reveal that the specific gender factors identified are consistent with those highlighted by previous studies on women's entrepreneurship. These include the unequal distribution of household and care tasks, the unsuitability of an entrepreneurial career for women, the challenge of reconciling professional and personal lives, and motherhood (Aldrich and Cliff, 2003; Bruni et al., 2004; Brush et al., 2009). Yet, it is the overlap between the gender factors and academic factors that condition women that provides the best space for analysing why the increasing number of women entrepreneurs in the business environment is not reflected equally in the academic environment.

First, in considering the traditional roles assigned to women, academic jobs seem to be a much better employment option than entrepreneurship. This is one of the main reasons used to explain the lack of entrepreneurial orientation of many female academics. In fact, the attitudes of the academic women entrepreneurs who have children are different from the women who do not. The presence of children makes it more difficult to distribute time between work, family responsibilities and the additional responsibility of business tasks. Consequently, it may be not only the smaller number of women academics in certain fields that explains the low levels of women's engagement in spin-off or start-up creation, but also gender factors, especially when women have family responsibilities.

Second, the universities seem to reflect the beliefs and general culture of their macro-environment. Women are hardly present in the higher ranks of academia and have only minimal participation on representative bodies in the university; this environment is also still dominated by masculine role models. In the universities, men's attitudes remain restricted to the premises of equal conditions and rules, and a gradual long-term natural process of woman's incorporation into relevant academic and business activities. A lack of awareness of the additional difficulties of reconciling family and professional life thus only perpetuates the social construction of gender roles, and explains the lack of specific measures for overcoming this situation.

This limited perspective prevents the development of specific measures necessary to encourage greater participation of women in knowledge commercialization activities. The smaller presence of women in specific research areas associated with knowledge transfer activities seems sufficient to justify their lower participation. It is simply a question that has not been addressed specifically. To summarize, women also remain invisible in the universities' transfer activities. Neither of the two universities studied had specific policies to facilitate the participation of women in commercialization activities or in the creation of spin-offs.

This fact raises the question of whether the current support systems for the commercialization of knowledge through spin-off or start-up creation are really effective, and whether universities are missing an opportunity to generate wealth by exploiting the research results of academic women. In other words, are universities perpetuating the tendency of women to remain in less productive sectors of the economy? Greater advances in the macro-environment regarding new roles for women in contemporary society will probably lead to more active measures in universities for achieving more egalitarian incorporation of academic women into knowledge transfer activities (through the creation of spin-offs).

On the other hand, the factors identified at the meso-level, or in the area of the universities, have shown that firm creation by women academics is not positively related to the universities' resources and trajectory in activities for knowledge and technology commercialization. Contrary to our expectations, this could involve more demanding standards in the selection of initiatives, thereby limiting firm creation in social areas in which there are more academics. Other factors, such as collaboration with other institutions for the promotion of entrepreneurship, may contribute to increasing the number of firms created by women.

In relation to previous studies on academic women's entrepreneurship, this research shows that individual-level study alone (based on the characteristics of academic women) does not adequately explain the entrepreneurial process in universities. A consideration of the institutional perspective provides a more comprehensive theoretical framework for the specific analysis of this type of entrepreneur. This work thus corroborates the suggestion of Brush et al. (2009) and uses two levels of analysis for the institutional factors.

As we expected, women academics involved in knowledge transfer activities through the creation of spin-offs continue to constitute a very small proportion of the participation in this activity. We therefore propose that universities adopt a social leadership role to counteract the possible negative effects produced by the macro-level. Consequently, the keys to reducing these negative forces, and in attempting to cushion the negative influences from the macro level, are to be found within the academic environment itself. The current university policies for encouraging the creation of spin-offs are oriented towards the search for investors, the creation of company incubators and a search for commercial applications of patents. Few projects adequately utilize the human capital embodied in women academics, however. More initiatives are necessary. An example of a positive initiative is the MEETS programme from the University of Cambridge for women in science, engineering and technology, which aimed at raising awareness of commercialization options for academic and Science, Engineering and Technology (SET)-educated women working elsewhere in the economy. Lack of awareness among those responsible for the universities' commercialization policies concerning the restrictions imposed by the macro-level reinforces unequal conditions for academic women by not taking into account any part of the entrepreneurial process. If universities seek to create wealth through activities that commercialize knowledge, they should not forget the knowledge created by women academics. They must recognize the diversity in the social and work contexts of these women and, consequently, the diversity of these women's needs. University policy-makers must work to adapt their policies to these specific needs in order to value the knowledge created by women and make the best use of it.

Future research should be oriented towards identifying more academic women entrepreneurs at other institutions in order to provide more evidence for these findings. Further research should address the question of what policy measures might be adopted to enhance the levels of spin-outs or start-ups; more specifically, it should also identify the number of women pursuing this career path, either as full-time entrepreneurs or as academics with their research firmly grounded in commercial reality.

NOTES

*   The authors gratefully acknowledge the financial support from the Ministry of Science and Innovation of Spain (FEM2009-08511).

1. See, for example, the Organic Law of Measures for Integral Protection against Gender Violence 1/2004, the Organic Law for Effective Equality between Women and Men 3/2007, the Strategic Plan for Equal Opportunities between Women and Men 2008–2011,

and the creation of new governing boards such as the State Secretary for the Politics of Equality and the Ministry for Equality.
2. In both countries, the statistics show positive evolution of women's incorporation into the job market, rates of employment for women, self-employment, and reduction of the pay gap.
3. See the Annual Report on Gender Equality Scheme of the Scottish government: 'Inequality between men and women still exists. Women are still over represented in the lower paid, less skilled jobs and occupations and underrepresented in decision-making. Women are disproportionately the victims of domestic abuse, rape and sexual assault. They have the main responsibility for childcare and caring and gender stereotypes about men and women's roles are still common (Scottish Government, 2010).

REFERENCES

Alcalá Cortijo, P., M. Bordons, M.L. García de Cortázar, M. Griñón, A. Guil, A.M. Muñoz Muñoz, E. Pérez Sedeño and M.J. Santesmases (2007), *Women and Science: The Situation of Women Researchers in the Spanish System of Science and Technology*, Madrid: Spanish Foundation for the Science and Technology.

Aldrich, H.E. and J. Cliff (2003), 'The pervasive effects of family on entrepreneurship: toward a family embeddedness perspective', *Journal of Business Venturing*, **18**, 573–96.

Aldrich, J. (1989), 'Networking among women entrepreneurs', in O. Hagen, C. Rivchum and D. Sexton (eds), *Women Owned Businesses*, New York: Praeger, pp. 103–32.

Allen, S.D., A.N. Link and D.T. Rosenbaum (2007), 'Entrepreneurship and human capital: evidence of patenting activity from the academic sector', *Entrepreneurship Theory and Practice*, November, 937–51.

Babcock, L. and S. Laschever (2003), *Women Don't Ask*, Princeton, NJ: Princeton University Press.

Bailyn, L. (2003) 'Academic careers and gender equity: lessons learned from MIT', *Gender, Work and Organization*, **10** (2), 137–53.

Bates, T. (2002), 'Restricted access to markets characterizes women-owned businesses', *Journal of Business Venturing*, **17**, 313–24.

Birley, S. (1989), 'Female entrepreneurs: are they really any different?', *Journal of Small Business Management*, **27** (1), 32–7.

Blau, F., M. Ferber and A. Winkler (2002), *The Economics of Women, Men and Work*, 4th edn, Englewood Cliffs. NJ: Prentice Hall.

Bruni, A., S. Gherardi and B. Poggio (2004), 'Entrepreneur-mentality, gender and the study of women entrepreneurs', *Journal of Organizational Change Management*, **17** (3), 256–68.

Brush, C.G., A. de Bruin and F. Welter (2009), 'A gender-aware framework for women´s entrepreneurship', *International Journal of Gender and Entrepreneurship*, **1** (1), 8–24.

Bunker-Whittington, K. and L. Smith-Doerr (2005), 'Gender and commercial science: women's patenting in the life sciences', *Journal of Technology Transfer*, **30**, 355–70.

Cunningham, J.B. and J. Lischeron (1991), 'Defining entrepreneurship', *Journal of Small Business Management*, **29** (1), 45–61.

Delbridge, R. and T. Edwards (2007), 'Reflections on developments in institutional theory', *Scandinavian Journal of Management*, **23** (2), 191–205.

Eisenhardt, K. (1989), 'Building theories from case study research', *Academy of Management Review*, **14** (4), 532–50.

Eisenhardt, K.M. and M.E. Graebner (2007), 'Theory building from cases: Opportunities and Challenges', *Academy of Management Journal*, **50** (1), 25–32.

Emirbayer, M. and A. Mische (1998), 'What is agency?', *American Journal of Sociology*, **4**, 962–1023.

Etzkowitz, H., C. Kemelgor and B. Uzzi (2000), *Athena Unbound: The Advancement of Women in Science and Technology*, Cambridge: Cambridge University Press.

Forster, N. (2000), 'A case study of women academics' views on equal opportunities, career prospects and work–family conflicts in a British university', *Women in Management Review*, **15** (7), 316–30.

Greenwood, R. and R. Suddaby (2006), 'Institutional entrepreneurship in mature fields: The big five accounting firms', *Academy of Management Journal*, **49** (1), 27–48.

Kantor, P. (2002), 'Gender, microenterprise success and cultural context: the case of South Asia', *Entrepreneurship Theory and Practice*, **26**, 131–43.

Landry, R., N. Amara and I. Rherrad (2006), 'Why are some university researchers more likely to create spin-offs than others? Evidence from Canadian universities', *Research Policy*, **35** (10), 1599–615.

Ledin, A., L. Bornmann, F. Gannon and G. Wallon (2007), 'A persistent problem: traditional gender roles hold back female scientists', *EMBO Reports*, **8** (11), 982–7.

Lituchy, T.R., M.A. Reavley and P. Bryer (2003), 'Women entrepreneurs: an international comparison', A*dvances in the Study of Entrepreneurship, Innovation & Economic Growth*, **14**, 161–93.

Lowe, R.A and C. González-Brambila (2007), 'Faculty entrepreneurs and research productivity', *Journal of Technology Transfer*, **32** (3), 173–94.

Morley, L. (1994), 'Glass ceiling or iron cage: women in UK academia', *Gender, Work and Organisation*, **1** (4), 194–204.

Mosey, S. and M. Wright (2008), 'From human capital to social capital: a longitudinal study of technology-based academic entrepreneurs', *Entrepreneurship Theory and Practice*, November, 909–35.

Murray, F. and L. Graham (2007), 'Buying science and selling science: gender differences in the market for commercial science', *Industrial and Corporate Change*, **16**, 657–89.

Niederle, M. and L. Vesterlund (2005), 'Do women shy away from competition? Do men compete too much?', National Bureau of Economic Research Working Paper no. 11474.

Noordenbos, G. (2002), 'Women in academies of sciences: from exclusion to exception', *Women's Studies International Forum*, **25** (1), 127–37.

North, D.C. (1990), *Institutions, Institutional Change and Economic Performance*, New York: Cambridge University Press.

Olm, K., A. Carsrud and L. Alvey (1988), 'The role of networks in new venture funding for the female entrepreneur: a continuing analysis', in B.A. Kirchoff, W.A. Long, W.E. McMullan, K.H. Vesper and W.E.Wetzel (eds), *Frontiers of Entrepreneurship Research*, Wellesley, MA: Babson College, pp. 43–55.

Rhodes, E. (1994), 'Women academics in Europe', *Equal Opportunities International*, **13** (3/5), 67–73.

Rosa, P. and A. Dawson (2006), 'Gender and the commercialization of university science: academic founders of spinout companies', *Entrepreneurship & Regional Development*, **18**, 341–66.

Rosser, S.V. and E.O. Lane (2002), 'Key barriers for academic institutions seeking to retain female scientists and engineers: family-unfriendly policies, low numbers, sterotypes, and harassment', *Journal of Women and Minorities in Science and Engineering*, **8**, 161–89.

Scott, W.R. (2001), *Institutions and Organizations*, Thousand Oaks, CA: Sage.

Scottish Government (2010), 'Gender equality scheme of the Scottish Government', Annual Report, Edinburgh: Scottish Government. Available at: www.scotland. gov.uk.

Shane, S. (2004), *Academic entrepreneurship: University Spinoffs and Wealth Creation*, Cheltenham, UK and Northampton, MA, USA: Edward Elgar.

Shaw, S. and C. Cassell (2007), '"That's not how I see it": female and male perspectives on the academic role', *Women in Management Review*, **22** (6), 497–515.

Steffensen, M., E.M. Rogers and K. Speakman (1999), 'Spin-off from research centers at a research university', *Journal of Business Venturing*, **15**, 93–111.

Stephan, P.E. and A. El-Ganainy (2007), 'The entrepreneurial puzzle: explaining the gender gap', *Journal of Technology Transfer*, **32**, 475–87.

Vanawelst, I., B. Clarysse, M. Wright, A. Lockett, N. Moray and R. S'Jegers (2006), 'Entrepreneurial team development in academic spinouts: an examination of team heterogeneity', *Entrepreneurship Theory and Practice*, **30** (2), 249–71.

Vohora, A., M. Wright and A. Lockett (2004), 'Critical junctures in the development of university high-tech spinout companies', *Research Policy*, **33**, 147–74.

Yin, R.K. (2003), *Case Study Research: Design and Methods*, 3rd edn, Applied Social Research Methods Series, vol. 5, Thousand Oakes, CA: Sage Publications.

Wright, M., B. Clarysse, P. Mustar and A. Lockett (2007), *Academic Entrepreneurship in Europe*, Cheltenham, UK and Northampton, MA, USA: Edward Elgar Publishing.

4. Gender-based firm performance differences in the United States: examining the roles of financial capital and motivations

Susan Coleman and Alicia Robb

INTRODUCTION

Women-owned firms represent an important segment of the small business sector. According to the latest available data from the US Census Bureau (2010), there were 7.8 million privately held women-owned firms in the USA in 2007 (*2007 Survey of Business Owners*). These firms generated an estimated US$1.3 trillion in sales and employed 7.6 million people. Although women-owned firms still comprise a minority of all firms (28.7 percent), the number of women-owned firms increased by 44 percent from 1997 to 2007, compared with a growth rate of 30 percent for US firms overall. However, while the number of women-owned businesses grew at twice the rate of all firms over the period 1997–2002, their number grew just slightly faster than the rate of firms overall for the 2002–07 period.

Additionally, women-owned firms have lagged men-owned firms in a number of traditional economic performance measures. From 1997 to 2007, revenues for women-owned firms increased by 45.7 percent, compared with 62.7 percent for all US firms. Similarly, employment by women-owned firms grew by only 7.2 percent, compared with a growth rate of 14.8 percent for US firms overall. Finally, payroll grew by 46.3 percent for women-owned firms, compared with 66.4 percent for all US firms. These statistics, provided by the US Census Bureau, reveal that the relative performance of women-owned firms as measured by sales, employment and payroll actually declined for the 1997–2007 period.

A number of studies have examined the relative underperformance of women-owned firms with conflicting results. A second and smaller group of studies has sought to establish a link between the motivations of women entrepreneurs, their financing strategies and firm performance. This chapter seeks to extend these lines of inquiry by examining the relationship between the motivations and expectations of the entrepreneur, the amount of startup capital raised and firm performance for newly established women- and men-owned firms. To our knowledge, this is the first study to use longitudinal data to explore the impact of motivation and financing on performance, by gender, for new firms.

THEORETICAL FOUNDATION

Women-owned Firms and Financing

A growing number of studies have examined women business owners' use of various sources of financing. Prior research suggests both supply and demand side issues in the acquisition of capital. Supply-side factors include the investor preference for specific types of industries, firms, or entrepreneurs. Conversely, demand-side issues include the preference of the entrepreneur for growth, profits, industry sector, risk and control.

Prior research has revealed that women are less likely to use both external debt and external equity than men (Carter et al., 2003; Chaganti et al., 1996; Cole and Mehran, 2008; Coleman, 2002, 2008; Coleman and Robb, 2009; Scott et al., 2003; Orser et al., 2006). In the area of debt financing, women continue to report difficulty in securing bank loans and dealing with lenders (Constantinidis et al., 2006; Fabowale et al., 1995; Walker and Joyner, 1999). This is troubling given that most studies indicate that women are no more likely to be turned down for loans than men (Coleman, 2002; Orser et al., 2006; Treichel and Scott, 2006). Women were more reluctant to apply, however, and were also more likely to anticipate denial (Cole, 2008; Coleman, 2002; Treichel and Scott, 2006). Several researchers have observed that women entrepreneurs rely more heavily on credit cards than men, possibly to avoid having to borrow from a bank (Robb and Wolken, 2002; Scott et al., 2003).

There is considerably less research on women entrepreneurs' use of equity. Findings reveal, however, that women rely heavily on internal sources of equity, while only a small percentage of firms actually use external equity in the form of angel investments or venture capital (Becker-Blease and Sohl, 2007; Brush et al., 2001b; Carter et al., 2003; Chaganti et al., 1996; Coleman and Robb, 2009; Haynes et al., 2000; Orser et al., 2006). Taken together, these studies suggest that women entrepreneurs may be more risk averse than men and more concerned with maintaining control of their firms. These characteristics would cause women to avoid both external debt and external equity. Alternately, as suggested by some researchers, women entrepreneurs may be closed out of male-dominated networks, particularly those that provide access to external equity capital (Brush et al., 2001b, 2004).

One consensus arising from several studies examining women entrepreneurs' use of both debt and equity is that whatever the source of capital, women raise a lot less of it (Alsos et al., 2006; Amatucci and Sohl, 2004; Coleman and Robb, 2009; Treichel and Scott, 2006). This lower level of capital can constrain the firm's ability to grow, as well as increase the risk of financial distress, particularly if the firm does not have sufficient liquidity to weather periods of adversity.

Women-owned Firms and Performance

A number of studies have examined various aspects of performance for women-owned firms, including survival, firm size, growth rates, earnings and profits. In general, these studies have had mixed results regarding performance, as well as conflicting theories for performance differences between women- and men-owned firms. Most studies have been consistent in finding that women-owned firms are smaller than firms owned by men (Loscocco et al., 1991; Rosa et al., 1996). A growing number of researchers attribute this size discrepancy to differences in the motivations of women entrepreneurs (Cliff, 1998; Orser and Hogarth-Scott, 2002; Watson, 2006). These studies suggest that women entrepreneurs prefer controlled rather than rapid growth. Nevertheless, Brush et al. (2001b) challenged the 'myth' that women do not want high growth firms by focusing on growth-oriented firms that participated in the Springboard forums, while Menzies et al. (2004) surveyed nascent entrepreneurs in Canada and determined there were no significant differences between men and women in terms of the desired future size of the business.

Gender differences in areas of performance aside from size and growth have also shown conflicting results. Several studies have examined firm survival to find no differences between women- and men-owned firms (Cooper et al., 1994; Kelleberg and Leicht, 1991; Robb and Watson, 2010), while others have found that women-owned firms are more likely to close than firms owned by men (Robb, 2002; Watson, 2003). In terms of profits and other measures of financial success, most studies found few differences between women- and men-owned firms when they controlled for other variables (Du Rietz and Henrekson, 2000; Kepler and Shane, 2007; Watson and Robinson, 2003). Nevertheless, several studies have noted that women entrepreneurs were less motivated by measures of financial success (Anna et al., 1999; Carter et al., 2003).

A growing number of studies attest to the link between financial capital and firm performance (Alsos et al., 2006; Carter and Allen, 1997; Carter et al., 1997; Coleman, 2007; Fairlie and Robb, 2009; Gundry and Welsch, 2001; Morris et al., 2006). While the findings of these studies are mixed, they do suggest that financial capital is related to firm performance, as measured by survival and growth in revenues and profits. In particular, firms with higher levels of financial capital experienced improved prospects. In spite of these results, however, there are some indications that women entrepreneurs may not be motivated by the same measures of success as men. Rather than striving for the goals of firm size and rapid growth, women may place a higher value on controlled and moderate growth that allows them to minimize their risks and maintain control of the firm. In this chapter, we build upon the current body of literature by examining the links between financial capital, owner motivations and expectations, and new firm performance, by gender.

STATEMENT OF HYPOTHESES

This research is based upon two major theories of the entrepreneurial firm. The first of these is resource-based theory. Well developed and documented, resource-based theory states that the task of the entrepreneur is to assemble, develop and transform needed resources in order to generate unique capabilities that will give her a competitive advantage (Amit and Schoemaker, 1993; Kor and Mahoney, 2000; Penrose, 1959; Rugman and Verbeke, 2002; Wernerfelt, 1984). Included in these resources are financial capital, human capital (education and experience), and social capital (contacts and networks) (Sirmon and Hitt, 2003). Resource-based theory also contends that those firms that muster and apply their resources most effectively will also be those that enjoy superior performance (Brush et al., 2001a; Sirmon and Hitt, 2003). Since financial capital is one of the key resource inputs for new firms, supply problems might be expected to have a negative effect on performance outcomes.

The second theory is less developed. We will refer to it as motivational theory. This theory is based upon a small, but growing body of research which contends that women entrepreneurs are motivated by different measures of success and performance outcomes than men (Cliff, 1998; Orser and Hogarth-Scott, 2002; Morris et al., 2006; Watson, 2006). In particular, women may prefer slower and more controlled growth, which allows them to balance competing priorities, minimize the risk of failure and maintain control. If this is the case, women-owned firms will demand lower levels of financial capital to finance correspondingly lower levels of firm size and growth.

Motivational theory is grounded in expectancy theory. This theory states that individuals will take actions that lead to expected and desired outcomes (Olson et al., 1996; Vroom, 1964). Expectancy theory, appropriated from psychology literature, has been applied to the field of entrepreneurship to explain the motivations and behaviours of entrepreneurs. Specifically, entrepreneurs take the action of starting a firm in order to achieve expected and desired outcomes, such as self-realization, status, autonomy and financial success (Gatewood et al., 2002; Manolova et al., 2008). In the case of women entrepreneurs, prior researchers have noted that women and men may have different expectations and desired outcomes for their firms. Thus, the actions they take to achieve those outcomes may also differ (Hughes, 2006; Manolova et al., 2008). This body of work is consistent with our motivational theory, which states that the different motivations of women and men entrepreneurs lead to different measures of success.

Our first hypothesis relates to performance differences between women- and men-owned firms. Prior research demonstrates fairly consistently that women start smaller firms and produce less growth-oriented firms than men (Loscocco et al., 1991; Rosa et al., 1996). However, there is less consistency in other measures of performance such as profits, employment and survival (Du Rietz and Henrekson, 2000; Kelleberg and Leicht, 1991; Kepler and Shane, 2007; Watson and Robinson, 2003). We can test these theories using data from the Kauffman Firm Survey, which is unique in that it provides data on a cohort of new women- and men-owned firms established at the same time and in the same economic environment. While no single measure captures performance perfectly, we examine a number of different outcomes which together provide us with a good picture of firm success overall. Our hypothesis for performance is as follows:

Hypothesis 1:   Women-owned firms will underperform firms owned by men in the early years of operation (in terms of sales, assets, profits, employment and survival).

Our second hypothesis relates to financing differences between women- and men-owned firms. The studies cited above highlight that women entrepreneurs continue to experience difficulties in the acquisition of external sources of capital, both debt and equity (Brush et al., 2001b, 2004; Constantinidis et al., 2006; Fabowale et al., 1995; Gatewood et al., 2009; Walker and Joyner, 1999). This finding is significant because financial capital has been identified as one of the key resource inputs for entrepreneurial firms (Alsos et al., 2006; Cooper et al., 1994; Fairlie and Robb, 2009; Orser et al., 2006; Watson, 2002). Although prior research has revealed financing differences between women- and men-owned firms, most studies to date have focused on established firms rather than nascent firms. One of the major contributions of this research is that it will allow for us to test for financing differences using a large sample of new firms. Our second hypothesis is as follows:

Hypothesis 2:   Women-owned firms are less likely to use outside debt or outside equity as financing sources at startup than men.

A third set of studies, also consistent with resource-based theory, has attempted to tie together the impact of financial capital and firm performance. Prior research has noted that key inputs such as financial, human and social capital are critical for the success of entrepreneurial firms. In the realm of financial capital in particular, previous studies have sought to establish a link between financial capital and growth, profitability and survival. In general, these studies have found that firms raising smaller amounts of capital have lower levels of performance (Alsos et al., 2006; Carter and Allen, 1997; Coleman, 2007; Fairlie and Robb, 2009; Gundry and Welsch, 2001). The value-added from this study is that it controls for the level of startup capital and initial firm size to determine if performance differences between women- and men-owned firms persist over time. If they do, it suggests that financial capital is not the only factor driving performance. Alternatively, and consistent with motivational theory, it is possible that women entrepreneurs are motivated by other factors and have different goals not captured by traditional measures of performance. Thus, our hypothesis is as follows:

Hypothesis 3:   In controlling for the level of startup financing, women-owned firms will still underperform firms owned by men after four years of operation (in terms of sales, assets, profits, employment and survival).

Finally, a fourth, smaller number of studies attests that differences in motivation have an impact on the financing strategies of women- and men-owned firms. Specifically, women entrepreneurs are less motivated by firm size, growth and personal wealth (Carter et al., 2003; Cliff, 1998; Orser and Hogarth-Scott, 2002). Alternatively, they prefer greater security, less risk of failure and controlled rather than rapid growth (Morris et al., 2006; Watson, 2006). Based on these studies, which form the basis of our motivational theory, our final hypothesis is as follows:

Hypothesis 4:   After four years of operation, women-owned firms will have lower expectations for firm growth than men, but similar levels of satisfaction with their firm's performance to date.

DATA

The Kauffman Firm Survey (KFS) is a survey of new businesses in the USA. This survey collects information on 4928 firms that started in 2004 and surveys them annually. This cohort is the first large national sample of firm startups to be tracked over time. The data contain detailed information on both the firm and up to ten business owners per firm. In addition to the 2004 baseline year data, there are four years of follow-up data (2005, 2006, 2007 and 2008) now available. Three additional years are planned.

A subset of the KFS data, firms surviving over the 2004–08 period and those firms that have been verified as going out of business over that period, is used in this research. This reduces the sample size to 4022 businesses. To assign owner demographics at the firm level, the primary owner was defined. For firms with multiple owners (35 percent of the sample), the primary owner was designated as the individual with the largest equity share. In cases where two or more owners owned equal shares, hours worked and a series of other variables were used to rank owners and define a primary owner.[1] Firms with a female primary owner are classified as women-owned firms. All empirical analyses used sample weights provided, which adjust for non-response and over-sampling of high-technology firms.

DESCRIPTIVE STATISTICS

Table 4.1 provides descriptive statistics, by gender, for firms included in the KFS. In terms of performance outcomes, it reveals that men-owned firms were significantly larger than women-owned firms in terms of total revenues and total assets in both 2004 and 2008. The difference in net profit by gender was not statistically significant in 2004, and women-owned firms actually had smaller losses than men-owned firms in the first year of operation. By 2008, however, men-owned firms had a significantly higher level of net profits than women-owned firms. Similarly, there were no significant differences between women- and men-owned firms in terms of return on assets in 2004, but men-owned firms were significantly more profitable by 2008 (12.09 percent vs 0.97 percent). Descriptive statistics (not shown) also reveal that a significantly higher percentage of men-owned firms had employees in both 2004 (42.7 percent vs 35.3 percent) and in 2008 (57.9 percent vs 50.0 percent). For those firms that had employees, men-owned firms also had a significantly larger number of employees on average. In terms of firm survival, approximately 62 percent of firms owned by women and by men survived through 2008. These descriptive statistics provide

Table 4.1 *Performance measures, startup capital, and owner motivations by gender*

	2004		2008	
	Female	Male	Female	Male
Outcomes				
Revenues	$56 506	$105 549***	$248 746	$537 548***
Net profits	$(1919)	$(4527)	$13 996	$28 509*
Assets	$78 244	$151 038**	$178 462	$341 495**
Return on assets	−0.87	−0.02	0.97	12.09*
Return on assets – bounded	0.58	0.73	1.72	12.74*
Survival through 2008			61.7%	62.8%
Initial startup capital				
Owner equity	$23 948	$36 697***	33.5%	27.4%***
Insider equity	$1876	$2088	2.6%	1.6%
Outsider equity	$935	$25 980***	1.3%	19.4%***
Owner debt	$3897	$5412	5.5%	4.0%
Insider debt	$4771	$7772*	6.7%	5.8%*
Outsider debt	$36 057	$56 191**	50.4%	41.9%**
Total financial	$71 484	$134 139***	100.0%	100.0%***
Motivations				
Met/exceeded expectations for performance (04–08)			47.2%	44.8%
High growth expectations (30+%)			17.3%	23.6%***
Optimist			40.4%	30.3%***
Average hours worked (week)	40.3	43.3**	40.9	44.4**
Previous startup experience	36.8%	44.9%**	38.3%	44.8%**
Previous industry work experience	9.1	13.1**	9.8	13.7**

Source: Kauffman Firm Survey microdata.

limited support for Hypothesis 1 at startup, but somewhat more consistent support for performance differences after four years of operation.

Table 4.1 provides a snapshot of the initial capital structure, by gender, of firms included in the KFS. It reveals that outsider debt (bank loans, credit lines, and so on) was the dominant form of financing for both women and men (50.4 percent vs 41.9 percent), followed by owner-provided equity (33.5 percent vs 27.4 percent). Nevertheless, women-owned firms were significantly more reliant on both sources than firms owned by men. Together, outsider debt and owner equity represented 83.9 percent of startup financing for women and 69.3 percent for men. Women were also significantly more reliant on debt provided by other insiders (spouse, family, employees) than men (6.7 percent vs 5.8 percent). Conversely, men-owned firms demonstrated a significantly higher level of reliance on external equity than women-owned firms (19.4 percent vs 1.3 percent), consistent with prior research. Overall, women started their firms with significantly less financial capital than men. Women invested an average of about US$71 000, compared with more than US$134 000 for men. This funding gap, particularly in the early stages of the firm's development, could affect the performance outcomes of women-owned firms in terms of their ability to survive, grow, generate earnings and hire employees. The link between financial capital and performance is a focal point of this research.

RESULTS FROM MULTIVARIATE ANALYSIS

Our discussion up to this point has revealed that women raised significantly smaller amounts of capital than men at startup, and that they were more dependent on internal, rather than external, sources of financing. In particular, women-owned firms raised dramatically lower amounts of external equity than men-owned firms. Descriptive statistics also showed that women-owned firms underperformed firms owned by men in traditional performance measures of size, profitability and employment after four years of operation. Multivariate analysis allows us to determine whether or not there is a link between the lower level of financial inputs for women-owned firms and their lower levels of performance output, controlling for other factors.

Financing Differences between Women- and Men-owned Firms

We now turn to the task of explaining the observed variation in capital structure choice. Table 4.2 provides the results of regression analyses; we regressed four different capital structure ratios against various owner

Table 4.2   OLS regressions of financing ratios of startup capital (2004)

	Owner financing/total financial capital	Insider financing/ total financial capital	Outside debt/total financial capital	Outside equity/total financial capital
Female	0.0277*	−0.00406	−0.0110	−0.0126***
	(0.0162)	(0.00898)	(0.0147)	(0.00420)
Ave. hours worked (week)	−0.00113***	0.000701***	0.000491*	−5.85e-05
In startup year – 2004	(0.000301)	(0.000160)	(0.000267)	(8.70e-05)
Some college	0.0241	−0.0215	−0.00917	0.00662
	(0.0230)	(0.0141)	(0.0207)	(0.00508)
College degree	0.0628***	−0.0396***	−0.0260	0.00286
	(0.0243)	(0.0143)	(0.0220)	(0.00597)
Graduate degree	0.0252	−0.0290*	−0.00648	0.0102
	(0.0272)	(0.0155)	(0.0246)	(0.00771)
Previous industry exp. (years)	0.00201***	−0.000632*	−0.00123*	−0.000145
	(0.000726)	(0.000356)	(0.000670)	(0.000242)
Previous startup exp.	−0.00224	−0.00924	0.00267	0.00881**
	(0.0144)	(0.00761)	(0.0131)	(0.00442)
Team ownership	−0.0164	−0.0177*	0.0213	0.0127**
	(0.0163)	(0.00910)	(0.0145)	(0.00578)
Incorporated	−0.0555***	−0.00167	0.0410***	0.0161***
	(0.0161)	(0.00949)	(0.0142)	(0.00494)
Home based	0.0992***	−0.0353***	−0.0512***	−0.0127***
	(0.0152)	(0.00867)	(0.0135)	(0.00440)
Intellectual property	0.00433	0.00897	−0.0222	0.00888
	(0.0168)	(0.00975)	(0.0147)	(0.00571)
High credit score	−0.0352	−0.00896	0.0407	0.00343
	(0.0278)	(0.0158)	(0.0254)	(0.00975)
Low credit score	0.0729***	−0.0314***	−0.0386***	−0.00288
	(0.0149)	(0.00845)	(0.0135)	(0.00409)
Technology based	0.0415*	−0.0155	−0.0472**	0.0212*
	(0.0224)	(0.0103)	(0.0187)	(0.0125)
Constant	0.833***	0.264***	−0.0445	−0.0524**
	(0.104)	(0.0656)	(0.0904)	(0.0264)
Observations	3466	3466	3466	3466
R-squared	0.085	0.057	0.052	0.039

Notes:
Owner race, ethnicity, and age were also controlled for in this anaylsis, as well as two-digit industry codes.
Standard errors in parentheses.
*** $p < 0.01$, ** $p < 0.05$, * $p < 0.1$.

and firm characteristics. Dependent variables include the ratios of (1) owner financing/total financial capital, (2) insider financing/total financial capital, (3) external debt/total financial capital, and (4) external equity/ total financial capital. Owner financing includes owner provided sources of debt and equity. Insider financing includes debt or equity provided by other non-owner insiders (that is, parent, spouse, other family members or employees). External debt includes bank loans used for the business (both business and personal), lines of credit, business credit cards, government business loans and other loans for the business. Finally, external equity includes angel, venture capital, business, or government equity financing.

Independent variables were selected to include measures that prior research has shown are related to firm performance. These include owner gender as well as human capital variables such as owner education, years of previous industry experience and previous startup experience. Social capital was captured by a variable representing team ownership. Variables representing differences in motivation, such as average hours worked in the business, whether or not the firm is home-based, organizational form and the presence of intellectual property (patents, copyrights, trademarks) were also included. Finally, firm riskiness, as measured by credit score, was included, as well as a dummy variable distinguishing between technology-based and non-technology-based firms.[2]

After controlling for all of these owner and firm characteristics, the coefficient for female was still positive and statistically significant in the owner financing equation and negative and statistically significant in the external equity equation. Although the coefficient for female was not significant in the outside debt model, it was negative as anticipated. Thus, we find support for Hypothesis 2, which states that women are less likely to use external sources of financing.

Performance Differences between Women- and Men-owned Firms

Table 4.3 provides results from OLS regressions on firm outcomes using the log of 2008 sales, the log of 2008 assets, 2008 net profits and the log of 2008 employment. The independent variables mimic those from the previous table. In addition, we added the log of 2004 total financial capital as an independent variable to determine if the level of startup capital had an effect on subsequent performance outcomes. While controlling for a variety of firm and owner characteristics, our results reveal that women-owned firms were still significantly smaller than firms owned by men in terms of revenues. The independent variable representing gender was not significant for the performance models using assets, profits, or employment as dependent variables. These multivariate results provide only

Table 4.3   OLS outcome regressions

Variables	Log of 2008 sales	Log of 2008 assets	2008 net profits	Log of 2008 empl.
Female	−0.616**	−0.330	−7186	−0.0716
	(0.280)	(0.234)	(7116)	(0.0469)
Some college	−0.448	0.314	7805	−0.00998
	(0.397)	(0.326)	(7146)	(0.0625)
College degree	0.940**	0.896***	8299	0.105
	(0.406)	(0.346)	(9339)	(0.0684)
Graduate	0.500	0.678*	34949**	0.0317
degree	(0.456)	(0.384)	(14959)	(0.0746)
Previous	0.0182	0.0345***	1032**	0.00415*
industry exp.	(0.0125)	(0.0107)	(410.5)	(0.00219)
Startup	0.226	−0.00574	−6454	0.0607
experience	(0.238)	(0.210)	(7500)	(0.0414)
Team	0.702**	0.260	8012	0.176***
ownership	(0.278)	(0.240)	(9668)	(0.0507)
Incorporated	0.514*	−0.393*	1898	0.133***
	(0.273)	(0.229)	(6505)	(0.0451)
Home based	−1.215***	−0.335	−13054	−0.492***
	(0.254)	(0.222)	(8998)	(0.0448)
Intellectual	−0.362	0.356	−27780**	0.0698
property	(0.295)	(0.261)	(11443)	(0.0542)
High credit	0.403	0.741*	−5909	0.136*
score	(0.426)	(0.384)	(16852)	(0.0788)
Low credit	−0.234	−0.809***	−6159	−0.104**
score	(0.259)	(0.218)	(7204)	(0.0434)
Technology	0.622	0.203	−27414	0.256***
based	(0.380)	(0.361)	(18377)	(0.0689)
Log of 2004	0.0573	0.116***	2605	0.0298***
financial	(0.0382)	(0.0321)	(1665)	(0.00693)
capital				
Hours worked	0.0309***	0.0159***	331.2	0.00464***
	(0.00548)	(0.00463)	(213.2)	(0.000983)
Constant	0.963	−0.538	8746	0.741**
	(2.126)	(1.629)	(48428)	(0.329)
Observations	2347	3866	2489	2510
R-squared	0.166	0.060	0.039	0.242

Notes:
Owner race, ethnicity, and age were also controlled for in this anaylsis, as well as two-digit industry codes.
Standard errors in parentheses.
*** $p < 0.01$, ** $p < 0.05$, * $p < 0.1$.

weak support for Hypothesis 3, which states that women-owned firms underperform firms owned by men after four years of operation.

Table 4.3 also reveals that a higher level of 2004 startup capital was associated with higher levels of all of the performance outcomes and was statistically significant in the asset and employment specifications. Thus, consistent with resource-based theory, the level of financial capital at startup was an important factor in determining some performance outcomes in subsequent years. Nevertheless, it does not explain all of the differences between new women- and men-owned firms, specifically those relating to size and growth. Rather, these findings suggest that differences in motivations and goals may play a role in explaining differences in performance, thereby giving credence to what we have referred to as motivational theory.

The Kauffman Firm Survey added several additional questions related to motivations and goals in the latest round of data (calendar year 2008). The descriptive statistics for these responses are also found in Table 4.1. Unfortunately, data are only available for firms that survived through 2008 and responded to the survey. Nevertheless, in terms of gender, there are some striking differences between surviving firms in 2008. Table 4.1 reveals that a significantly higher percentage of men expected growth in excess of 30 percent per year for their firms (23.6 percent vs 17.3 percent). Similarly, male owners worked significantly more hours per week and had higher levels of previous startup and work experience. Conversely, a significantly higher percentage of women owners indicated that they were optimistic about the prospects for their firm (40.4 percent vs 30.3 percent). There were no significant differences between the percentage of women and men owners who stated that, after four years of operation, the firm's performance had met or exceeded their expectations (47.2 percent vs 44.8 percent). This finding suggests that women owners were equally happy with the performance of their firms in spite of their lower growth expectations. These results provide support for Hypothesis 4, which states that women owners are satisfied with their firm's level of performance in spite of their lower expectations for growth. Additionally, these findings are also consistent with motivational theory, which suggests that women may be motivated by different measures of success than men.

SUMMARY AND CONCLUSIONS

This chapter explores the link between financial capital, motivations and expectations, and firm performance for a large sample of new women- and men-owned firms. Multivariate results reveal that women had a significantly higher probability of using owner financing and a lower probability of using external equity than men in 2004. Nevertheless, our multivariate results for 2008 demonstrate substantial differences between women- and men-owned firms in only one of the five outcomes measured (log of 2008 sales). The coefficient for the female variable was negative, but not significant in the equations involving assets, profits, employment and survival. With regard to performance, these findings provide some support for prior research that identifies few differences between women- and men-owned firms, when controlling for other variables such as firm size (Du Reitz and Henrekson, 2000; Kepler and Shane, 2007; Watson and Robinson, 2003).

Simultaneously, however, our findings provide evidence that differentials in the outcome measuring firm size are driven in part by gender differences in levels of startup capital, even after controlling for a number of other firm and owner characteristics. This finding is consistent with resource-based theory, which contends that differences in resource inputs will lead to differences in performance outputs. Our findings are also consistent, however, with Penrose's (1959) contention that the entrepreneur's objective is profitable growth. Although women-owned firms in our study were smaller than firms owned by men, there were no significant differences in the area of profitability. This finding suggests that, from a resource-based perspective, women entrepreneurs were managing their resource inputs as productively as men.

Our results also provide evidence that gender differences in motivation could play an important role in determining performance outcomes. As suggested by prior research, women may place less value on firm size and growth than men-owned firms (Cliff, 1998; Orser and Hogarth-Scott, 2002). Our findings indicate that women were significantly more likely to organize as sole proprietorships; they also devoted fewer hours to their startups than men. Additionally, women have a higher level of risk aversion than men for the perceived risks associated with firm size, growth and a possible loss of control. Our findings reveal that women relied on a lower level of external equity, which could relate to a loss of control and the risks associated with sharing ownership.

This study also indicates that for surviving firms, there were no statistically significant differences between men- and women-owned firms in terms of meeting or exceeding their expectations for firm performance over the 2004–08 period. Although women had a lower level of performance in the area of firm size, they were just as likely to be satisfied with that outcome. This suggests that these women were motivated by factors other than traditional economic measures of firm size and growth. We also found significant differences between women and men in terms of expectations for future growth. Men owners were significantly more likely to have expectations of growth of 30 percent or more over the ensuing three years than women. This finding, again, suggests that women were less likely to be motivated by rapid growth than men, and possibly more oriented toward profitable growth, rather than growth for growth's sake (Du Rietz and Henrekson, 2000).

Finally, women were significantly more likely to be optimistic about the future of the firm compared to men, even though they had lower growth expectations. Taken together, these findings suggest that women entrepreneurs had alternative motivations and expectations for their firms than men. Consistent with motivational theory, these differences may account for differences between women and men in financing strategy and performance outcomes. In closing, it should be noted that in this study we have examined differences in firm performance, financial capital and motivation for a broad sample of women- and men-owned firms. Going forward it would also be fruitful to pursue the line of inquiry initiated by the Diana scholars (Brush et al., 2001b) by studying a sub-sample of growth-oriented women- and men-owned firms. This would allow for an exploration of differences in performance, financial capital and motivation for a subset of firms that is becoming increasingly attractive and accessible to women entrepreneurs.

NOTES

1. For more information on this methodology see Robb et al. (2009).
2. Detailed variable names and descriptions are available upon request.

REFERENCES

Alsos, G.A., E.J. Isaksen and E. Ljunggren (2006), 'New venture financing and sub-sequent business growth in men- and women-led businesses', *Entrepreneurship Theory and Practice*, September 6, 667–86.

Amatucci, F.M. and J.E. Sohl (2004), 'Women entrepreneurs securing business angel financing: tales from the field', *Venture Capital*, **6** (2/3), 181–96.

Amit, R. and P. Schoemaker (1993), 'Strategic assets and organizational rent', *Strategic Management Journal*, **14** (1), 33–46.

Anna, A.L., G.N. Chandler, E. Jansen and N.P. Mero (1999), 'Women business owners in traditional and non-traditional industries', *Journal of Business Venturing*, **15**, 279–303.

Becker-Blease, J.R. and J.E. Sohl (2007), 'Do women-owned businesses have equal access to angel capital?', *Journal of Business Venturing*, **22** (4), 503–21.

Brush, C., N. Carter, E. Gatewood, P. Greene and M. Hart (2001b), *The Diana*

Project: Women Business Owners and Equity Capital: The Myths Dispelled, Kansas City, MI: Kauffman Center for Entrepreneurial Leadership.

Brush, C., N. Carter, E. Gatewood, P. Greene and M. Hart (2004), *Gatekeepers of Venture Growth: A Diana Project Report on the Role and Participation of Women in the Venture Capital Industry*, Kansas City, MI: Kauffman Center for Entrepreneurial Leadership.

Brush, C.G., P.G. Greene and M.M. Hart (2001a), 'From initial idea to unique advantage: the entrepreneurial challenge of constructing a resource base', *Academy of Management Executive*, **15** (1), 64–78.

Carter, N.M. and K.R. Allen (1997), 'Size determinants of women-owned businesses: choice or barriers to resources', *Entrepreneurship & Regional Development*, **9**, 211–29.

Carter, N.M., W.B. Gartner, K.G. Shaver and E.J. Gatewood (2003), 'The career reasons of nascent entrepreneurs', *Journal of Business Venturing*, **18**, 13–39.

Carter, N.M., M. Williams and P.D. Reynolds (1997), 'Discontinuance among new firms in retail: the influence of initial resources, strategy, and gender', *Journal of Business Venturing*, **12**, 125–45.

Chaganti, R., D. DeCarolis and D. Deeds (1996), 'Predictors of capital structure in small ventures', *Entrepreneurship Theory and Practice*, **20** (2), 7–18.

Cliff, J.E. (1998), 'Does one size fit all? Exploring the relationship between attitudes toward growth, gender, and business size', *Journal of Business Venturing*, **13**, 523–42.

Cole, R. and H. Mehran (2008), 'Gender and the availability of credit to privately held firms', paper presented at the Kauffman Foundation-Cleveland Federal Reserve Bank Pre-Conference on Entrepreneurial Finance, Kansas City, Missouri, 11–12 March.

Coleman, S. (2002), 'Characteristics and borrowing behavior of small, women-owned firms: evidence from the 1998 Survey of Small Business Finances', *Journal of Business and Entrepreneurship*, **14** (2), 151–66.

Coleman, S. (2007), 'Women-owned firms and growth', *Journal of Business and Entrepreneurship*, **19** (2), 31–44.

Coleman, S. and A. Robb (2009),'A comparison of new firm financing by gender: evidence from the Kauffman Firm Survey data', *Small Business Economics*, **33**, 397–411.

Constantinidis, C., A. Cornet and S. Asandei (2006), 'Financing of women-owned ventures: the impact of gender and other owner- and firm-related variables', *Venture Capital*, **8** (2), 133–57.

Cooper, A.C., J.F. Gimeno-Gascon and C.Y. Woo (1994), 'Initial human and financial capital as predictors of new venture performance', *Journal of Business Venturing*, **9**, 371–95.

Du Rietz, D. and A. Henrekson (2000), 'Testing the female underperformance hypothesis', *Small Business Economics*, **14**, 1–10.

Fabowale, L., B. Orser and A.Riding (1995), 'Gender, structural factors, and credit terms between Canadian small businesses and financial institutions', *Entrepreneurship Theory and Practice*, **19** (4), 41–66.

Fairlie, R.W. and A.M. Robb (2009), 'Gender differences in business performance: evidence from the characteristics of business owners survey', *Small Business Economics*, **33**, 375–95.

Gatewood, E.J., C.G. Brush, N.M. Carter, P.G. Greene and M.M. Hart (2009),

'Diana: a symbol of women entrepreneurs' hunt for knowledge, money, and the rewards of entrepreneurship', *Small Business Economics*, **32**, 129–44.

Gatewood, E.J., K.J. Shaver, J.B. Powers and W.B. Gartner (2002), 'Entrepreneurial expectancy, task effort and performance', *Entrepreneurship Theory and Practice*, **27** (2), 187–206.

Gundry, L.K. and H.P. Welsch (2001), 'The ambitious entrepreneur: high growth strategies of women-owned enterprises', *Journal of Business Venturing*, **16**, 453–70.

Haynes, G.W., B.R. Rowe, R. Walker and G. Hong (2000),'The differences in financial structure between women- and men-owned family businesses', *Journal of Family and Economic Issues*, **21** (3), 209–26.

Hughes, K. (2006), 'Does Motivation Matter? Women's Entrepreneurship and Economic Success', paper presented at the Annual Meeting of the American Sociological Association, Montreal, Canada, 10 August.

Kelleberg, A.L. and K.T. Leicht (1991), 'Gender and organizational performance: determinants of small business survival and success', *Academy of Management Journal*, **34** (1), 136–61.

Kepler, E. and S. Shane (2007), *Are Male and Female Entrepreneurs Really That Different?*, SBA Office of Advocacy, available at: http://www.sba.gov/advo/research/rs309tot.pdf (accessed 15 December 2010).

Kor, Y.Y. and J.T. Mahoney (2000), 'Penrose's resource-based approach: the process and product of research creativity', *Journal of Management Studies*, **37** (1), 109–39.

Loscocco, K.A., J. Robinson, R.H. Hall and J.K. Allen (1991), 'Gender and small business success: an inquiry into women's relative disadvantage', *Social Forces*, **70** (1), 65–85.

Manolova, T.S.,C.G. Brush and L.F. Edelman (2008), 'What do women entrepreneurs want?', *Strategic Change*, **17**, 68–82.

Menzies, T.V., M. Diochon and Y. Gasse (2004), 'Examining venture-related myths concerning women entrepreneurs', *Journal of Developmental Entrepreneurship*, **9** (2), 89–107.

Morris, M.H., N.N. Miyasaki, C.E. Watters and S.M. Coombes (2006), 'The dilemma of growth: understanding venture size choices of women entrepreneurs', *Journal of Small Business Management*, **44** (2), 221–44.

Olson, J.M., N.J. Roese and M.P. Zanna (1996), 'Expectancies', in E.T. Higgins and A.W. Kuglanski (eds), *Social Psychology: Handbook of Basic Principles*, New York: Guilford Press, pp. 211–38.

Orser, B. and S. Hogarth-Scott (2002), 'Opting for growth: gender dimensions of choosing enterprise development', *Canadian Journal of Administrative Sciences*, **19** (3), 284–300.

Orser, B.J., A.L. Riding and K. Manley (2006),'Women entrepreneurs and financial capital', *Entrepreneurship Theory and Practice*, September 6, 643–65.

Penrose, E.T. (1959), *The Theory of the Growth of the Firm*, New York: John Wiley.

Robb, A.M. (2002), 'Entrepreneurial performance by women and minorities: the case of new firms', *Journal of Developmental Entrepreneurship*, **7** (4), 383–97.

Robb, A.M. and J. Watson (2010), 'Comparing the performance of female- and male-controlled SMEs: evidence from the United States', unpublished working paper.

Robb, A.M. and J. Wolken (2002), 'Firm, owner, and financing characteristics: differences between female- and male-owned small businesses', Federal Reserve Working Paper Series, 2002-2018.

Robb, A., J. Ballou, T. Barton, D. DesRoches, F. Potter, E.J. Reedy and Z. Zhao (2009), *An Overview of the Kauffman Firm Survey: Results from the 2004–2007 Data*, Kansas City, MI: Kauffman Foundation.

Rosa, P., S. Carter and D. Hamilton (1996), 'Gender as a determinant of small business performance: insights from a British study', *Small Business Economics*, **8**, 463–78.

Rugman, A.M. and A. Verbeke (2002), 'Edith Penrose's contribution to the resource-based view of strategic management', *Strategic Management Journal*, **23** (8), 769–80.

Scott, J., W. Dunkelberg and W. Dennis (2003), *Credit, Banks and Small Business – The New Century*, Washington, DC: National Federation of Independent Businesses.

Sirmon, D.G. and M.A. Hitt (2003), 'Managing resources: linking unique resources, management, and wealth creation in family firms', *Entrepreneurship Theory and Practice*, Summer, 339–58.

Treichel, M.Z. and J.A. Scott (2006), 'Women-owned businesses and access to bank credit: evidence from three surveys since 1987', *Venture Capital*, **8** (1), 51–67.

US Census Bureau (2010), *2007 Survey of Business Owners*, available at: http://www.census.gov/econ/sbo/ (accessed 15 December 2010).

Vroom, V.H. (1964), *Work and Motivation*, New York: John Wiley and Sons.

Walker, D. and B.E. Joyner (1999), 'Female entrepreneurship and the market process: gender-based public policy considerations', *Journal of Developmental Entrepreneurship*, **4** (2), 95–116.

Watson, J. (2002), 'Comparing the performance of male- and female-controlled businesses: relating outputs to inputs', *Entrepreneurship Theory and Practice*, **26**, 91–100.

Watson, J. (2003), 'Failure rates for female-controlled businesses: are they any different?', *Journal of Small Business Management*, **41** (3), 262–77.

Watson, J. (2006), 'External funding and firm growth: comparing female- and male-controlled SMEs', *Venture Capital*, **8** (1), 33–49.

Watson, J. and S. Robinson (2003), 'Adjusting for risk in comparing the performances of male- and female-controlled SMEs', *Journal of Business Venturing*, **18** (6), 773–88.

Wernerfelt, B. (1984), 'A resource-based view of the firm', *Strategic Management Journal*, **5**, 171–80.

PART II

Diverse Questions

5. How do social welfare and support systems influence the attitudes of female entrepreneurs towards risk and options?

Nicholas C. Fairclough

INTRODUCTION

Over the last ten years the field of entrepreneurship has become a distinct and valued field of managerial research. As a consequence, entrepreneurs, entrepreneurial behaviour and characteristics, and the success and failure of new ventures, have been the subject of increasing amounts of academic research, theory-building and empirical testing. However, the majority of this research, valuable though it is, has been predominantly focused on North American individuals, practices, organizations and phenomena. Admittedly, there is a small, and growing, corpus of research which is concerned with data from Western Europe, transitional economies, and the Far East. However, with taking this research into account, the picture is still heavily skewed in favour of North American data and research sites. Because of the preponderance of North American literature, country-specific factors have been lost or ignored. Thus, the power of institutions, cultures and national traits, and their role in entrepreneurial behaviour, success and failure, have not been properly researched or appreciated.

Contextual information (country-specific information) is lacking as a meaningful component of current entrepreneurial thinking and theory-building. As Shane and Venkataraman (2000: 220) write, 'to have entrepreneurship, you must first have entrepreneurial opportunities'; however, different societies, cultures, and legal and political systems will provide different opportunities, on different terms and at different times. As North (1990: vii) notes, 'History matters . . . the present and the future are connected to the past by the continuity of a society's institutions'. Understanding some of the factors that might affect these varied entrepreneurial settings will help improve the overall understanding of the field of entrepreneurship. At the same time, it will also help define some of the more salient characteristics of a particular society or setting which are beneficial in aiding or hindering the development of entrepreneurial behaviour and impacting the success or failure of entrepreneurial ventures.

On the economic flank of entrepreneurial research, there is an increasing recognition that institutions matter a great deal. Minniti and Lévesque (2008: 606) argue, 'economists are somewhat moving from *Homo Economicus* to *Homo Sapiens*, and the distance between economics and other social and management sciences is declining'. There has been some work done on the role of institutions in forming the entrepreneurial environment (Baumol, 1990; Sobel, 2008), but with roots in the economic view of institutionalism (North, 1990; Williamson, 1998) it fails to give depth to the role, history and traditions of institutions and culture in particular countries. I suggest that to give nuance to our understanding of the role of institutions in entrepreneurship, we should be adopting a more sociologically oriented lens and addressing not simply the regulatory institutions in a particular economy, but also the normative and cultural-cognitive institutions (Scott, 2008).

To an institutionalist, institutions exhibit distinctive properties; they are relatively resistant to change (Jepperson, 1991). They also tend to be transmitted from generation to generation, and are thus maintained and reproduced (Zucker, 1977). Finally, institutions are 'the more enduring features of social life . . . giving solidarity to [social systems] across time and space' (Giddens, 1984: 24). As Scott suggests, 'to an institutionalist, knowledge of what has gone before is vital information' (Scott, 2008: 47).

This chapter addresses one specific societal-level institutional characteristic: the level of social welfare and the degree of social support provided to women in a society. Through an examination and analysis that focuses on social welfare, I adapt an established typology (Esping-Andersen, 1990) from the field of political science to identify and categorize various shades of welfare regime. I then develop an argument to illustrate how the risk-reward calculation and a real options perspective (McGrath, 1999) will be affected by the specific climate prevailing in a particular country. I suggest that generous social welfare regimes, driven by political ideology and a real options logic, will encourage the development of a more vibrant entrepreneurial environment (where risk and endeavour are rewarded). I also suggest that the provision of a strong social welfare safety net can both promote entrepreneurial venture, but also be detrimental to the creation of a strong entrepreneurial ethic. More specifically, in addressing the specific issues of women's entrepreneurship and a female entrepreneur's motivation and behaviour, I examine what role attitudes towards welfare provision and the formation of social welfare policy might have on women's entrepreneurship attitudes, activity and aspirations. Further, what role might different social welfare policy approaches play in encouraging women entrepreneurs to achieve success and persevere through the often difficult early years, when failure rates are the highest (Shepherd et al., 2000)? I will then consider the role of exogenous support in mediating the role of social welfare in women's entrepreneurial decision-making, and address the question of work–family conflict and family-specific factors (Jennings and McDougald, 2007). Finally, this chapter speaks to the literature on necessity and opportunity entrepreneurship (Smallbone and Welter, 2001), and how welfare benefits and women's entrepreneurship might be understood in this context.

THE IMPORTANCE AND RELEVANCE OF COUNTRY-SPECIFIC ATTRIBUTES TO THE FIELD OF ENTREPRENEURSHIP

Varieties of Capitalism

Over the last 30 years, writers in political sociology (Hall and Soskice, 2001) and public policy (Korpi, 1983) have begun a discussion about 'varieties of capitalism,' and several typologies have developed. More recently, management scholars have begun to acknowledge the importance of country specific characteristics in their research (Dobbin, 2004; Guillen, 1994). Further, March and Olsen (1989) introduced the importance of national characteristics and culture into institution theory.

Latterly, some areas of entrepreneurial research are beginning to acknowledge the fact that different economic systems exist in different countries – and these diverse economic systems can and do have an important bearing on the level and type of entrepreneurial activity that exists at the national level (Sobel, 2008). Indeed, the systematic country level research carried out by the Global Entrepreneurship Monitor (GEM) project has, for the first time (GEM, 2008), adopted a typology of country-specific economic development based on Porter et al.'s (2002) distinction between 'factor-driven economies,' 'efficiency-driven economies' and 'innovation-driven economies'. However, in this chapter I have adopted and adapted a typology from the field of political science which is more relevant to industrialized nations, where attitudes towards tax and welfare policies are well established and culturally embedded, and the democratic process is well defined. This typology is particularly well suited to an analysis of the focal institutional factor (the existence and degree of availability of social welfare benefits) and provides a convenient, well-respected framework for theory-building.

DEVELOPING A TYPOLOGY OF SOCIAL WELFARE REGIMES

The provision of social benefits to a citizenry is a fundamental role of governments across all types of economic systems, both developed and developing. However, social welfare and social services have to be paid for; thus, governments of all political persuasions impose taxes in order to elicit the funds necessary to allow a society to function adequately. However, taxation levels imposed by national governments vary enormously from country to country. Different societies and national cultures have different attitudes towards taxation, including who and what should be taxed as well as how tax revenues should be spent. In some countries the inclusion of free or subsidized healthcare is an integral part of what the state should provide, while in other countries responsibility for healthcare lies beyond the state.

State spending on welfare and social programs is a particularly strongly demarked area of national difference even among the most developed nations, such as members of the G7 and G20 (Adema and Ladaique, 2009). Because higher spending on social welfare provision requires the imposition of higher levels of taxation – both on individuals and organizations – the question of the extant degree of welfare provision in a particular society and whether it is likely to change (to a greater or lesser degree) is one that has both political and cultural implications. From 1945 through to the 1970s, there was a seeming consensus in Western Europe that the ideas of welfare state full employment and expanding social citizenship rights (effected in many states following the Second World War) had achieved a condition of permanency (Korpi, 2003). However, the large-scale unemployment of the 1970s began a process of retrenchment in welfare provision and spending that has been further affected by 'greying' populations, changing family dynamics, an increasing share of women in the labour force and expanding service sectors in countries that have experienced decreasing economic growth rates (Pierson, 2001a, 2001b). Further, over the last 30 years new discourses have developed which have begun to question long-held ideals and expectations about the role of the state and the breadth of provision of social welfare, such that concepts central to the idea of a welfare state, such as universality and solidarity (Marshall, 1981), are being replaced by notions such as targeting and selectivity, and an increased emphasis on individual responsibility (Andersen, 2005; Cox, 1998). This has produced more defined differences in welfare regimes and the idea of 'universality' in particular jurisdictions. Academics might disagree as to how and why these divergent paths developed (i.e. post-industrial causes (Pierson, 2001a, 2001b) versus power conflicts between class-related groups and political parties (Esping-Andersen, 1990; Huber and Stephens, 2001)), but there is little disagreement that these differences do exist (Korpi, 2003).

This chapter adopts the typology developed by the Danish political scientist Esping-Andersen (1990), which divides nations into three categories for the purposes of addressing their respective populations' attitudes to social welfare provision. This typology was chosen in preference to several other possible welfare state categorizations (e.g., Korpi and Palme, 1998; Leibfried, 1992; Siaroff, 1994) because it specifically identifies and addresses the relationship between the state, the market and the family in its analysis. All of these factors are important to the propositions developed below.

The Esping-Anderson Welfare State Typology

Esping-Andersen's (1990) typology distils countries into three essential types: 'liberal,' 'conservative' and 'social democratic.' Typical examples of each are the US, Germany and Sweden, respectively (see Table 5.1). Esping-Andersen argues that the classification is best conceptualized as groupings of states rather than along a particular spectrum from 'strong' to 'no' welfare state. The theory, and subsequent typology, is based on the concept of 'de-commodification,' which refers to the extent to which access and rights to welfare benefits in a society are automatic and universal. Esping-Andersen writes, 'de-commodification occurs when a service is rendered as a matter of a right, and when a person can maintain a livelihood without reliance on the market' (1990: 141).

However, the mere provision of social welfare does not necessarily equate to high 'de-commodification' if, ultimately, individuals still have some dependence on the market. Means-tested benefits may possibly offer a safety net to individuals with the most dire need; however, if those benefits are minimal, and society attaches social stigma to claiming them, then all but the poorest or most desperate individuals in that society will seek to participate in the market. Thus, Esping-Andersen defines a de-commodifying welfare state as one that 'must entail that citizens can freely, and without potential loss of job, income or general welfare, opt out of work when they themselves consider it necessary' (1990: 143). In this typology the Scandinavian welfare states tend to be the most de-commodyfying, and the Anglo-Saxon states the least.

De-commodification is therefore a widely debated and hugely contested concept in the welfare state development (Esping-Andersen, 1990). Countries have developed different attitudes to the question of de-commodification and exhibit differences in the degree to which the concept

Table 5.1   Esping-Andersen's typology

Regime type	Characteristics	Example countries
Liberal	Means-tested assistance, modest universal transfer payments, modest social insurance plans	USA, Canada, Australia
	Benefits mainly for low-income, usually working class, state dependants	
	The limits of welfare equal the marginal propensity to opt for welfare instead of work	
	Entitlement rules strict, often associated with stigma, benefits typically modest	
Conservative or corporatist regime	State is primary provider of welfare, private insurances and occupational fringe benefits play a marginal role	Austria, France, Germany, Italy
	Rights associated with class and status. State's emphasis on upholding status differences mean redistributive impact is negligible	
	Typically shaped by the Church, hence strongly committed to preservation of traditional family	
	Social insurance specifically excludes non-working wives; family benefits encourage motherhood	
	Daycare, and similar family services, are conspicuously underdeveloped	
Social democratic	Principles of welfare state are extended to the middle classes, promotion of equality of highest standards not minimum needs, one universal insurance system	Sweden, Denmark, Norway, Finland
	Services and benefits at levels commensurate with tastes of the middle classes; equality provided by guaranteeing workers full participation in quality of rights enjoyed by the better-off	
	All benefit, all are dependent and all will presumably feel obliged to pay	
	State grants transfers directly to children, takes direct responsibility of caring for children, the aged and the helpless	
	Commitment to allowing women to choose to work rather than the household	

is developed within their own particular societies. Taking as examples the three countries cited above, the differences become apparent.

Liberal regime: the United States

In the United States, welfare provision is not automatic, entitlement to unemployment benefits is not routine, and the state does not play an active role in the provision of healthcare and retirement benefits.

Conservative regime: Germany

Under Bismarck in the 1880s, Germany was the pioneer of social insurance with the introduction of state insurances to cover workers' health and disability, and the first real old-age pension provision. However, over the course of the twentieth century, Germany's attitude towards social welfare has not moved towards the de-commodification model, with benefits to workers depending almost exclusively on their contributions into the system made through taxes; thus, the availability of benefits, though generous, are dependent upon previous work and employment.

Social democratic regime: Sweden

In contrast to Germany and the US, in Sweden unemployment and sickness benefits are universally available and generous, healthcare is of a consistently high standard and free to those in need, and retirement benefit provision is managed and guaranteed by the state. However, the generosity of these systems does come without a price. Because of the enhanced levels of benefits, and their universal application, it is clear that the Swedish system must necessarily involve higher levels of government spending. Therefore, taxation rates are much higher than in the US. Indeed, figures for 2008 indicate that income tax rates in the US ranged from 10 per cent to 35 per cent, while in Germany rates ranged from zero to 45 per cent and in Sweden from 28.9 per cent to 59 per cent (OECD, 2010).

The US and Sweden are thus two countries with markedly different approaches to the provision of welfare to their citizens. The Swedish welfare model provides automatic rights to unemployment benefits, child support, and healthcare and daycare, all of which would be deemed generous (and highly unusual) by US standards. In Sweden unemployment benefits are a minimum of $50 per day for everyone over the age of 20, and can, in most circumstances, rise to as much as 80 per cent of the claimant's previous salary (capped at $108 per day); these benefits can be paid for up to 18 months before falling to the minimum. There are also generous provisions for children, with childcare payments when a child is sick or disabled and generous provisions if a parent becomes sick or suffers from a long-term illness (Försäkringskassan, 2011). In contrast, the US benefits system is far from universal; around 65 per cent of those out of work do not qualify for unemployment benefits (exceedingly few self-employed individuals actually do qualify). Further, US childcare provisions vary wildly in quantity and quality, and have to be paid for by individuals (with limited exceptions) (US Department of Health and Human Services, 2010). Hence, the Swedish system provides a well-developed and reliable safety net, without the need for contributions or the imposition of a threshold means-test. In this system women entrepreneurs can be sure of adequate income and support in the case of business failure and help to cover the costs of illness and looking after children. The US system does not have this type of coverage; healthcare and childcare provisions are normally provided by an employer (not the state), if provided at all.

There are critics of the Esping-Andersen typology. Some point to the fact that it fails to adequately categorize some countries, such as the UK and the Mediterranean European countries, because they have characteristics which fall into more than one of the regime types (Arts and Gelissen, 2002). Others suggest that a fourth regime type should be added to cover countries such as Australia and New Zealand (Castles and Mitchell, 1993). Furthermore, some point to the fact that the typology does not take gender into account (Orloff, 1993). Lastly, critics note that countries falling within the same regime type can have demonstrable variations in their levels and extent of social welfare provisions (Leira, 1992). However, despite these critiques the typology provides a valuable comparative backdrop on which to examine the interplay of social welfare provision and women's entrepreneurial thinking and behaviour.

The Effects of Welfare and Social Service Provision on Women's Entrepreneurship

Having established a typology of welfare regimes and highlighted cultural attitudes towards them, how is this helpful for our understanding of how a particular state's approach to welfare provision interacts with the creation of an entrepreneurial culture for women? Some of the tangible differences between the states that have been outlined above illustrate how social benefits and social provisions vary from country to country. However, what effect does this have on women entrepreneurs and their proclivity to develop from nascent to actual entrepreneurship?

The conventional use of the term 'entrepreneur' refers to individuals who take the risk of founding an organization (Aldrich, 2005). Having identified an entrepreneurial opportunity, a budding female entrepreneur must take the positive and decisive step to found a business venture and manage it. Taking this step necessarily entails the tacit recognition and acceptance of all the risks that go with it, including the recognition of a priori irreducible uncertainty (Venkataraman, 1997). Nascent female entrepreneurs are cognisant of the fact that new businesses can fail (and do so in great numbers). Thus, one potential outcome of their venture is failure. However, even if a business does not fail, it should be recognized that, at the very least, the business is likely to experience temporal variations in returns to the owner and any investors. Therefore, a nascent female entrepreneur will carefully weigh the pros and cons of investing personal and social capital in a new venture, and will consider the alternatives available.

As McGrath writes, 'a complete accounting of a real option's worth requires an understanding of the other options in play' (1999: 15). Consequently, a decision to become a practising entrepreneur will invariably involve the conscious rejection of other employment opportunities and, most likely, the investment of the individual's capital (and perhaps her family's capital) in the venture. The entrepreneur will form some view of the likely success of the venture, and will need to balance the risk of success against failure.

Giving up a position of steady employment in favour of the uncertainty of pursuing an entrepreneurial venture could have negative financial consequences, especially when a woman trades the certainty of income from employment (and perhaps the associated benefits of childcare and health insurance) for the uncertainties associated with entrepreneurial venturing. Therefore, adopting McGrath's real options approach (1999), in Sweden nascent women entrepreneurs have to balance the options of beginning a new venture or retaining an employee position. They would know that should a new business fail they can rely on the generous state benefits to adequately fill the resultant gap in earnings; also, crucially, they can rely on the state to provide the childcare and child healthcare that they would have lost by giving up an employed position. Further, a Swedish stay-at-home mother who has to care for her children but wishes to start a new business will be aware of the state's provision of free healthcare and childcare. Consequently, her choice to pursue entrepreneurship is not constrained by the need to cover these costs (and she does not have to worry about having to pay for them out of the new venture's early revenues).

The environment for intending US women entrepreneurs differs greatly from that of Sweden. The US counterpart would have to make provisions – both financially and practically – for childcare, and for personal and child healthcare. She would also know the cost of entrepreneurial failure and how her financial position would be affected (no unemployment benefits, no healthcare). Therefore, one could argue that the decision whether to start a business will be moderated by the levels of welfare provision accorded by the state. This leads to my first proposition:

Proposition 1: A nascent female entrepreneur's decision of whether to create a new venture will depend upon the social welfare system prevailing in the national economy, such that, all things being equal: (a) nascent entrepreneurs in 'social democratic' states (e.g., Sweden) will be more likely to embark on an entrepreneurial venture than their equivalents in 'liberal' (e.g., United States) and 'corporatist' (e.g., Germany) states; and (b) those in corporatist states, will be more likely to embark on an entrepreneurial venture than their equivalents in liberal states.

Further, an entrepreneur facing difficulties with her business (from low profits or low growth, to losses or negative growth) will constantly be contemplating whether to continue a business with a poor prognosis; she may continue with a hope of turning the corner, or throw in the towel, liquidate the business and try again in the near future. Ultimately, the provision of welfare will be a factor. A Swedish entrepreneur knows that she will be entitled to healthcare benefits, free high-quality childcare and generous unemployment benefits should she decide to close her business; her US counterpart might be compelled to continue, despite the signals, because the alternative could be no income, childcare or healthcare.

Proposition 2: An entrepreneur's decision about whether to continue with a poorly performing business will depend upon the social welfare system prevailing in the national economy, such that, all things being equal: (a) an entrepreneur in a liberal state is more likely to persevere with her underperforming venture than her counterparts in social democratic and corporatist states; and (b) an entrepreneur in a corporatist state is more likely to persevere with her underperforming venture than her counterpart in a social democratic state.

Corporatist or conservative states generally have more generous welfare regimes. However, the cultural focus of the regime is more family focused, with family benefits favouring motherhood. For example, in the corporatist state of France the tax system rewards the family unit by aggregating family incomes and dividing by a quotient depending on marital status and number of children, such that the most generous tax rates are available to married couples with three children. Indeed, child benefits are only available to families with two or more children (O'Donoghue and Sutherland, 1999). In addition, the question as to whether an individual has or will have access to personal welfare benefits, such as unemployment benefits, tends to be dependent on the extent to which that individual has 'paid into' the system during previous employment. In the case of mothers who have never worked, or have spent significant time out of the work-force while raising children, it is possible that they will not be entitled to unemployment support and other welfare benefits (because they have not made sufficient contributions into the system).

Therefore, in corporatist states a nascent female entrepreneur will have to consider whether she will be entitled to social benefits if her business fails. If she is currently out of the employment market, she is unlikely to qualify in the future unless the new venture lasts long enough for her to make the requisite contributions. If she is currently in a position as a sala-ried employee she will have to weigh up the risks of giving up guaranteed employment (with associated benefits) against her desire and belief that her new venture has a credible future.

Proposition 3:   In corporatist states, a nascent entrepreneur's decision as to whether to create a new venture will depend upon the extent to which she is entitled to social welfare benefits in the event her business fails.

Exogenous Support

Until now the focus has been on the decision-making and behaviour of an 'average' female entrepreneur – though it is difficult to define precisely what the term 'average' actually denotes. Nevertheless, I can give the term some context by acknowledging the huge diversity in personal circum-stances of women entrepreneurs (Ahl, 2006; Hughes, 2005; Jennings and Provorny Cash, 2006). Women entrepreneurs are diverse in terms of their age, experience, education, personal wealth, whether or not they have children (if so how many and how old), whether they are married, have a partner or are single, and whether they can look to family, friends or other sources of support in the event they need help with their business or family (e.g., childcare).

However, if one is to consider an above-average individual, in terms of income and access to capital, then the propositions set out above are less relevant. A woman (and mother) of above-average means is less likely to have to consider the kinds of issues outlined above. She may have independent means, have sufficient savings or capital not to have to worry about income in the event of business failure; she may perhaps have sufficient alternative income or support to negate any significant concerns about health insurance and the provision of quality childcare. An obvious source of such resources is a working husband or spousal partner. Alternatively, a woman who earns a low income, whether working or not, will be more concerned with the degree to which her home state's welfare regime provides childcare support, child benefits and healthcare. Therefore, I posit that the degree to which the first two propositions have merit will in turn be moderated by the degree to which the nascent female entrepreneur has access to her own savings, capital or alternative monetary support. I will refer to such independent means as 'exogenous support.'

Proposition 4: The relevance of a particular social welfare system to a nascent female entrepreneur's decision as to whether to create a new venture will be moderated by the extent of the exogenous support available to that nascent entrepreneur, such that those with more exogenous support will be less concerned with social welfare considerations.

Work–family Conflict

On the basis that women entrepreneurs are often drawn to new venture creation because of the benefits of more autonomy and greater flexibility when it comes to managing household time demands and work–family conflict (Jennings and McDougald, 2007), how might the likelihood of female entrepreneurial start-up be impacted by family specific factors? Studies have shown that in most Organisation for Economic Co-operation and Development (OECD) countries there is a consensus that childcare should be subsidized, to a greater or lesser extent, by the state (Blau, 2000; Schofield et al. 1996). Whilst in some countries daycare subsidies are intended to promote female employment, in other places the focus is more on redressing social imbalances by committing resources to children from low-income backgrounds (who may be below the poverty line). This perspective sees childcare as an investment in future human capital. Whatever the theoretical underpinnings, childcare costs are generally considered as being, effectively, a 'tax' on female wages (Heckman, 1974) and thus are presumed to reduce a woman's propensity to work in the labour market. Therefore, the extent to which childcare or daycare is made available by the state, and the degree to which it is funded (through the public or private sector), is important to both nascent and active women entrepreneurs.

Jennings and McDougald (2007) highlight the significance of work–family interface considerations and indicate that it is often the mother who takes responsibility for childcare and managing the household. Milkie and Peltola (1999) demonstrated that young children have a negative effect on women's perceptions of work–family balance; therefore, if a mother who is also a nascent entrepreneur is able to rely on the provision of free, high-quality childcare, she is arguably more likely to be willing to take the next steps in new venture creation.

In Sweden, a social democratic regime, childcare is regarded as hugely important. Since the mid-1960s Sweden has had a free, high-quality childcare system with nationally set standards. It is specifically designed to cater for working parents. Centres provide a hot lunch for children; they are open until 6.00 p.m. and, in some communities, are open to cover evening work by the parents (Canadian Union of Public Employees, 2009; OECD, 2001). A Swedish mother considering embarking on an entrepreneurial venture will not have to concern herself about the cost, availability or quality of the childcare she will require.

In Germany, a corporatist regime, childcare is provided by local municipalities. Due to heavy regulations, high market barriers to entry and the dominance of public providers, there are few private suppliers in the market. Childcare is not free, however; the fee is supposed to take into account the parents' income, though research suggests that, in reality, there is little correlation between income and fees paid (Kreyenfeld et al., 2000). Data from the German Socio-Economic Panel suggests that in the mid-1990s the monthly fee for a pre-schooler in all-day childcare was the equivalent of USD80. In the US, during the same period, the average monthly fee paid for childcare by parents was US$240, about three times the amount in Germany (Anderson and Levine, 1999). Furthermore, a US mother will not only have to pay for childcare (and she may have to pay a great deal to find a provider she is happy with), she is also unlikely to find many options for childcare after 5 p.m. Consequently, a US mother has to consider how she will pay for childcare in weighing the possibility of leaving her job to become self-employed (as paid employment might have a childcare provision in her contract).

Proposition 5:   The decision by a mother and nascent entrepreneur on whether to start a new venture will depend upon the cost, quality and hourly coverage of childcare available to her, such that, all things being equal: (a) a female entrepreneur in a social democratic state is more likely to start a new business venture than her counterpart in a conservative or liberal state; and (b) a female entrepreneur in a conservative state is more likely to start a new business venture than her counterpart in a liberal state.

Necessity and Opportunity Entrepreneurship

Women entrepreneurs make an important contribution to the development of national economies, particularly developing and middle-income countries; however, it is recognized that there are varying reasons why an individual may decide to embark upon an entrepreneurial venture. An area of recent research focus is on the distinction between those who are motivated by what they perceive as the chance to exploit a valid entrepreneurial opportunity and those who embark upon an entrepreneurial venture due to necessity, because other options for work are scarce or unavailable (Smallbone and Welter, 2001).

In those countries where welfare benefits are more universally available, and in Esping-Andersen's terminology 'de-commodified', the notion of necessity entrepreneurship should be less prevalent (since the availability of welfare should be sufficient to obviate any need to start a business purely due to the need for income). However, to the extent an individual prefers to work but there are few employment opportunities, the availability of universal benefits would not preclude an individual feeling a 'need' to start her own business.

As discussed above, in corporatist states the amount of welfare payable to someone unemployed is dependent on the amount of money they earned in their previous employment. If there is no previous employment then the amount of welfare paid is *de minimis*; for a woman who has been out of the workforce for some time this is relevant. In liberal states, such as the US and Canada, welfare is means-tested and modest, the qualification rules are strict, and claiming welfare is often associated with stigma. In these countries, when alternative work is scarce or unavailable an individual is arguably more likely to consider an entrepreneurial venture as a means of improving their earning capacity and providing for their family.

Proposition 6:   The degree to which an entrepreneur decides to pursue an entrepreneurial opportunity because other options for work are absent or unsatisfactory will depend upon the welfare regime in which she resides, such that a female entrepreneur in a liberal state is more likely to start a new business venture than her counterparts in corporatist or social democratic states.

DISCUSSION

As the OECD notes, 'It is abundantly clear that entrepreneurship is important for economic growth, productivity, innovation and employment, and many OECD countries have made entrepreneurship an explicit policy priority' (OECD, 2009: 5). However, it is important to recognize that different countries provide different environments for entrepreneurs, some more munificent than others.

The foregoing has provided an introductory level of analysis which has indicated the importance of country-specific factors to the field of women's entrepreneurship research; in addition, I have examined one particular (highly country-specific) institutional factor as a focal factor – that being the existence and degree of availability of social welfare benefits. I have argued that this is an important factor in determining and influencing the behaviour and decision-making of both nascent female entrepreneurs and women entrepreneurs managing underperforming ventures.

However, I have merely scratched the surface in properly exploring both this factor and institutional factors more widely. There is much more work and theory-building that can be done. What is clear is that social welfare regimes, cultural attitudes to the notion of welfare, and attitudes to its availability and those that claim it, are strong institutional factors in any society. Added to this is the fact that men and women are not always equal in the eyes of social benefit systems. Further, some welfare systems are more 'equal' than others.

With regard to public policy, it should be recognized that women find themselves approaching entrepreneurship with different perceptions, expectations and needs. Many social welfare systems trace their roots back to the post-war period; their institutional underpinnings are based on societal make-up and culture that existed then. Societies have changed significantly since that time, however, with the role of motherhood changing and marriage rates falling in many Western countries.[1] Nevertheless, studies still demonstrate that women spend more time caring for children than men (Williams, 2004). A further consideration is the fact that different ethnic groups within countries have different patterns with regard to income, marriage, family make-up and family structure. In the UK, for example, South Asian households are more likely to contain a married couple, and Afro-Caribbean households are least likely to contain a married couple (Walby, 1997).

Public policy should recognize these differences and seek to develop customized and targeted policies. The manner in which a state chooses to provide a safety net to nascent female entrepreneurs is one option that could be usefully examined. The provision of childcare is also clearly an important criterion in developing a munificent environment for potential and already practising women entrepreneurs.

NOTE

1. In the UK the number of women marrying per 1000 unmarried females fell from 48 in 1980 to 21.6 in 2005 (ONS, 2007).

REFERENCES

Adema, W. and M. Ladaique (2009), 'How expensive is the welfare state? Gross and net indicators in the OECD social expenditure database (socx)', OECD Social, Employment and Migration Working Papers no. 92

Ahl, H. (2006), 'Why research on women entrepreneurs needs new directions', *Entrepreneurship Theory And Practice*, **30**, 595–621.

Aldrich, H.E. (2005), 'Entrepreneurship', in N. Smelser and R. Swedberg (eds), *The Handbook of Economic Sociology*, 2nd edn, Princeton, NJ: Princeton University Press, pp. 451–77.

Andersen, J.G. (2005), 'Citizenship, unemployment, and welfare policy', in J.G. Andersen, A.M. Guillemard, P.H. Jensen and B. Pfau-Effinger (eds), *The Changing Face of Welfare: Consequences and Outcomes from a Citizenship Perspective*. Bristol: Policy Press, pp. 75–91.

Anderson, P.M. and P.B. Levine (1999), 'Child care and mothers' employment decisions', NBER Working Paper No. 7058, Cambridge, MA: National Bureau of Economic Research.

Arts, W. and J. Gelissen (2002), 'Three worlds of welfare capitalism or more? A state-of-the-art report', *Journal of European Social Policy*, **12** (2), 137–58.

Baumol, W.J. (1990), 'Entrepreneurship: productive, unproductive and destructive', *Journal of Political Economy*, **98** (5), 893–921.

Blau, D. (2000), 'Child care subsidy programs', NBER Working Paper 7806, Cambridge, MA: National Bureau of Economic Research

Canadian Union of Public Employees, (2009), *Public Child Care Profile: Sweden*, available at: http://cupe.ca/updir/Public_profile_Sweden.pdf (accessed 25 May 2011).

Castles, F.G. and D. Mitchell (1993), 'Worlds of welfare and families of nations', in F.G. Castles (ed.), *Families of Nations: Patterns of Public Policy in Western Democracies*, Aldershot: Dartmouth, pp. 93–128.

Cox, R.H. (1998), 'The consequences of welfare reform: how conceptions of social rights are changing', *Journal of Social Policy*, **27** (1), 1–16.

Dobbin, F. (2004), 'How institutions create ideas: railroad finance and the construction of public and private in France and the United States', available at: http://escholarship.org/uc/item/94n62948#page-2 (accessed 20 May 2011).

Esping-Andersen, G. (1990), *The Three Worlds of Welfare Capitalism*, Cambridge: Polity Press.

Försäkringskassan (2011), 'Social insurance', available at: http://www.forsakring-skassan.se/irj/go/km/docs/fk_publishing/Dokument/Publikationer/broschyrer/Basbroschyrer/basbroschyrer_andra_sprak/social_insurance.pdf (accessed 26 May 2011).

Giddens, A. (1984), *The Constitution of Society: Outline of the Theory of Structuration*, Berkeley, CA: University of California Press.

Global Entrepreneurship Monitor (GEM) (2008), *Executive Report*, N. Bosman, Z.J. Acs, E. Autio, A. Coduras and J. Levie (eds), Babson Park, MA and London: Global Entrepreneurship Research Association.

Guillen, M.F. (1994), *Models and Management: Work, Authority, and Organization in a Comparative Perspective*, Chicago, IL: University of Chicago Press.

Hall, P. and D. Soskice (2001), *Varieties of Capitalism: The Institutional Foundations of Comparative Advantage*, Oxford: Oxford University Press.

Heckman, J.J. (1974), 'Effects of child-care programs on women's work effort', *Journal of Political Economy*, **82**, S136–S169.

Huber, E. and J.D. Stephens (2001), *Development and Crisis of the Welfare State: Parties and Policies in Global Markets*, Chicago, IL: Chicago University Press.

Hughes, K.D. (2005), *Female Enterprise in the New Economy*, Toronto: University of Toronto Press.

Jennings, J.E. and M.S. McDougald (2007), 'Work–family interface experiences and coping strategies: implications for entrepreneurship research and practice', *Academy of Management Review*, **32**, 747–60.

Jennings, J.E. and M. Provorny Cash (2006), 'Women's entrepreneurship in Canada: progress, puzzles and priorities', in C.G. Brush, N.M. Carter, E.J. Gatewood, P.G. Greene and M.M. Hart (eds), *Growth-oriented Women Entrepreneurs and Their Businesses: A Global Research Perspective*, Cheltenham, UK and Northampton, MA, USA: Edward Elgar, pp. 53–87.

Jepperson, R. (1991), 'Institutions, institutional effects, and institutionalism', in P.J. DiMaggio and W.W. Powell (eds), *The New Institutionalism in Organizational Analysis*, Chicago, IL: University of Chicago Press, pp. 143–63.

Korpi, W. (1983), *The Democratic Class Struggle*, London: Routledge.

Korpi, W. (2003), 'Welfare-state regress in Western Europe: politics, institutions, globalization, and europeanization', *Annual Review of Sociology*, **29**, 589–609.

Korpi, W. and J. Palme (1998), 'The paradox of redistribution and strategies of equality: welfare state institutions, inequality and poverty in the Western countries', *American Sociological Review*, **63** (5), 661–87.

Kreyenfeld, M., C.K. Spiess and G.G. Wagner (2000), 'A forgotten issue: distributional effects of day care subsidies in Germany', Discussion Paper No. 198, Bonn: Institute for the Study of Labor (IZA).

Leibfried, S. (1992), 'Towards a European welfare state? On integrating poverty regimes into the European Community', in Z. Ferge and J.E. Kolberg (eds), *Social Policy in a Changing Europe*, Frankfurt am Main: Campus Verlag, pp. 245–79.

Leira, A. (1992), *Welfare States and Working Mothers: The Scandinavian Experience*, New York: Cambridge University Press.

March, J. and J. Olsen (1989), *Rediscovering Institutions: The Organizational Basis of Politics*, New York: Free Press.

Marshall, T.H. (1981), 'The right to welfare,' and 'Afterthought on the right to welfare', in T.H. Marshall (ed.), *The Right to Welfare and Other Essays*, London: Heinemann, pp. 83–103.

McGrath, R.G. (1999), 'Falling forward: real options reasoning and entrepreneurial failure', *Academy of Management Review*, **24** (1), 13–30.

Milkie, M.A. and P. Peltola (1999), 'Playing all the roles: gender and the work–family balancing act', *Journal of Marriage and the Family*, **61**, 476–90.

Minniti, M. and M. Lévesque (2008), 'Recent developments in the economics of entrepreneurship', *Journal of Business Venturing*, **23**, 603–12.

North, D.C. (1990), *Institutions, Institutional Change and Economic Performance*, New York: Cambridge University Press.

O'Donoghue, C. and H. Sutherland (1999), 'Accounting for the family in European income tax systems', *Cambridge Journal of Economics*, **23**, 565–98.

Office for National Statistics (ONS) (2007), 'Marriage rates fall to lowest on record', Office for National Statistics news release, available at: http://www. statistics.gov.uk/pdfdir/mar0207.pdf (accessed on 24 May 2011).

Organisation for Economic Co-operation and Development (OECD) (2001), 'Starting Strong: Early Childhood Education and Care – Sweden', Organisation for Economic Co-operation and Development, available at http://www.oecd. org/dataoecd/44/16/1942365.pdf (accessed on 25 May 2011).

Organisation for Economic Co-operation and Development (OECD) (2009), *Measuring Entrepreneurship: A Collection of Indicators*, Paris: OECD Statistics Directorate.

Organisation for Economic Co-operation and Development (OECD) (2010), 'Public finance – Taxes', *OECD Factbook 2010: Economic, Environmental and Social Statistics*, Paris: OECD.

Orloff, A.S. (1993), 'Gender and the social rights of citizenship: the comparative analysis of gender relations and welfare states', *American Sociological Review*, **58**, 303–328.

Pierson, P. (2001a), 'Coping with permanent austerity: welfare state restructuring in affluent democracies', in P. Pierson (ed.), *The New Politics of the Welfare State*, Oxford: Oxford University Press, pp. 410–56.

Pierson, P. (2001b), 'Post-industrial pressures on the mature welfare states', in P. Pierson (ed.), *The New Politics of the Welfare State*, Oxford: Oxford University Press, pp. 80–104.

Porter, M.E., J.J. Sachs and J. McArthur (2002), 'Executive summary: competitiveness and stages of economic development', in M. Porter, J. Sachs, P.K. Cornelius, J.W. McArthur and K. Schwab (eds), *The Global Competitiveness Report 2001–2002*, New York: Oxford University Press, pp. 16–25.

Schofield, D., P. Josh and A. Hardin (1996), 'Modelling child care services and subsidies', National Centre For Social And Economic Modelling (eds), *NATSEM* Technical paper, no. 10.

Scott, W.R. (2008), *Institutions and Organizations: Ideas and Interests*, 3rd edn, Thousand Oaks, CA: Sage.

Shane, S. and S. Venkataraman (2000), 'The promise of entrepreneurship as a field of research', *Academy of Management Review*, **25**, 217–26.

Shepherd, D., E. Douglas and M. Shanley (2000), 'New venture survival: ignorance, external shocks, and risk reduction strategies', *Journal of Business Venturing*, **15**, 393–410.

Siaroff, A. (1994), 'Work, welfare and gender equality: a new typology', in D. Sainsbury (ed.), *Gendering Welfare States*, London: Sage, pp. 82–100.

Smallbone, D. and F. Welter. (2001), 'The distinctiveness of entrepreneurship in transitional economies', *Small Business Economics*, **16**, 249–62.

Sobel, R.S. (2008), 'Testing Baumol: institutional quality and the productivity of entrepreneurship', *Journal of Business Venturing*, **23**, 641–55.

US Department of Health and Human Services. (2010), 'About the Child Care and Development Fund', accessible at: http://www.acf.hhs.gov/programs/ccb/ccdf/index.htm (accessed 26 May 2011).

Venkataraman, S. (1997), 'The distinctive domain of entrepreneurship research', in J. Katz and R. Brockhaus (eds), *Advances in Entrepreneurship, Firm Emergence, and Growth*, Greenwich, CT: JAI Press, pp 119–38.

Walby, S. (1997), *Gender Transformations*, London: Routledge.

Williams, D.R. (2004), 'Effects of childcare activities on the duration of self-employment in Europe', *Entrepreneurship Theory and Practice*, **28**, 467–85.

Williamson, O.E. (1998), 'The institutions of governance', *The American Economic Review*, **88** (2), 75–9.

Zucker, L.G. (1977), 'The role of institutionalization in cultural persistence', *American Sociological Review*, **42**, 726–43.

6. Should women go into business with their family partner?

Manely Sharifian, P. Devereaux Jennings and Jennifer E. Jennings*

INTRODUCTION

This study investigates outcomes pertinent to a growing yet under-investigated subcategory of female entrepreneurs: the 'copreneurial women' who operate businesses with their spouse or significant other. In North America, copreneurship represents a sizeable and increasing segment of the small business sector. Ruef et al. (2003), for example, found that over half (53 per cent) of the multi-member founding teams in their US sample were comprised of married couples or cohabiting partners. In Canada, more than two-thirds (68 per cent) of the country's dual self-employed couples were in business together in 1998 (Marshall, 1999). Indeed, copreneurial firms have been touted as the fastest-growing segment of not only family-based businesses (Gardner, 1991) but also the small business sector as a whole (Eggertson, 2007).

Despite their increasing prevalence, surprisingly limited academic research has been conducted on copreneurs. This oversight is likely attributable to the individualistic orientation that permeates both the entrepreneurship literature in general (as noted by Gartner et al., 1994) and women's entrepreneurship research in particular (as identified by Ahl, 2006). Although work on entrepreneurial teams is starting to appear (for a review see Blatt, 2009), this, too, tends to ignore the impact of spousal relationships on team dynamics and outcomes. This is so even within studies examining such constructs as sex composition (Godwin et al. 2006), family membership (Ucbasaran et al., 2003) or cohesion and conflict (Ensley et al. 2002). Ruef et al.'s (2003) investigation represents a notable exception, but its focus was on the factors that influenced the initial composition of entrepreneurial founding teams rather than the subsequent outcomes.

Those interested in knowing whether married couples or cohabiting partners who run businesses together experience different outcomes (for example, business performance, job satisfaction and family satisfaction) than other entrepreneurs would be hard-pressed to find a definitive answer, even within the small corpus of research conducted explicitly on copreneurs. As noted by Marshack (1993), early work consisted of anecdotal accounts or single-case studies with limited generalizability. Moreover, subsequent work conducted by Marshack (1994) and others (Baines and Wheelock, 1998, 2000; Baines et al., 2003; Millman and Martin, 2007; Ponthieu and Caudill, 1993) has focused primarily on the internal processes within copreneurial teams, detailing how roles and responsibilities are distributed and negotiated between the marital partners. Although some studies have examined basic outcomes of interest to entrepreneurship scholars – such as firm survival, business performance and/or subjective indicators of entrepreneurial satisfaction (Davidsson, 2004; Shane and Venkataraman, 2000) – their number is very small. This is likely attributable to the difficulties inherent in convincing copreneurial couples to discuss their perceived and actual success (or failure) within the business and family spheres. Those researchers who have been able to overcome this challenge have tended to examine copreneur-only samples (Cole and Johnson, 2007; Smith, 2000) or have compared copreneurs to either non-entrepreneurial, dual-career couples (Marshack, 1994) or to other types of family-run firms (Fitzgerald and Muske, 2002; Muske and Fitzgerald, 2006). As a result, we possess a limited understanding of whether members of married or cohabiting couples who run businesses together experience different outcomes than other entrepreneurs more broadly (and if so, why). We approach this question from a family embeddedness perspective (Aldrich and Cliff, 2003; Jennings and McDougald, 2007), which suggests that entrepreneurs must manage both the business and family spheres in order to be successful. Drawing on Stafford et al.'s (1999) sustainable family business model in particular, we suggest that a greater overlap between these two spheres is likely to result in lower business performance and satisfaction – but higher family satisfaction – in the case of copreneurial teams. We further suggest that fundamental decisions within each domain (particularly the actual or perceived equity, or inequity, of such decisions) will be especially influential on the objective and subjective outcomes experienced by married couples or cohabiting partners who run businesses together.

To test these ideas, we examined previously collected survey data on 163 small business owners in a Western Canadian province, 51 (31 per cent) of whom were part of a copreneurial couple. Multivariate analyses of the full sample of entrepreneurs, and of copreneurs as a subsample, confirmed that copreneurs experience different outcomes in the family domain than other entrepreneurs. Our analysis also revealed that inequity is often present in copreneurial relationships; this inequity has negative implications for both the business and family domains (but not in equal measure). As such, our study helps address not so much an old question about female entrepreneurs as a new one: should women go into business with their family partner?

A FAMILY EMBEDDEDNESS PERSPECTIVE ON COPRENEURIAL OUTCOMES

Copreneurs have recently been defined as couples who share a personal and work relationship in the creation or operation of a new venture of small business (Fitzgerald and Muske, 2002: 1). This definition is consistent with early views of copreneurs as married couples 'who share ownership of, commitment to, and responsibility for a business' (Marshack, 1993: 356; see also Ponthieu and Caudill, 1993). The more recent definition, however, does not require that the couples be legally married, or that both partners hold an ownership stake in the business. As such, it represents a more inclusive view of the term 'copreneur' that exhibits greater compatibility with the evolving notion of family (Aldrich and Cliff, 2003). Moreover, the emphasis on the shared *operation* of the business, rather than shared ownership, helps ensure that situations in which one marital partner is a silent shareholder (likely for tax reasons) and does not participate in the day-to-day operations of the firm are not deemed to be instances of copreneurship.

According to the family embeddedness perspective, the operations and outcomes of copreneurial ventures, like those of any new ventures, will be affected by the nature of the family (Aldrich and Cliff, 2003). Stafford et al.'s (1999) sustainable family business (SFB) model further specifies that the family and the business spheres operate simultaneously and partially overlap. The resources and interpersonal transactions within each sphere influence business and family success, both in objective and subjective terms. Moreover, characteristics and dynamics associated with the family sphere are deemed to be just as influential as those associated with the business sphere. Olson et al.'s (2003) study of enterprising households offers preliminary support for these central arguments.

When applying the SFB framework to copreneurial couples, two fundamental issues arise. These pertain to the specification of the key inputs within each sphere as well as the most pertinent outcomes. On the input side, the above-noted theoretical and empirical work on the SFB model suggests that the division of roles, responsibilities and resources between the partners within both the business and family spheres is essential (along with strategies for handling trade-offs between the two domains). From the standpoint of entrepreneurship theory, dividing up roles, responsibilities and resources is essentially a governance issue (Shane, 2003; Williamson, 1986). Partnerships that arrange their transactions and implicit (or explicit) contracts such that the partners are rewarded relative to their contributions (that is, those that use good governance) should outperform other types of simpler start-up firm forms (Jobin, 2008). Partnerships may be inferior to other forms, however, when the division of roles, responsibilities and resources is not handled effectively. In the family sphere, governance is deemed to be more normative and implicit, but still involves the division of labour and the sharing of tasks (Marshack, 1993; Stafford et al., 1999). In addition, governance in the family is strongly affected by other norms such as the need for harmonious operation and long-term commitment (Marshack, 1993). As a result, equity in the arrangement of family tasks (whether actual or perceived) is likely to be a particularly salient and influential input (Marshack, 1994; Olson et al., 2003), just as it is in the business sphere.

Turning from inputs to outcomes, a family embeddedness approach in general, and the SFB model in particular, call attention to the importance of examining not only business-related outcomes but also family-related outcomes in studies of entrepreneurship (Aldrich and Cliff, 2003; Olson et al., 2003; Stafford et al., 1999). This line of work also emphasizes the value of investigating subjective as well as objective outcome indicators. This is consistent with calls in women's entrepreneurship research (Ahl, 2006; Brush, 1992; Cliff, 1998) and the entrepreneurship literature more broadly (Calás et al., 2009; Davidsson, 2004; Shane and Venkataraman, 2000). We therefore incorporate objective and subjective outcomes related to both the business and family spheres within our ensuing theorizing and analysis.

THE EFFECTS OF COPRENEURSHIP ON BUSINESS AND FAMILY OUTCOMES

We focus first upon the direct effect of copreneurship on the above-noted outcomes. In contrast to those comparing copreneurs to dual-career couples (Marshack, 1994; Marshall, 1999) or to other forms of family-run businesses (Muske and Fitzgerald, 2006), our comparison group consists entirely of small business owners who are not part of a copreneurial couple. These can include sole proprietors as well as members of entrepreneurial teams comprised of non-family members and/or family members other than marital partners (for example, parent–child teams). These other entrepreneurs may (or may not) have spouses or significant others with (or without) jobs, careers or businesses of their own.

Some scholars have argued that firms run by copreneurs are likely to outperform others (especially sole proprietorships) because of the pooling of resources and time on behalf of the marital partners (Millman and Martin, 2007). However, the majority of researchers agree with the original insights of Barnett and Barnett: 'Copreneurs are not empire builders – they are dream builders . . . ' (1988: 202). As such, instead of optimizing the firm's outcomes, copreneurs often operate their businesses as a means of sharing resources and responsibilities between the firm and the household. Olson et al. (2003), for example, demonstrated that members of business families tend to pursue several trade-off (resolution) strategies between the firm and the household, such as shifting time and money between the two (even from the former to the latter). Fitzgerald and Muske (2002) further demonstrated that, from the outset, copreneurs have fewer financial resources, make lower salaries and view their business as less successful than non-copreneurs in other types of family firms. Furthermore, Baines et al. (1997) demonstrated that businesses co-owned by spouses tend to perform worse than other co-owned businesses. We therefore hypothesize that:

Hypothesis 1:   Firms led by copreneurs will exhibit poorer business performance than those led by other entrepreneurs.

The implications for business satisfaction are not as straightforward. In general, research on self-employment shows that self-employed individuals have more job satisfaction compared to those who work for an organization, typically because of the autonomy and flexibility they experience in their jobs (Hughes, 2005; Hundley, 2001). But if copreneurial businesses underperform their counterparts in financial terms, satisfaction research (Porter et al., 2003) seems to suggest that copreneurs will express less satisfaction within the business sphere than other entrepreneurs. That said, Barnett and Barnett's (1988) more focused research revealed that marital partners are typically motivated to launch business ventures for very different (and often non-economic) reasons than other entrepreneurs. As such, they are likely to be less troubled by any substandard financial performance, especially if their business is profitable. Moreover, the increased work–life flexibility, sharing of tasks and psychic understanding between copreneurial couples is likely to compensate for any dissatisfaction with their firm's financial performance relative to others. As a result of these counterbalancing mechanisms, then, we hypothesize that:

Hypothesis 2: Copreneurs will exhibit no observable differences relative to other entrepreneurs in terms of their satisfaction within the business sphere.

In turning to family satisfaction, we expect that clear differences will emerge between copreneurs and other small business owners. One of the commonly observed problems facing working women is finding time to balance the household and work tasks. To overcome this problem, some working women decide to start a business with their spouse or significant other in order to have more flexibility in both family and business domains (Epstein, 2002; Millman and Martin, 2007). Indeed, a qualitative study of 20 Australian copreneurs showed that family management was enhanced by copreneurship, due to the flexibility it provided individuals for handling tasks at work and home (Smith, 2000). Apart from these practical benefits, copreneurship is likely to result in psychic benefits within the family sphere. For example, due to their closer connection with the demands faced by their spouse or significant other, copreneurs are likely to be more empathetic and experience less guilt than other entrepreneurs about the amount of time that they are investing into the business. For both practical and psychic reasons, then, we expect that:

Hypothesis 3: Copreneurs will express greater satisfaction with respect to the family sphere than other entrepreneurs.

Even though copreneurs are likely to be more satisfied than other small business owners in the family domain, we nevertheless suspect that they will fare less well on a key objective outcome indicator pertinent to this sphere – household income (Marshall, 1999; Olson et al., 2003). This expectation derives from Hypothesis 1, which predicts that firms led by copreneurs will experience poorer economic performance than those led by other entrepreneurs. Moreover, many of those non-copreneurs are likely to have spouses with jobs, careers or even businesses of their own, which further increases the income-generating capability of their households. As such, we expect that:

Hypothesis 4: Copreneurs will experience lower levels of family performance (that is, household income) than other entrepreneurs.

THE EFFECTS OF BUSINESS AND FAMILY EQUITY ON WITHIN-SPHERE OUTCOMES

Having argued that copreneurial outcomes are likely to differ from those of non-copreneurial firms, our next theory-building step is to discuss how equity in the business and family spheres affects the outcomes experienced by copreneurs.[1] While it would be possible to examine the effects of equity for other entrepreneurs as well, we will limit ourselves here to theorizing only about the world of copreneurs. We do this for two reasons. First, research on entrepreneurship has recently emphasized the heterogeneity of new venture types (for example, Davidsson, 2004); hence, it is crucial to understand each type in its own right (a claim evident within the women's entrepreneurship community as well). Second, much of the research on copreneurs has focused on the internal operations of copreneurial firms as a distinct group, rather than on their operations relative to non-copreneurial firms. To speak to these claims and findings, we need the same starting point.

According to the SFB model, and work–family research more broadly, the equity experienced by a copreneur within the business and family spheres is likely to impact outcomes not only in each sphere but also across them. Within the business sphere, objective perceptions of governance are presumed to make a difference for business outcomes, even if the firm is family owned (Ahl, 2006; Stafford et al., 1999). Objective perceptions are based on how equity is arranged in terms of ownership rights and responsibilities (Williamson, 1986). The more equal the rights and responsibilities between partners, the more likely each will be motivated to perform well (Jobin, 2008; see also Adams, 1965). Motivation theory also teaches us that the higher the perceived equity, the higher the satisfaction and performance (Porter et al., 2003). We therefore hypothesize that:

Hypothesis 5:   Among copreneurs, those who perceive greater equity in the business sphere will exhibit: (a) greater performance, and (b) greater satisfaction in the business sphere.

Similarly, greater equity in the division of resources and responsibilities within the family domain is likely to have positive consequences within that sphere. Several studies have shown that the sharing of household tasks is an important feature of copreneurial firms (Barnett and Barnett, 1988; Millman and Martin, 2007; Muske and Fitzgerald, 2006). While female copreneurs are known to employ strategies for perceiving unequal sharing of tasks as acceptable, a rough equity of shared tasks obviates this (Jennings and McDougald, 2007). Of course, a sceptic might maintain that males in an 'equitable' arrangement would find the situation less acceptable, and consequently family satisfaction would decline. But recent studies have shown that in the post-millennial era men are more amenable to split loads at home and work (Epstein, 2002), and women now demand more sharing (Millman & Martin, 2007). Moreover, a more equitable division of household labour enables both partners to contribute more equally to the business, thereby potentially increasing the income available to the household. We therefore expect that:

Hypothesis 6:   Among copreneurs, those who perceive greater equity in the family sphere will experience: (a) greater satisfaction, and (b) greater performance in the family sphere.

SPILLOVER EFFECTS OF BUSINESS AND FAMILY EQUITY ON ACROSS-SPHERE OUTCOMES

Given the SFB model's emphasis on overlap and the copreneurship literature's findings about integration, spillover from one sphere of life to another (as a result of greater equity) is likely to be experienced among copreneurs. Research suggests that a more equitable division of responsibilities between couples can decrease tension between business partners (Goffee and Scase, 1985). Olson et al. (2003) also showed that decreased tension can move from one sphere to another. Indeed, Foley and Powell (1997) suggest that the perceived equity within the family domain can reduce work–family conflict and improve the quality of the marital relationship, which might subsequently increase the success of the business (whether measured in objective or subjective terms). We thus explore whether:

Hypothesis 7:   Among copreneurs, those who perceive greater equity in the family sphere will also experience: (a) greater performance, and (b) greater satisfaction in the business sphere.

   Whether equity in the business domain will enhance satisfaction at home for copreneurs, however, is more debatable. On the face of it, equity in the business sphere would seem to imply more satisfaction at home, due to the positive spillovers that have been documented between work and family (for example, Greenhaus and Powell, 2006; Rothbard, 2001). However, if there is equity of resources and responsibilities among copreneurs at work, there may also be a larger burden put on the male spouse at home; this could consequently create problems with the traditional division of labour that is known to exist in such relationships (Marshack, 1994). On the other hand, if there is *in*equity at work – whether in the male or female's favour – one partner may not be at home as much as the other, again decreasing satisfaction. A final consideration is that inequalities existent within the business domain may not automatically spillover into the family dimension (Jennings and McDougald, 2007). Some researchers have found, for example, that copreneurs tend to possess strong role boundaries and compartmentalization abilities (Cole and Johnson, 2007; Marshack, 1993, 1994), particularly where negative, tension-inducing issues are concerned. We thus offer this final conjecture as more of an avenue for exploration:

Hypothesis 8:   Among copreneurs, those who experience greater equity in the business sphere will also experience: (a) greater satisfaction, and (b) greater performance in the family sphere.

METHODS

Data

To test our claims, we relied on quantitative data on the operations and performance of 163 small business owners; this data was collected by one of the researchers for a related project. Six hundred firms were sampled from the *Alberta Business Directory* from *InfoCanada*,[2] 200 in each of the following categories: (1) manufacturing firms; (2) retail, wholesale or general service firms; and (3) professional service firms. Franchises were excluded due to their dependence on parent firms. For each of the three industry sectors we selected all businesses headed by women and randomly chose 100 firms headed by men located within the province's two largest metropolitan districts of Edmonton and Calgary. We received completed questionnaires from the primary active owner-manager of 163 firms, for an overall response rate of 27 per cent. Among this group of 163 firms, 51 were run by copreneurs. Apart from hypothesized performance differences, the copreneur subsample was remarkably similar to the non-copreneur sample on all of the control variables. Following the survey, quantitative data on performance was updated annually between 2005 and 2007 using the *InfoCanada* database.

MEASURES

Dependent Variables

Business sphere performance was measured by average sales and by firm average growth in sales from 2004 to 2007. *Business sphere satisfaction* was measured by combining two Likert scale items comprised of the statements, 'Overall, I am very satisfied with being a business owner-manager' and 'I am generally satisfied with the work I do as a business owner-manager'. The items, which were mean centered (Baron and Kenny, 1986), possessed a Cronbach's alpha of 0.72. As a validity check, we calculated the correlation between the business satisfaction scale and a single question capturing perceived success in the business domain. The correlation was positive and significant ($r = 0.47$; $p < .01$), providing evidence of the scale's validity. *Family sphere satisfaction* was measured by a mean-centred factor combining three Likert-type scale questions from the survey: (1) 'Overall, I am very satisfied with my family situation'; (2) 'I am generally satisfied with my family situation'; and (3) 'I frequently think that I would like to change my family situation' (reverse scored). The Cronbach's alpha of the construct was 0.82. As a validity check, we calculated the correlation between the family satisfaction scale and a single question about perceived success in family domain. The correlation was positive and significant ($r = 0.71$; $p < .01$). *Family household income* was measured using a nominal variable with values of one to nine for earnings ranging from under CA$25 000 to over CA$200 000, each variable value representing a CA$25 000 increment.

Independent Variables

Our measure of *copreneurship* was based on the response to the question, 'Does your spouse primarily work in your business?', with a response of yes coded as one and no as zero. *Business sphere equity* was measured objectively by the proportion of shareholder equity held by each member of the copreneurial couple. A differential of zero represented a situation of complete business sphere equity, whereas a differential of 100 represented a situation of complete business sphere inequity. *Family sphere equity* was also based on a relatively objective measure, the participant's response to the question, 'What share of the household and family related tasks would you say that you perform?' We created a nominal categorical variable, with responses of 'none' or 'all' coded as one (that is, low family equity), a response of 'about half' coded as four (that is, high family equity), and answers between these qualitative descriptors coded as either two or three (that is, moderate family equity).

Control Variables

We controlled for several variables in our analyses. Organizational-level controls included firm age, size, complexity and industry. *Firm age* was measured as the number of years in business, as reported by the participant. *Firm size* was measured by the number of employees working in the business at the time of the survey, again according to the survey respondent. *Firm complexity* was measured by the percentage of the business owned by individuals other than the respondent and his or her marital partner. *Industry* was captured by dummy variables, with manufacturing and professional services as the included dummies, and wholesale-retail as the excluded baseline.

Individual- or couple-level controls included the owner's sex, age and the existence of dependents in his or her household. *Owner sex* was coded one for female owners. *Owner age* was measured using the following categories from the survey: one for people under 30 years old, two for those aged 31 to 40, three for those aged 41 to 50, four for those aged 51 to 60 and five for those over 60. The *existence of household dependents* was measured by a dummy variable with at least one dependent at home coded as one (zero if none).

RESULTS

Our hypotheses regarding the main effects of copreneurship on business and family outcomes were tested via OLS regression, as reported in Table 6.1.[3] As shown in Models 1 and 2, we found no significant difference between copreneurial and non-copreneurial firms in terms of business performance. We therefore found no support for Hypothesis 1, that copreneurial firms will underperform relative to non-copreneurial firms. As reported in Model 3 of Table 6.1, however, we found that copreneurship did not influence business satisfaction, thereby supporting Hypothesis 2. Thus, contrary to some prior research (Baines et al., 1997; Fitzgerald and Muske, 2002), it appears that copreneurs do not satisfice when it comes to business outcomes.

Differences between copreneurs and non-copreneurs were more observable in the family sphere. Models 4 and 5 report the effects of copreneurship on family satisfaction and family performance. Copreneurs appear to be more satisfied with their family life than non-copreneurs ($p < 0.10$), lending marginal support for Hypothesis 3. But the effect of copreneurship does not seem to translate into family household income differentials. In Model 5, the total household income of non-copreneurs and copreneurs,

Table 6.1   *The effects of copreneurship on business and family performance and satisfaction*

Variable	Model 1 Bus. avg sales		Model 2 Bus. avg growth		Model 3 Bus. satisfaction		Model 4 Fam. satisfaction		Model 5 Fam. hshld income	
	Coeff.	(St. err.)	Coeff.	(St. err.)	Coeff.	(St. err.)	Coeff.	(St. err.)	Coeff.	(St. err.)
Copreneur	.717	(.883)	.064	(.080)	.101	(.128)	.210	(.164)†	−.318	(.403)
Firm age	.039	(.031)	−.003	(.003)	.000	(.004)	.010	(.006)†	.009	(.014)
Firm size	.079	(.016)***	.009	(.001)***	.004	(.002)	.003	(.003)	.023	(.007)*
% owned others	1.958	(1.481)	−.064	(.138)	.178	(.216)	.316	(.276)	.451	(.665)
Manufacturing	2.691	(1.074)*	−.089	(.097)	.328	(.156)	−.136	(.200)	−1.260	(.493)*
Prof. services	−.501	(1.183)	.083	(.115)	.133	(.172)	−.039	(.218)	.283	(.527)
Female	−.323	(.864)	−.021	(.078)	−.049	(.126)	.025	(.161)	−.769	(.394)*
Owner age	.291	(.494)	−.025	(.044)	.056	(.072)	−.002	(.092)	−.160	(.221)
Dependent(s)	−.703	(.912)	.074	(.082)	−.063	(.133)	.108	(.170)	.501	(.413)
R²	.287		.272		.096		0.065		.201	
F (N)	6.568*** (157)		5.613*** (145)		1.714† (155)		1.110 (154)		3.889 (149)	

Note: † $p < .10$, * $p < .05$, ** $p < .01$, *** $p < .001$ (one-tailed for main variables; two-tailed for control variables).

Table 6.2 Within-sphere effects of business and family equity

Variables	Model 6 Bus. avg sales		Model 7 Bus. avg growth		Model 8 Bus. satisfaction		Model 9 Fam. satisfaction		Model 10 Fam. hshld income	
	Coeff.	(St. err.)	Coeff.	(St. err.)	Coeff.	(St. err.)	Coeff.	(St. err.)	Coeff.	(St. err.)
Business equity	.843	(3.000)	.388	(.222)*	.166	(0.266)	.145	(.112)†	−.805	(.355)*
Family equity	.020	(.073)	.003	(.005)	−.002	(.006)	.013	(.007)†	.022	(.021)
Firm age	.107	(.046)*	.002	(.004)	.006	(.004)	.011	(.004)*	.032	(.014)*
Firm size	6.522	(4.701)	.036	(.354)	.017	(.416)	−.510	(.440)	.712	(1.350)
% owned others	3.618	(2.858)	−.315	(.210)	.519	(.253)*	−.221	(.269)	−1.303	(.864)
Manufacturing	−1.056	(3.585)	−.228	(.295)	.033	(.317)	.154	(.349)	−.076	(1.066)
Prof. services	.369	(2.493)	.167	(.178)	−.063	(.221)	.305	(.232)	.168	(.732)
Female	.778	(1.549)	.029	(.109)	.140	(.137)	−.029	(.136)	.044	(.423)
Owner age	−.125	(2.510)	.080	(.178)	.049	(.222)	.047	(.233)	.373	(.736)
Dependent(s)										
R²	.315		.193		.276		.197		.335	
F (N)	2.095* (51)		.982 (47)		1.739† (51)		1.119 (51)		2.128* (48)	

Note: † p < .10, * p < .05, ** p < .01, *** p < .001 (one-tailed for main variables; two-tailed for control variables).

net of other important factors like business size, are not significantly different. Indeed, simple mean difference tests of copreneurial versus noncopreneurial subgroups showed no significant differences in household family income. Thus, Hypothesis 4 is not supported.

Table 6.2 presents our analysis of the within-sphere effects of business and family equity on copreneurial operations. While business equity has no observable effect on the performance of copreneurial firms when measured by average sales level (Model 6), it does exert a positive impact when measured by average sales growth ($p < .05$ in Model 7), thus supporting Hypothesis 5a. Nevertheless, the effect of equity within the business sphere does not translate into business satisfaction (Model 8), lending little support to Hypothesis 5b.

The within-sphere effect of equity is more noticeable within the family domain. In Model 9, family equity, as measured by shared household duties, has a positive and significant impact on perceived family satisfaction ($p < .10$). This lends some support to Hypothesis 6a. In addition, as shown in Model 10, family equity has a significant effect on family performance, as measured by household income; however, the effect is negative rather than positive, which runs counter to Hypothesis 6b.

Our hypotheses regarding the across-sphere spillover effects of family and business equity are tested in Table 6.3. While we find no observable effect of family equity on average sales, family equity does influence the average sales growth (Model 12) and business satisfaction (Model 13). However, it actually *lowers* rather than enhances them, supporting the opposite of Hypotheses 7a and 7b. These are rather suggestive exploratory findings, observations more in line with the darker view of work-family resolution or trade-off strategies (Jennings and McDougald, 2007; Marshack, 1994; Olson et al., 2003) than the lighter, more benevolent, view of copreneuring that is typically portrayed within that literature (Barnett and Barnett, 1988; Millman and Martin, 2007).

Turning to the spillover of effects of business equity on the family sphere, we find no evidence in Models 14 and 15 for Hypotheses 8a and 8b that equal ownership among copreneurs influences either family satisfaction or household family income. This could be due to the poor measurement of business equity; however, this counterargument seems to be incorrect. In additional (unreported) analyses, we found that business equity affected family satisfaction under some conditions. It seems more likely, then, as some researchers have suggested (Jennings and McDougald, 2007; Olson et al., 2003), that the use of conflict-resolution strategies and trade-offs by copreneurs seals off the family sphere from spillover from the business sphere.

Table 6.3 *Across-sphere effects of family and business equity*

Variables	Model 11 Bus. avg sales		Model 12 Bus. avg growth		Model 13 Bus. satisfaction		Model 14 Fam. satisfaction		Model 15 Fam. hshld income	
	Coeff.	(St. err.)	Coeff.	(St. err.)	Coeff.	(St. err.)	Coeff.	(St. err.)	Coeff.	(St. err.)
Family equity	.155	(1.188)	-.198	(.082)*	-.170	(.102)*				
Business equity							.036	(.288)	.007	(1.016)
Firm age	.013	(.070)	.000	(.005)	-.003	(.006)	.013	(.007)†	.018	(.023)
Firm size	.109	(.047)*	.000	(.004)	.004	(.004)	.009	(.004)*	.040	(.014)*
% owned others	6.660	(4.671)	.149	(.341)	.091	(.402)	-.484	(.452)	.498	(1.444)
Manufacturing	3.669	(2.859)	-.302	(.201)	.511	(.246)*	-.236	(.275)	-1.191	(.919)
Prof. services	-1.111	(3.706)	-.553	(.281)†	-.180	(.319)	.018	(.345)	.652	(1.127)
Female	.505	(2.468)	.196	(.171)	-.066	(.212)	.278	(.240)	.310	(.787)
Owner age	.961	(1.440)	.094	(.101)	.162	(.124)	-.045	(.149)	.138	(.501)
Dependent(s)	-.235	(2.475)	.013	(.172)	.006	(.213)	.037	(.241)	.421	(.794)
R²	.314		.246		.315		.165		.245	
F (N)	2.085*(51)		1.340 (47)		2.099*(51)		.898 (51)		1.374 (48)	

Note: † $p < .10$, * $p < .05$, ** $p < .01$, *** $p < .001$ (one-tailed for main variables; two-tailed for control variables).

128

DISCUSSION

Contrary to our expectations and to some prior research (Baines et al., 1997; Fitzgerald and Muske, 2002), our study revealed no observable differences between the business performance of copreneurial firms and other entrepreneurial ventures, in economic terms. Consistent with our expectations, however, we found that copreneurs tend to have higher levels of family satisfaction than other small business owners. In addition, we found that equity in the family sphere for copreneurs (that is, the sharing of household tasks) positively affected family satisfaction as an outcome and spilled over into the business sphere; although, contrary to our expectations, it *negatively* affected average sales growth and business satisfaction. Finally, we discovered that business equity (that is, ownership equality) influenced the average sales growth of copreneurial ventures, but had no other observable within- or across-sphere effects.

The first contribution of our theory building and findings is to research on copreneurs. Our study partially confirmed prior research, such as that by Barnett and Barnett (1988), Fitzgerald and Muske (2002) and Olson et al. (2003). These studies documented cases of copreneurs emphasizing the importance of home over work, even to the point of shifting resources from the business sphere to the family domain. At the same time, our findings challenges some recent, rosier views of copreneurship that argue in favour of copreneurship as a means of running the entrepreneurial venture compared to other new venture arrangements (for example, Cole and Johnson, 2007; Millman and Martin, 2007). We did not find evidence that flexibility at home and task sharing spilled over in a positive way into the business domain. Finally, we broadened an understanding of both copreneurship's drawbacks and advantages by specifying, in theoretical and empirical terms, how family and business sphere operations are linked to important outcomes in each domain.

Our second contribution is to the research on the family embeddedness perspective (Aldrich and Cliff, 2003), and the sustainable family business model (Stafford et al., 1999) that falls within this perspective. In keeping with the former, we found that social enmeshment at home and work affected outcomes in each sphere, if not in equal measure or directly. In accordance with the latter, the arrangement of tasks affected not just the outcomes in the family sphere, but also in the business sphere. Nevertheless, the fact that business equity positively influenced business performance, while family equity negatively influenced business performance, shows that there is no exact symmetry in processes associated with each domain. Stafford et al. (1999) discuss this possibility, but their SFB model does not go so far as to suggest an *absence* of effects of the business on the family. This strong mediation is more in keeping with the results found by Olson et al. (2003) and the theoretical model proposed by Jennings and McDougald (2007), which suggest that several work–family conflict resolution strategies may be employed by entrepreneurs. These strategies may be employed even to the point where inequities at work are either reframed as completely acceptable or not perceived at all.

Our third contribution is to the women's entrepreneurship literature. The call in recent years has been for theoretical specification of different contexts and processes in which female entrepreneurs engage (for example, Ahl, 2006; Brush et al., 2009; Hughes, 2005). Marshack (1994) examined copreneurial versus dual-career couple processes in the business and family sphere, and Ruef et al. (2003) examined the composition of founding teams in terms of their homophily and spousal relationships. In a limited way, our study combines elements from these two studies; it also links them to entrepreneurial outcomes, something neither do. We examined female entrepreneurs who were part of a copreneurial team, compared them to entrepreneurs who were not (for example, solo male or female entrepreneurs, unrelated business partners, and so on), and demonstrated the impact of this arrangement on business and family outcomes in firms that spanned three main industry categories. In addition, we theorized how equity (business ownership and household responsibility), as a form of entrepreneurial firm and family governance, was shared within these teams and tested the impacts on both objective and subjective outcomes. We argue that new work in women's entrepreneurship will move in a similar direction; that is, it will specify contexts and mechanisms in a tighter fashion, and then demonstrate their impact on a broad array of outcomes.

Nevertheless, we feel that there are substantial limitations to our work, especially in the context of the women's entrepreneurship literature. We did not explicitly theorize and test the strategies used by female entrepreneurs in different situations to manage the often competing goals of their work and family lives. New work must be more explicit about how these mechanisms and strategies operate in female-led firms, and how they vary by context. Nor did we theorize how different categories of non-copreneurs, many of whom were women, would behave and thus perform as a comparison group to women who were part of copreneurial teams. Instead, we were forced to assume a great deal about such processes and outcomes based on a slim set of theoretical and empirical studies. Again, future work must develop slightly broader theory that details mechanisms across categories of entrepreneurial firms in which women participate, then demonstrates the workings of those mechanisms and identifies strategies needed to improve them. Finally, we were only able to test our model on a limited set of entre-preneurs and copreneurs at primarily one point in time. Recent work (Muske and Fitzgerald, 2006) has begun to move away from these static tests to more dynamic ones using large-scale panel data. We encourage women's entrepreneurship researchers to build and share longitudinal data sets in order to further our collective efforts, test our theories and corroborate our findings.

CONCLUSION

What, then, can our study tell us about our opening question, 'Should women go into business with their family partner?' On the surface, our results suggest that the answer would be 'yes'. Not only did the copreneur-ial businesses in our sample perform just as well as the non-copreneurial firms, but the household incomes of copreneurs and other business owners were also similar. Moreover, those running businesses with their spouses or significant others appear to be more satisfied within the family domain than their non-copreneurial counterparts, and just as satisfied within the business domain. If copreneurship is pursued through a more equitable division of household labour, however, the associated increase in family satisfaction may come at the expense of slower business growth, lower household income and reduced business satisfaction. The trade-offs asso-ciated with more equitable copreneurial arrangements definitely warrant greater exploration in future research.

NOTES

* The data collection for this chapter was supported by SSHRC grant number 501-2001-0017 awarded to Dr Jennifer Jennings. The authors would like to thank Karen Hughes for her valuable feedback on the initial draft.

1. It should be noted that equity does not mean equality. Women and men are likely to perceive equity differently because their sense of entitlement, especially within the family domain, is different. This sense of entitlement is closely linked to social norms and values that define the roles and responsibilities of women and men in the family (Major, 1993).
2. *InfoCanada* is the leading online supplier of business and consumer data in Canada. It is generally recognized as having high quality data, using external research audits to ensure accuracy.
3. Examination of the correlation matrix (available upon request) revealed that multi-collinearity was not an issue, given that no value was over .65. At the same time, the existence of several significant correlations lent support for our claims about the central constructs being independent yet related (Tabachnick and Fidell, 1996).

REFERENCES

Adams, J.S. (1965), 'Inequity in social exchange.', in L. Berkowitz's (ed.), *Advances in Experimental Social Psychology*' (vol. 2), New York: Academic Press, pp. 267–99.

Ahl, H. (2006), 'Why research on women entrepreneurs needs new directions', *Entrepreneurship Theory and Practice*, **30** (5), 595–621.

Aldrich, H.E. and J.E. Cliff (2003), 'The pervasive effects of family on entrepreneurship: toward a family embeddedness perspective', *Journal of Business Venturing*, **18** (5), 573–96.

Baines, S. and J. Wheelock (1998), 'Reinventing traditional solutions: job creation, gender and the micro-business household', *Work, Employment & Society*, **12** (4), 579–601.

Baines, S. and J. Wheelock (2000), 'Work and employment in small businesses: perpetuating and challenging gender solutions', *Gender, Work and Organization*, **7** (1), 45–56.

Baines, S., J. Wheelock and A. Abrams (1997), 'Microbusiness owner-managers in social context: household, family, and growth or non-growth', in D. Deakins, P. Jennings and C. Mason (eds), Small Firms: Entrepreneurship in the Nineties, London: Paul Chapman Publishing, pp. 47–60.

Baines, S., J. Wheelock and U. Gelder (2003), *Riding the Rollercoaster: Family Life and Self-employment*, Bristol: Joseph Rowntree Foundation/Policy Press.

Barnett, F. and S. Barnett (1988), *Working Together: Entrepreneurial Couples*, Berkley, CA: Ten Speed Press.

Baron, R.M. and D.A. Kenny (1986), 'The moderator-mediator variable distinction in social psychological research: conceptual, strategic and statistical considerations', *Journal of Personality and Social Psychology*, **51**, 1173–82.

Blatt, R. (2009), 'Tough love: how communal schemas and contracting practices build relational capital in entrepreneurial teams', *Academy of Management Review*, **34**, 533–51.

Brush, C. (1992), 'Research on women business owners: past trends, a new perspective, and future directions', *Entrepreneurship Theory and Practice*, **16**, 5–30.

Brush, C.G., A. de Bruin and F. Welter (2009), 'A gender-aware framework for women's entrepreneurship', *International Journal of Gender and Entrepreneurship*, **1**, 8–24.

Calás, M.B., L. Smircich and K.A. Bourne (2009), 'Extending the boundaries: reframing "entrepreneurship as social change" through feminist perspectives', *Academy of Management Review*, **34** (3), 552–69.

Cliff, J.E. (1998), 'Does one size fit all? Exploring the relationship between attitudes towards growth, gender, and business size', *Journal of Business Venturing*, **13**, 523–42.

Cole, P.M and K. Johnson (2007), 'An exploration of successful copreneurial relationships postdivorce', *Family Business Review*, **20** (3), 185–98.

Davidsson, P. (2004), *Researching Entrepreneurship*, Boston, MA: Springer.

Eggertson, L. (2007), 'In business for life', *The Globe and Mail*, available at: http://www.theglobeandmail.com/report-on-business/article777038.ece (accessed 19 August 2010).

Ensley, M.D., A.W. Pearson and A.C. Amason (2002), 'Understanding the dynamics of new venture top management teams: cohesion, conflict, and new venture performance', *Journal of Business Venturing*, **17** (4), 365–86.

Epstein, C.F. (2002), 'Wives and husbands working together', in M. Yalom and L.L. Carstensen (eds), *Inside the American Couple: New Thinking, New Challenges*, London: University of California Press, pp. 136–48.

Fitzgerald, M. and G. Muske (2002), 'Copreneurs: an exploration and comparison to other family businesses', *Family Business Review*, **15** (1), 1–16.

Foley, S. and G. Powell (1997), 'Re-conceptualizing work-family conflict for business/marriage partners: a theoretical model', *Journal of Small Business Management*, **35** (4), 36–47.

Gardner, A. (1991), 'Family matters', *The B.C. Home Business Report*, Summer, 8–11.

Gartner, W.B., K.G. Shaver, E. Gatewood and J.A. Katz (1994), 'Finding the entrepreneur in entrepreneurship', *Entrepreneurship Theory and Practice*, **18**, 5–10.

Godwin, L.N., C.E. Stevens and N.L. Brenner (2006), 'Forced to play by the rules? Theorizing how mixed-sex founding teams benefit women entrepreneurs in male-dominated contexts', *Entrepreneurship Theory and Practice*, **20**, 623–42.

Goffee, R. and R. Scase (1985), *Women in Charge: The Experience of Female Entrepreneurs*, London: George Allen and Unwin.

Greenhaus, J.H. and G.N. Powell (2006), 'When work and family are allies: a theory of work–family enrichment', *Academy of Management Review*, **31** (1), 72–92.

Hughes, K.D. (2005), *Risky Business? Women, Self-Employment and Small Business in Canada*, Toronto: University of Toronto Press.

Hundley, G. (2001), 'Why and when are the self-employed more satisfied with their work', *Industrial Relations*, **40** (2), 293–316.

Jennings, J. and D. McDougald (2007), 'Work-family interface experiences and coping strategies: implications for entrepreneurship research and practice', *Academy of Management Review*, **32** (3), 747–60.

Jobin, D. (2008), 'A transaction cost-based approach to partnership performance evaluation', *Evaluation*, **14**, 437–65.

Major, B. (1993), 'Gender, entitlement, and the distribution of family labour', *Journal of Social Issues*, **49** (3), 141–59.

Marshack, K. (1993), 'Copreneurial couples: a literature review on boundaries and transitions among copreneurs', *Family Business Review*, **6** (4), 355–69.

Marshack, K. (1994), 'Copreneurs and dual-career couples: are they different?', *Entrepreneurship Theory and Practice*, **19** (1), 49–69.

Marshall, K. (1999), 'Working together: self-employed couples', *Perspectives on Labour and Income* (Statistics Canada, Catalogue no. 75-001-XPE), **11** (4), 9–13.

Millman, C. and L. Martin (2007), 'Exploring small copreneurial food companies: female leadership perspective', *Women in Management Review*, **22** (3), 232–39.

Muske, G. and A. Fitzgerald (2006), 'A panel study of copreneurs in business: who enters, continues, and exits?', *Family Business Review*, **29** (3), 193–205.

Olson, P.D., V.S. Zuiker, S.M. Danes, K. Stafford, R.K.Z. Heck and K.A. Duncan (2003), 'The impact of the family and the business on family business sustainability', *Journal of Business Venturing*, **18** (5), 639–66.

Ponthieu, L. and H. Caudill (1993), 'Who's the boss? Responsibility and decision making in copreneurial ventures', *Family Business Review*, **6** (1), 3–17.

Porter, L.W., G. Bigley and R.M. Steers (2003), *Motivation and Work Behavior* (7th edn), New York: Irwin-McGraw-Hill.

Rothbard, N.P. (2001), 'Enriching or depleting? The dynamics of engagement in work and family roles', *Administrative Science Quarterly*, **46** (4), 655–84.

Ruef, M., H. Aldrich and N. Carter (2003), 'The structure of founding teams: homophily, strong ties, and isolation among U.S. entrepreneurs', *American Sociological Review*, **68** (2), 195–222.

Shane, S. (2003), *A General Theory of Entrepreneurship: The Individual-Opportunity Nexus*, Cheltenham, UK and Northhampton, MA, USA: Edward Elgar publishing.

Shane, S. and S. Venkataraman (2000), 'The promise of entrepreneurship as a field of research', *Academy of Management Review*, **25**, 217–26.

Smith, C.R. (2000), 'Managing work and family in small "copreneurial" businesses: an Australian study, *Women in Management Review*, **15**, 283–93.

Stafford, K., K. Duncan, S. Dane and M. Winter (1999), 'A research model of sustainable family business', *Family Business Review*, **7** (3), 197–208.

Tabachnick, B.G. and L.S. Fidell (1996), *Using Multivariate Statistics*, New York: HarperCollins.

Ucbasaran, D., A. Lockett, M. Wright and P. Westhead (2003), 'Entrepreneurial founder teams: factors associated with entry and exit', *Entrepreneurship Theory and Practice*, **28** (2), 107–27.

Williamson, O.E. (1986), *Economic Organization: Firms, Markets, and Policy Control*, New York: New York University Press.

7. Are women more likely to pursue social and environmental entrepreneurship?

Diana M. Hechavarria, Amy Ingram,
Rachida Justo and Siri Terjesen

INTRODUCTION

Little is known about whether social entrepreneurship and ecopreneurship are 'gendered' similar to the mainstream concept of entrepreneurship (Bruni et al., 2004a). This omission is surprising given that females seem to be key targets (Pestoff, 2000; Phillips, 2005; Zahra et al., 2009) and agents (Braun, 2010; McKya et al., 2010) of the social entrepreneurship and ecopreneurship strategies promoted around the globe. Moreover, scholars have recently claimed that adopting a feminist analytical lens can help reframe the current conceptualization of entrepreneurship from a mere economic activity to a more complex phenomenon and catalyst for social change (Calás et al., 2009).

De Bruin et al. (2007) call for female entrepreneurship research that incorporates a theoretical approach which emphasizes the role of personal ambitions, and normative and societal environments. This study seeks to fill these gaps by taking into account gender role theory and hegemonic masculinity to investigate the extent to which the social and environmental goals and practices of entrepreneurs are gendered.

To do so, we use a 52-country dataset drawn from the 2009 Global Entrepreneurship Monitor (GEM). We begin by describing how female entrepreneurs enact the common discourse that depicts entrepreneurship as embodying attributes of masculinity and economic rationality (Ahl, 2002; Bird and Brush, 2002; Mirchandani, 1999), what Bruni et al. (2004b) commonly describe under the concept of hegemonic masculinity. Because female entrepreneurs tend to deviate from mainstream entrepreneurship, we hypothesize that they will be less likely than male entrepreneurs to emphasize economic value creation as a goal of entrepreneurial activity. Secondly, based on gender role theory (Eagly, 1987), we suggest that female entrepreneurs are more likely than male entrepreneurs to emphasize social or environmental value creation. In so doing, female entrepreneurs conform to gender stereotypes typically attributed to females, specifically an interpersonal orientation as well as an inherent concern for social or environmental issues (Eagly and Crowley, 1986; Fortin, 2005; Zelezny et al., 2000). Our results show that these gender differences prevail in both entrepreneurs' discourse (that is, their stated goals for social or environmental value creation) and actual practices (the extent to which they create organizations with the main purpose of solving a social or environmental problem). We discuss the practical and theoretical implications of our findings and offer directions for future research.

THEORY AND HYPOTHESES

Gender Roles and Hegemony

Extant literature is replete with discussions about the existence of an entrepreneurial gender divide (Gupta et al., 2009). This divide is often examined through social role theory and its extension, gender role theory (Eagly, 1987; Eagly and Carli, 2003; Rigg and Sparrow, 1994). The latter posits that both sexes adopt stereotypical gender roles in order to gain societal acceptance. Males exhibit more dominant, achievement-oriented behaviours and females display more affiliative and nurturing behaviours. For instance, females 'take care' while males 'take charge' (Furst and Reeves, 2008).

Building upon gender role theory, we argue that hegemony stems from stereotypical gender roles. Hegemonic masculinity is depicted as the patterns of practice, beyond role expectations or identity, which enable male dominance to persist (Connell and Messerschmidt, 2005). However, this lens does not purport that there is a monolithic class of males who oppress females. Instead, hegemonic masculinity is a 'culturally idealized form of masculine character' (Connell, 1990: 83) in which men position themselves in dominant positions by normalizing a given discourse. Hegemonic masculinity is not necessarily the most prevalent masculinity, but rather the most socially endorsed masculinity.

Entrepreneurship depictions embody attributes of masculinity (Bird and Brush, 2002; Bruni et al., 2004a; Mirchandani, 1999), with entrepreneurs described in terms that are associated more with males than with females (Bruni et al., 2004b). Yet, there is limited theoretical understanding of how hegemonic masculinity relates to organizational emergence. This study applies the concept of hegemonic masculinity to advance our understanding of the entrepreneurship phenomena. Specifically, we suggest that a hegemonic masculinity lens sheds light on why male entrepreneurs are more likely than female entrepreneurs to exhibit goals aligned with economic value creation, and why female entrepreneurs are more likely than male entrepreneurs to emphasize social and environmental value creation.

Economic, Social and Environmental Value Creation in Entrepreneurship

Several scholars argue for a more holistic view of entrepreneurial value creation and entrepreneurs' motivations. Empirical findings consistently suggest that some entrepreneurs exhibit strong non-monetary values (Douglas and Shepherd, 2000; Filley and Aldag, 1978; Gorgievski et al., 2011; Low and MacMillan, 1988). For example, Amit and colleagues (2000) report that high technology entrepreneurs are more motivated by lifestyle and contribution than by wealth achievement. Contribution is articulated as 'helping others, making a difference to your organization, community, industry and creating opportunities' (Amit et al., 2000: 143). The present study develops Cohen et al.'s (2008) typology of entrepreneurial motives, extending the entrepreneurial-economic value creation juxtaposed with two other selected dimensions: entrepreneurial-social value creation and entrepreneurial-environmental value creation.

Economic value creation

Typically, work in an entrepreneurial environment is portrayed as a rational choice; emotional components to pursuing entrepreneurship are largely ignored or silenced (Bruni et al., 2004a). Mainstream entrepreneurship has marginalized females who are considered unable to participate due to their non-masculine traits and behaviours (and instead are engaged in domestic activities). Accordingly, we argue that female entrepreneurs will be less likely to identify with goals and motivations that are typical of mainstream entrepreneurs. One such goal is economic value creation.

Our arguments are based on the traditional depiction of mainstream entrepreneurship as an individualistic and profit-maximizing endeavour. Entrepreneurship is commonly defined as the utilization of productive factors for the creation of economic goods intended to increase the residual element in business income (namely, profits), or to achieve some other business gain (for example, power, efficiency, survival or growth) (Cole, 1946). In contrast, female entrepreneurs consistently emphasize non-monetary entrepreneurial motivations (Brush, 1992; Buttner and Moore, 1997; MacNabb et al., 1993; Romano, 1994; Walker and Brown, 2004). Subsequently, we propose:

Hypothesis 1a: Males are more likely than females to emphasize goals of economic value creation when pursing entrepreneurial activity.

Social value creation

Entrepreneurship's social value is widely recognized by scholars (Austin et al., 2006; Zahra et al., 2009), practitioners (Bornstein, 2005) and policy-makers (Korosec and Berman, 2006). We suggest that the concept of social entrepreneurship has been socially constructed to align entrepreneurship more appropriately with the stereotypically feminine domain. This is because social entrepreneurship departs from traditional entrepreneurship in that it does not focus necessarily on economic value; social value creation is explicit and central (Mair and Marti, 2006; Zahra et al., 2009). Successful social entrepreneurs' goals are conceptualized as a less efficient, less rational form of entrepreneurship, which matches the gendered stereotypes of female entrepreneurs. Since performing entrepreneurship involves a gender positioning, we suggest that social entrepreneurship provides an outlet for females to participate in the domain of entrepreneurship; in turn, social entrepreneurship actively reproduces societal expectations of male and female gender roles.

Our view is supported by extant research that posits females are more aligned with social rather than economic goals. Indeed, literature in the social science arena has demonstrated females' proclivity towards altruistic behaviour, spanning a wide range of institutional contexts and methodologies. For example, Eagly and Crowley (1986) report that females are more likely to exhibit long-term helping behaviour. Others find that compared to their male counterparts, females are more likely to engage in volunteer activities (DiMaggio and Louch, 1997) and volunteer more hours per week (Taniguchi, 2006). Furthermore, females' participation in the paid non-profit sector tends to be higher than their male counterparts, both in the USA (Conry and McDonald, 1994) and internationally (McCarthy, 2001). This is significant given that the nonprofit sector is characterized by lower wages, especially when compared with employment in government and business (Themudo, 2009). Similarly, Inglehart and Norris's study (2003), based on World Value Survey data, supports the claim that females display stronger altruistic and equity preferences. These findings reinforce that females tend to be more aligned with businesses that incorporate social well-being rather than economic well-being. Therefore, we propose:

Hypothesis 1b: Females are more likely than males to emphasize goals of social value creation when pursing entrepreneurial activity.

Environmental value creation

Environmental entrepreneurship, or ecopreneurship, is a class of start-up activities aimed to exploit market opportunities centring on environmental concerns (Keogh and Polonsky, 1998). The ecopreneurship literature challenges the conventional masculinity implicit in the traditional ethos and organizational practices of economic entrepreneurship. Ecopreneurship is based on strong green values (Keogh and Polonsky, 1998; Kirkwood and Walton, 2010) and has a powerful moral dimension. Isaak (2002: 81) describes ecopreneurship as 'an existential form of business behavior committed to sustainability'. The capacity to have feelings worth expressing, to be sensitive, to have some depth of emotion, and to care for people and for nature (Connell, 1990) contradict the dominant form of masculine attributes associated with mainstream entrepreneurial activity.

Hence, we expect female entrepreneurs to be more likely to emphasize environmental value creation and exhibit goals that are more compatible with stereotypically feminine values. Indeed, scholars reiterate that female entrepreneurs are more likely to emphasize environmental issues, as compared with their male counterparts. For instance, Davidson and Freudenberg (1996) demonstrate that females have stronger environmental attitudes and behaviours, and Zelezny et al.'s (2000) literature review reveals that these results hold across a broad range of social contexts.

Of special relevance to the subject of our study, Borden and Francis (1978) find that females with high environmental concern are significantly more extraverted ('leader-types') than females with low environmental concern; the opposite relation is true for males. Accordingly, the positive association between entrepreneurship, leadership and extraversion (Vecchio, 2003) suggests that female entrepreneurs are prone to exhibit high environmental concerns, as reflected in their goals for value creation. The contrary could be expected for male entrepreneurs. Braun's (2010) recent study lends additional support to this suggestion, as females participating in green entrepreneurship programmes have stronger environmental attitudes and commitment than do males. Based on the above arguments, we propose:

Hypothesis 1c: Females are more likely than males to emphasize goals of environmental value creation when pursuing entrepreneurial activity.

Goals versus activity

Furthermore, we are interested in investigating whether females actually engage in social or environmental entrepreneurship activity at a higher rate than males, rather than simply espousing an emphasis on social or environmental goals. This analysis offers insight into whether sex differences found in entrepreneurial behaviour studies are due to the usage of a gender-stereotypic rhetoric rather than observations of actual practices (Cliff et al., 2005; Rosener, 1990).

In a study of 229 Canadian businesses, Cliff and colleagues (2005) find that while male and female business owners tend to implement a mix of masculine and feminine organizational characteristics in their firms, there is a disconnect between narrative and practice. Specifically, when asked the question 'what are your goals for the businesses', female entrepreneurs are more likely than male entrepreneurs to report stereotypically feminine objectives (such as building strong interpersonal relationships or attaining life–work balance). In turn, male entrepreneurs are more likely than female entrepreneurs to mention stereotypically masculine objectives (such as increasing their status and wealth). The authors conclude that business owners might not be 'walking the talk' and encourage more systematic research on the subject. It is plausible that female entrepreneurs describe their goals as being more socially oriented and less economically driven than their male counterparts; however, their actions are not aligned with their spoken goals. Based on the above, we explore whether:

Hypothesis 2a: The proportion of females to males in social entrepreneurial activity is greater than the proportion of females to males in economic entrepreneurial activity.

Hypothesis 2b: The proportion of females to males in environmental entrepreneurial activity is greater than the proportion of females to males in economic entrepreneurial activity.

METHODS

To test our hypotheses, we utilize GEM data[1] from 52 countries for 2009. GEM interviews were conducted between May and October 2009; our sample includes only those individuals who were identified as either nascent entrepreneurs or owner managers of young firms (for example, baby businesses), and for whom we have all the data for the key variables of interest. Within this sample, we select three types of respondents: (1) total entrepreneurial activity (TEA) respondents, who are entrepreneurs actively involved in a mainstream business activity; (2) social entrepreneurial activity (SEA) respondents; and (3) environmental entrepreneurial activity (EEA) respondents. The last two groups consist of entrepreneurs actively involved in the creation or development of a social or environmental organization. The total sample of 10362 respondents is weighted according to census adult labour force population (age 18 to 64) data for the respective countries, and centred to adjust for the sample size (the sum of the weights equals the sum of the cases).

Variables

Dependent variables

In order to test Hypotheses 1a, 1b and 1c, we utilize three dependent variables: *economic value goals*, *social value goals* and *environmental value goals*. These measures correspond to TEA respondents who were read the statement 'Organizations may have goals according to the ability to generate economic value, societal value, and environmental value', and then asked to 'Please allocate a total of 100 points across these *three* categories as it pertains to your goals'. Based on their highest response to the goals question, entrepreneurs were categorized as economic, social or environmental TEA participants.

Hypotheses 2a and 2b are tested using SEA and EEA measures, respectively. Specifically, social or environmental entrepreneurship is indicated by a positive response to the following question:

> Are you, alone or with others, currently trying to start or currently owning and managing any kind of activity, organization or initiative that has a particularly social, environmental or community objective? This might include providing services or training to socially deprived or disabled persons, using profits for socially oriented purposes, organizing self-help groups for community action, and so on.

A series of follow-up questions further helped to identify whether the activities were mainly social-oriented (SEA) or environmental-oriented (EEA).

Independent variables

The respondents' self-reported biological sex (male or female) is coded as the bivariate *gender* variable.

Control variables

We control for respondents' age, household income, education and home country. *Age* is often identified as a factor that influences entrepreneurial activity (Gartner et al., 2004), as well as social entrepreneurship intentions (Nga and Shamuganathan, 2010) and environmental attitudes (Zelezny et al., 2000). Past studies also indicate that education levels influence entrepreneurial activity (Autio et al., 2001; Honig, 2004; Krueger, 1993; Peterman and Kennedy, 2003). We measure *education* as an ordinal variable harmonized with the United Nations coding scheme: pre-primary, primary, lower secondary, higher secondary, post-secondary, first stage of tertiary education and second stage of tertiary education. As availability of resources may influence the organizational emphasis of the start-up or young firm, we include household income. *Household income* is recoded into an ordinal variable to represent the lowest third percentile, middle third percentile and the highest third percentile of reported household income among respondents. Individual values vary with a country's cultural and institutional framework (Schwartz and Rubel-Lifschitz, 2009). Accordingly, we control for *country* utilizing a nominal variable to represent the respondent's country of origin.[2] Finally, respondent answers to SIC industry were coded into the nominal variable *industry* to represent four major industry categories: extractive, transforming, business services and consumer oriented services.

RESULTS

Descriptive statistics for the sample (n = 10362) can be found in Table 7.1. The sample is 49.3 per cent male and 50.7 per cent female. On average respondents are 38.6 years old; 69.8 per cent have completed post-secondary non-tertiary education or higher, and 47.4 per cent are in the upper third percentile for household income. The industry split is as follows: 8.3 per cent extractive, 21.4 per cent transforming, 12 per cent business services and 58.4 per cent consumer-oriented. Respondents rate organizational value on average as 65.6 per cent economic, 22.2 per cent social and 14.0 per cent environmental. See Table 7.1 for the mean, standard deviations and correlations.

A one-way multivariate analysis of variance (MANOVA) was conducted to test all hypotheses. In order to employ the MANOVA procedure, the dependent variables must be normally distributed. Since the dependent variables for this analysis were negatively skewed, normal scores were generated using the Tukey procedure to normalize responses. Significant differences were found for gender and industry. For gender, the test statistics show Wilks Λ = .999 F = 4.74, df = 3; p = .003. The multivariate η^2 for gender indicates that about 1 per cent of the multivariate variance in the dependent variables is associated with gender. Based on the multivariate test statistics we can conclude that the independent variables have a significant impact on at least one of the dependent variables. We can also reject the hypothesis that the population means on the dependent variables are the same for gender.

The between-subject effects test applies an F test of significance to the

Table 7.1 *Descriptive and bivariate correlations*

Variable	Mean	S.D.	1	2	3	4	5	6	7	8	9	10	11	12	13	14
1. Education	3.14	1.26	1													
2. Household income	2.26	0.78	.272**	1												
3. Age	38.57	13	−.084**	−.053**	1											
4. Gender	0.51	0.5	.043**	.098**	−.018**	1										
5. Extractive industry	0.07	0.26	−.140**	−.128**	.031**	0.016	1									
6. Transforming industry	0.19	0.39	.023**	.058**	.028**	.072**	−.136**	1								
7. Business service industry	0.11	0.31	.175**	.059**	−0.013	.062**	−.097**	−.166**	1							
8. Consumer oriented industry	0.52	0.5	−.126**	−.028**	−.049**	−.137**	−.291**	−.499**	−.356**	1						
9. Economic value emphasis	65.62	25.84	−.029**	.060**	.016**	.113**	.042**	0.009	−.018*	0.001	1					
10. Social value emphasis	22.2	18.84	.022**	.053**	.010**	.080**	−.063**	−0.013	.023**	−0.01	.439**	1				
11. Environmental value emphasis	14.02	14.84	.009**	.044**	.015**	.079**	0.012	0.011	0.013	−0.003	.368**	.544**	1			
12. Economic TEA	0.64	0.25	−.008**	.036**	−.058**	−0.067**	.239**	−0.008	.357**	.261**	.586**	.225**	−.126**	1		
13. Social TEA	0.02	0.05	.017**	−.003	0.007**	0.008**	.026**	−0.001	0.030**	0.035**	.062**	−.188**	−.008**	−.012**	1	
14. Environmental TEA	0.01	0.04	.013**	0.004	0.001	0.006**	0.018**	0.01	0.041**	0.040**	.050**	−.165**	.218**	−.010**	−.002	1

Note: ** Correlation is significant at the 0.01 level (2-tailed). * Correlation is significant at the 0.05 level (2-tailed).

relationship of each covariate (age, education, household income) and factor (gender, industry, country) to each dependent variable (economic value, social value, environmental value). The tests of between-subjects factors show that gender is a significant factor influencing economic value $F(1, 10249) = 6.57$ $p = .010$ $\eta^2 = .01$ and social value $F(2, 10249) = 13.22$ $p < .0001$ $\eta^2 = .01$ (see Table 7.2). Therefore we find support for Hypothesis 1a and Hypothesis 1b. On the other hand, there is no support for Hypothesis 1c.

Subsequently, we use a z test for two proportions to examine the differences in proportion of females (P_f/P_m) in TEA, SEA and EEA (see Table 7.3). Testing the proportion of females in TEA against the proportion of females in SEA, we confirm Hypothesis 2a. The portion of women to men in SEA ($P_f/P_m = .68$) is higher than the proportion of women to men in TEA ($P_f/P_m = .58$) ($z = -3.76$, $p < .0001$). The difference in proportions of TEA and SEA for women is 10 per cent, with a 5.3 per cent margin of error. Computing the relative risk, women are 1.17 times more likely to pursue SEA initiatives than TEA initiatives. Therefore, there is sufficient evidence to conclude that women engage in SEA more readily than in TEA.

Finally, using a z test for two proportions, the data shows that the proportion of women to men TEA ($P_f/P_m = .58$) is less than that of women to men in EEA ($P_f/P_m = .70$) ($z = -3.96$, $p < .0001$), supporting Hypothesis 2b. The difference in proportions of TEA and EEA for women is about 12 per cent, with a 6 per cent margin of error. Computing the relative risk, women are 1.23 times more likely to pursue EEA initiatives than TEA initiatives. Consequently, there is sufficient evidence to conclude that women engage in EEA more readily than in TEA.

DISCUSSION

Our findings provide support for the gender divide occurring in economic and social entrepreneurial activity. Specifically, males are more likely to pursue traditional economic entrepreneurial activity than females; additionally, females are more likely to engage in social and environmental entrepreneurial activity than males. Consequently, hegemonic masculinity may advance our understanding of the entrepreneurship phenomena because it can help explain why there are more male entrepreneurs emphasizing traditional mainstream economic value creation than female entrepreneurs.

This chapter makes several contributions to the female entrepreneurship literature. First, we answer calls for multi-country and multi-level research

Table 7.2   MANOVA between subject effects for economic, social and environmental value goals

| Effect | Multivariate Test | | | Between-subject effects | | | | | | | | |
| | Wilks Λ | F | Sig. | Economic | | | Social | | | Environmental | | |
				F	Sig.	df	F	Sig.	df	F	Sig.	df
Corrected model	n/a	n/a	n/a	16.69	0	112	4.5	0.001	112	21.14	0	112
Intercept	0.565	2630.5	0	3269.74	0	1	679.51	0	1	517.39	0	1
Education	0.995	16.61	0	1.1	0.295	1	42.86	0	1	2.44	0.118	1
Household income	0.999	3.52	.014	0.383	0.536	1	6.23	0.013	1	7.53	0.007	1
Age	0.999	3.02	0.028	2.56	0.11	1	5.27	0.022	1	7.53	0.006	1
Country	0.727	22.58	0	27.71	0	51	27.82	0	51	36.51	0	51
Industry	0.994	6.91	0	6.67	0	3	3.33	0.016	3	6.65	0	3
Gender	0.999	4.74	0.003	6.57	0	1	13.22	0	1	1.79	0.181	1

Table 7.3   Test statistics for two proportions of economic, social and environmental entrepreneurial activity

Hypotheses		z value	p value	95% CI	
				Lower	Upper
H2a	P_f/P_m TEA $<$ P_f/P_m SEA	-3.76	$<.0001$	-0.15	-0.05
H2b	P_f/P_m TEA $<$ P_f/P_m EEA	-4.15	$<.0001$	-0.19	-0.07

in female entrepreneurship (De Bruin et al., 2007; Langowitz and Minniti, 2007). Second, we link gender participation in the entrepreneurial process to hegemonic masculinity and gender roles. The cross-sectional nature of the data makes it impossible to determine causality among the variables in this study; however, our study does indicate that the emergence of female entrepreneurs is increasing because the idealized characteristics of the 'best' entrepreneur are changing (with feminine and masculine qualities merging). Yet, the pervasive gendered stereotypes and discourses are neither changing nor improving; however, the contexts in which the discourses are embedded are changing. Instead of challenging feminine ideologies, females are actually perpetuating and driving the hegemony with their emergence as social or environmental entrepreneurs (versus the traditional, for-profit masculine entrepreneurs). Future research with a longitudinal dataset could investigate relationships over time and enable casual inferences. Our study also extends research on female entrepreneurship by highlighting females' contribution to social value creation. The field of entrepreneurship has recently moved beyond a traditional focus on economic performance and towards social wealth (Calás et al., 2009; Short, et al., 2009) and environmental sustainability (Cohen and Winn, 2007; Cohen et al., 2008). Our study demonstrates that females play a prominent role in extending the value creation logic to the realm of social and environmental entrepreneurship.

Our results also offer important policy implications. The past decades have seen a concerted effort to increase women's participation in entrepreneurial activity. Resulting policy reforms were justified on the grounds of increasing equity and economic growth, as female entrepreneurs were found to contribute as much as men to economic value creation (Verheul, 2005). If female entrepreneurs contribute to higher social value creation then the global trend towards narrowing the gender gap in entrepreneurship is creating an increasingly favourable environment for social entrepreneurship and socially responsible venturing. Using cross-national data, Themudo (2009) finds empirical evidence of a strong association between female empowerment and nonprofit sector development, a relationship he credits to females' higher concern with the common good and their more altruistic behaviour. Supply-side theories (James, 1987; Young, 1983), also indicate that the social sector develops as entrepreneurs with social or environmental goals create new organizations or reshape existing ones. Extending this rationale to the field of entrepreneurship, we argue that to the extent that female entrepreneurs clearly place a higher value on social value creation than do males, then supporting female entrepreneurship would not only boost the economy and foster gender equality, it will also play a fundamental role in improving society.

Our study suggests a number of promising directions for future research. First, longitudinal data would allow an examination of gendered entrepreneurial values across time. Researchers could explore how values may change prior to and during the start-up process. Second, future research could examine gender and value differences for other types of entrepreneurial activity (for example necessity and opportunity-motivated entrepreneurship). Such exploration could enable an understanding of the impact of whether necessity-based entrepreneurs are more likely to prioritize personal economic goals over social and environmental goals. Finally, cross-national investigations could explore variances across both developed and developing country contexts.

NOTES

1. Detailed descriptions of the methods and sampling frame used to generate the GEM database are reported in Reynolds et al. (2005).
2. Information on the countries included in this study can be found in the 2009 Global Report, www.gemconsortium.org.

REFERENCES

Ahl, H.J. (2002), 'The making of the female entrepreneur. A discourse analysis of research texts on women's entrepreneurship', unpublished doctoral thesis, Jönköping University, Jönköping.

Amit, R., K.R. MacCrimmon and C. Zietsma (2000), 'Does money matter? Wealth attainment as the motive for initiating growth oriented technology ventures', *Journal of Business Venturing*, **16**, 119–43.

Austin, J., H. Stevenson and J. Wei-Skillern (2006), 'Social and commercial entrepreneurship: same, different, or both?', *Entrepreneurship Theory and Practice*, **30** (1), 1–22.

Autio, E., R. Keeley, M. Klofsten, G. Parker and M. Hay (2001), 'Entrepreneurial intent among students in Scandinavia and in the USA', *Enterprise and Innovation Management Studies*, **2** (2), 145–60.

Bird, B. and C. Brush (2002), 'A gendered perspective on organizational creation', *Entrepreneurship Theory and Practice*, **26** (3), 41–66.

Borden, R.J. and J.L. Francis (1978), 'Who cares about ecology? Personality and sex differences in environmental concern', *Journal of Personality*, **46**, 190–203.

Bornstein, D. (2005), *How to Change the World: Social Entrepreneurs and the Power of New Ideas*, New Delhi: Penguin Books.

Braun, P. (2010), 'Going green: women entrepreneurs and the environment', *International Journal of Gender and Entrepreneurship*, **2** (3), 1–9.

Bruni, A., S. Gherardi and B. Poggio (2004a), 'Doing gender, doing entrepreneurship: an ethnographic account of intertwined practices', *Gender, Work & Organization*, **11** (4), 406–29.

Bruni, A., S. Gherardi and B. Poggio (2004b), 'Entrepreneur-mentality, gender and the study of women entrepreneurs', *Journal of Organizational Change Management*, **17** (3), 256–68.

Brush, C.G. (1992), 'Research on women business owners: past trends, a new perspective and future directions', *Entrepreneurship Theory and Practice*, **16** (4), 5–31.

Buttner, E.H. and D.P. Moore (1997), 'Women's organizational exodus to entrepreneurship: self-reported motivations and correlates with success', *Journal of Small Business Management*, **35** (1), 34–46.

Calás, M.B., L. Smircich and K.A. Bourne (2009), 'Extending the boundaries: reframing "entrepreneurship as social change" through feminist perspectives', *The Academy of Management Review*, **34** (3), 552–69.

Cliff, J.E., N. Langton and H.E. Aldrich (2005), 'Walking the talk? Gendered rhetoric vs. action in small Firms', *Organization Studies*, **26** (1), 63–91.

Cohen, B. and W.I. Winn (2007), 'Market imperfections, opportunity and sustainable entrepreneurship', *Journal of Business Venturing*, **22** (1), 29–49.

Cohen, B., B. Smith and R. Mitchell (2008), 'Toward a sustainable conceptualization of dependent variables in entrepreneurship research', *Business Strategy and the Environment*, **17** (2), 107–19.

Cole, A.H. (1946), 'An approach to the study of entrepreneurship: a tribute to Edwin F. Gay', *Journal of Economic History*, Supplement VI, 1–15.

Connell, R.W. (1990), 'An iron man: the body and some contradictions of hegemonic masculinity', in M. Messner and D. Sabo (eds), *Sport, Men and the Gender Order*, Champaign, IL: Human Kinetics Books, pp. 83–95.

Connell, R.W. and J.W. Messerschmidt (2005), 'Hegemonic masculinity: rethinking the concept', *Gender and Society*, **19** (6), 829–59.

Conry, J.C. and J.E. McDonald (1994), 'Moving toward a matrix: gender and the nonprofit culture of the nineties', *New Directions for Philanthropic Fundraising*, **5**, 45–53.

Davidson, D.J. and W.R. Freudenburg (1996), 'Gender and environmental risk concerns', *Environment and Behavior*, **28** (3), 302–39.

De Bruin, A., C.G. Brush and F. Welter (2007), 'Advancing a framework for coherent research on women's entrepreneurship', *Entrepreneurship Theory and Practice*, **31** (3), 323–39.

DiMaggio, P. and H. Louch (1997), *Who Volunteers? Dominant and Relevant Statuses*, Washington, DC: Aspen Institute.

Douglas, E.J. and D. Shepherd (2000), 'Entrepreneurship as a utility-maximizing response', *Journal of Business Venturing*, **15**, 231–51.

Eagly, A. (1987), *Sex Differences in Social Behavior: A Social-role Interpretation*, Hillsdale, NJ: Erlbaum.

Eagly, A.H. and L.L. Carli (2003), 'The female leadership advantage: an evaluation of the evidence', *Leadership Quarterly*, **14**, 807–34.

Eagly, A.H. and M. Crowley (1986), 'Gender and helping behavior: a meta-analytic review of the social psychological literature', *Psychological Bulletin*, **100** (3), 283–308.

Filley, A. and R. Aldag (1978), 'Characteristics and measurement of an entrepreneurial typology', *Academy of Management Journal*, **21**, 578–91.

Fortin, N. (2005), 'Greed, altruism, and the gender wage gap', working paper, University of British Columbia.

Furst, S.A. and M. Reeves (2008), 'Queens of the hill: creative destruction and the emergence of women as organizational leaders', *Leadership Quarterly*, **19**, 372–84.

Gartner, W.B., K.G. Shaver, N.M. Carter and P.D. Reynolds (eds), (2004), *Handbook of Entrepreneurial Dynamics: The Process of Business Creation*, Thousand Oaks, CA: Sage.

Gorgievski, M.J., M.E. Ascalon and U. Stephan (2011), 'Small business owners' success criteria: a values approach to personal differences', *Journal of Small Business Management*, **49** (2), 207–32.

Gupta, V.K., D.B. Turban, S.A. Wasti and A. Sikdar (2009), 'The role of gender stereotypes in perceptions of entrepreneurs and intentions to become an entrepreneur', *Entrepreneurship Theory and Practice*, **33** (2), 397–417.

Honig, B. (2004), 'Entrepreneurship education: toward a model of contingency-based business planning', *Academy of Management Learning and Education*, **3** (3), 258–73.

Inglehart, R. and P. Norris (2003), *Rising Tide: Gender Equality and Cultural Change Around the World*, New York and Cambridge: Cambridge University Press.

Isaak, R. (2002), 'The making of the ecopreneur', *Greener Management International*, **38**, 81–91.

James, E. (1987), 'The nonprofit sector in comparative perspective', in W. Powell (ed.), *The Nonprofit Sector*, New Haven, CT: Yale University Press, pp. 397–415.

Keogh, P.D. and M.J. Polonsky (1998), 'Environmental commitment: a basis for environmental entrepreneurship?', *Journal of Organizational Change Management*, **11** (1), 38–49.

Kirkwood, J. and S. Walton (2010), 'What motivates ecopreneurs to start businesses?', *International Journal of Entrepreneurial Behaviour & Research*, **16** (3), 204–28.

Korosec, R.L. and E.M. Berman (2006), 'Municipal support for social entrepreneurship', *Public Administration Review*, **66** (3), 448–62.

Krueger, N. (1993), 'Impact of prior entrepreneurial exposure on perceptions of new venture feasibility and desirability', *Entrepreneurship Theory and Practice*, **18** (1), 5–21.

Langowitz, N. and M. Minniti (2007), 'The entrepreneurial propensity of women', *Entrepreneurship Theory and Practice*, **31** (3), 341–64.

Low, M. and I. MacMillan (1988), 'Entrepreneurship: past research and future challenges', *Journal of Management*, **14** (2), 139–61.

MacNabb, A., J. McCoy, P. Weinreich and M. Northover (1993), 'Using identity structure analysis (ISA) to investigate female entrepreneurship', *Entrepreneurship and Regional Development*, **5**, 301–13.

Mair, J. and I. Marti (2006), 'Social entrepreneurship research: a source of explanation, prediction, and delight', *Journal of World Business*, **41** (1), 36–44.

McCarthy, K.D. (ed.), (2001), *Women, Philanthropy and Civil Society*, Bloomington, IN: Indiana University Press.

McKya, S., J. Phillimore and S. Teasdale (2010), 'Exploring the gendered nature of social entrepreneurship: women's leadership, employment and participation in the third sector', paper presented at the 60th Political Studies Association Annual conference, Edinburgh.

Mirchandani, K. (1999), 'Feminist insight on gendered work: new directions in research on women and entrepreneurship', *Gender, Work & Organization*, **6** (4), 224–36.

Nga, J.K. and G. Shamuganathan (2010), 'The influence of personality traits and demographic factors on social entrepreneurship start up intentions', *Journal of Business Ethics*, **95**, 259–82.

Pestoff, V. (2000), 'Enriching Swedish women's work environment: the case of social enterprises in day care', *Economic & Industrial Democracy – an International Journal*, **21** (1), 39–70.

Peterman, N. and J. Kennedy (2003), 'Enterprise education: influencing students' perceptions of entrepreneurship', *Entrepreneurship Theory and Practice*, **28** (2), 129–44.

Phillips, S.D. (2005), 'Will the market set them free? Women, NGOs, and social enterprise in Ukraine', *Human Organization*, **64** (3), 251–64.

Reynolds, P., N. Bosma, E. Autio, S. Hunt, N. De Bono and I. Servaias (2005), 'Global Entrepreneurship Monitor: data collection design and implementation 1998–2003', *Small Business Economics*, **24**, 205–31.

Rigg, C. and J. Sparrow (1994), 'Gender, diversity and working styles', *Women in Management Review*, **9** (1), 9–16.

Romano, C. (1994), 'It looks like men are from Mars, women are from Venus', *Management Review*, **83** (10), 7.

Rosener, J. (1990), 'Ways women lead', *Harvard Business Review*, **68** (6), 119–25.

Schwartz, S.H. and T. Rubel-Lifschitz (2009), 'Cross-national variation in the size of sex differences in values: effects of gender equality', *Journal of Personality and Social Psychology*, **97** (1), 171–85.

Short, J.C., Moss, T.W. and G.T. Lumpkin (2009), 'Research in social entrepreneurship: past contributions and future opportunities', *Strategic Entrepreneurship Journal*, **3** (2), 161–94.

Taniguchi, H. (2006), 'Men's and women's volunteering: gender differences in the effects of employment and family characteristics', *Nonprofit and Voluntary Sector Quarterly*, **35** (1), 83–101.

Themudo, N.S. (2009), 'Gender and the nonprofit sector', *Nonprofit and Voluntary Sector Quarterly*, **38** (4), 663–83.

Vecchio, R.P. (2003), 'Entrepreneurship and leadership: common trends and common threads', *Human Resource Management Review*, **13** (2), 303–27.

Verheul, I. (2005), 'Is there a (fe)male approach?', unpublished doctoral thesis, Erasmus University of Rotterdam.

Walker, E. and A. Brown (2004), 'What success factors are important to small business owners?', *International Small Business Journal*, **22** (6), 577–94.

Young, D.R. (1983), *If Not For Profit, For What?*, Lexington, MA: D.C. Heath.

Zahra, S.A., E. Gedajlovic, D.O. Neubaum and J.M. Shulman (2009), 'A typology of social entrepreneurs: motives, search processes and ethical challenges', *Journal of Business Venturing*, **24** (5), 519–32.

Zelezny, E., P. Chua and C. Aldrich (2000), 'Elaborating on gender differences in environmentalism', *Journal of Social Issues*, **56** (3), 443–57.

8. Do highly accomplished female entrepreneurs tend to 'give away success'?

Mary Riebe

INTRODUCTION

Over the past three decades researchers such as Babcock and Laschever (2007), Chodorow (1978), Fels (2004), Gilligan (1982, 1990), Horner (1972) and others have described the ways in which women in the USA and else-where are systematically discouraged from achieving success. A significant body of research has demonstrated the inhibiting effect of socialization on women's beliefs regarding success. Based on Bandura's (1986) work on self-efficacy (the belief in one's ability to successfully perform career-related tasks) researchers have found that women tend to have a lower sense of confidence in their professional capabilities and more modest career goals than their male peers. This is particularly true in male-dominated fields or tasks (Betz and Hackett, 1981; Gist and Mitchell, 1992; Zeldin and Pajares, 2000). Building on Weiner's attribution theory (1985), researchers have also found that women are more likely than men to attribute their successes to luck or hard work than to ability (Försterling et al., 2007; Russo et al., 1991; Swim and Sanna, 1996). Such beliefs have been shown to have negative effects on women's self-esteem, aspirations, motivation, persistence and resilience (Abramson et al., 1978; Gist and Mitchell, 1992; Hirschy and Morris, 2002). These patterns have been found even among highly successful women (Dyke and Murphy, 2006; Zeldin and Pajares, 2000). This has lead to the most extreme form of what has been termed the imposter phenomenon, whereas woman is unable to internalize her own accomplishments and instead attributes them to luck, timing or the ability to fool others (Clance and Imes, 1978; Kumar and Jagacinski, 2006). In other words, beliefs profoundly shape behaviour and often lead to self-sabotaging thoughts and practices, which Schenkel (1984) terms 'giving away success.' This includes behaviours such as self-silencing, avoiding conflict and attributing success to luck rather than competence.

If the socialization process encourages such self-defeating behaviours even on the part of many talented and highly educated women, how are we to explain the remarkable success of increasing numbers of women entrepreneurs in the USA? Have these women somehow escaped these self-limiting beliefs and behaviours, or found ways to effectively manage and succeed despite them? What might this (successful) group of women be able to illuminate about the many ways in which women can give away or achieve success? What insights can they provide researchers, educators and practitioners to guide training, personal and professional growth, and the elimination of perceived barriers? These are the questions that motivated this preliminary study of highly successful, growth-oriented women entrepreneurs.

METHODS AND SAMPLE

The results discussed here were gathered as part of a larger research project. At this stage of the research, the data-gathering consisted of online questionnaires that were completed by a dozen successful women business owners. This group is defined for the purposes of this study as women who had founded a business that had been in operation for more than five years with a minimum of US$500000 in annual sales. All but one of the women who completed the questionnaire were also members of the Women Presidents' Organization (WPO),[1] indicating that their businesses generated more than US$1 million in revenue if it is in a service industry and more than US$2 million if it is in a non-service industry.

The respondents ranged in age from 35 to 63; their median age was 45, while their average age was 48. They owned and operated businesses within a wide range of industries, including catering, civil engineering, investment banking, accounting, communications, creative design, feed and seed, business-to-business marketing, inclusion and diversity consulting, translation services and industrial cleaning. Three women lived in western USA, one in southwest USA, and the rest lived in mid-west USA.

The participants answered a series of seven questions about whether they have found themselves engaging in the self-defeating behaviours described by Schenkel (1984) and others. The questions also addressed what effect, if any, these behaviours may have had on the success of their businesses, and how they have managed to avoid or work past those behaviours. Although this sample of successful women business owners is small (and the results of this survey must thus be considered preliminary), the responses both validate many of the previous research findings about women entrepreneurs and raise some interesting questions for future research.

FINDINGS

This section will discuss the results for each of the seven questions; it will be followed by a discussion of the relevance of these findings to the current literature on women entrepreneurs, as well as the implications of this study for future research.

Question 1: Motivation for Becoming Entrepreneurs

To better understand the beliefs and experiences that motivated the respondents to become entrepreneurs in the first place, they were first asked how far back they could trace their desire to run their own business and if they could identify the major factors that had inspired or shaped that desire. Although none of the participants reported that they had always wanted to be business owners, several responded that they had known at least by the time they were in college that they were not likely to be satisfied being just another employee in someone else's organization. The most frequent reasons cited for the decision to become a business owner included wanting to be a woman leader and wanting to have greater autonomy. As one respondent put it, 'I decided long ago that I would never be a member of a committee unless I could chair it. That's probably the basis of my entrepreneurship'.

In addition to these 'early deciders,' two individuals traced the genesis of their desire to start their own business to a dissatisfaction with the companies that they had begun their careers with. One wrote that after working for other companies in her chosen industry, she 'just knew it was time to try it myself. My struggles with other companies included issues around integrity, honesty, communication and business focus'. The other participant replied that she had 'loved the business but not the owner's ethics. I felt I had a better way to do it'.

At least half of the respondents reported becoming entrepreneurs almost by accident. Two said they had never planned on business owner-ship but had been pulled into it by their husbands. One woman, who had first joined her husband in the start-up phase of his business, echoed the responses of many of the women, saying she had soon 'realized that business ownership was a great fit for my maverick personality' and a way to 'express my individuality, create wealth and circumvent the limitations of being someone else's employee'. Striking a common theme among these 'accidental' entrepreneurs, she quoted a German adage that translates to 'the appetite comes with eating'. She said, 'after a year or two in business, my desire to be successful became overwhelming'.

The remaining participants had begun their entrepreneurial careers as independent contractors whose businesses had grown beyond their original expectations. One reported that she had started her catering business as a way to help support her family, but an opportunity to develop the food service programme at a private school had sparked her desire to form a larger company and later to add a deli. Similarly, another individual replied,

> My desire was to be a successful artist or designer. The business grew up under me – I kept getting more work and needed to add employees. I think it would be very different today if I was approaching it from the standpoint of wanting to own a business at the outset. My company grew organically and I was not focusing on how to grow the company as much as how to keep my clients happy.

Another participant even described herself as a 'reluctant entrepreneur', saying, 'I loved the work that I did; so by default that meant becoming a business owner'.

Question 2: Attributions of Success

In line with earlier attribution studies, question two asked respondents to what extent they attributed their success to: (a) ability; (b) hard work; (c) luck; or (d) something else. Unlike the earlier findings on women's socialization cited above, none of these women attributed much of their success to luck. The greater number, in fact, said explicitly that luck had had little or no bearing on their success; the others claimed responsibility for creating their own luck. As one respondent put it, 'luck is where opportunity meets preparation'. Several women mentioned 'being in the right place at the right time' as fortuitous, but added that, in the words of one woman entrepreneur, 'the hard work and preparation makes one able to see the opportunities when they present themselves'.

Although all of the women credited much of their success to hard work and a willingness to put in long hours, they all ranked ability as more important than hard work. Several specifically credited their success not only to the skills, talents and expertise that they had originally brought into the business, but also to the skills and knowledge they had since acquired. One participant, for example, noted, 'I have been told that I was a gifted freelancer and a gifted project manager [as the company grew]. I am trying very hard to be a gifted executive as well, with an MA and any specialized training I can find'. None of the women framed this continual learning as a sign of weakness or a doubt about their abilities, but rather suggested that it was the ability and willingness to learn itself that had contributed to their success. In fact, one woman attributed most of her success to what she called 'learned ability, knowing that I had always succeeded when I had put my mind to it'.

Among the four respondents who identified other factors that had contributed to their success, two cited hiring great people and two mentioned tenacity or persistence. One of these women defined tenacity as different than hard work, calling it 'a certain mental toughness and unwillingness to give up, even in the absence of other factors mentioned'. She noted that 'we have outlasted most of our customers, suppliers, and competitors because of this factor'.

Question 3: Silencing and Recognition

Because earlier research has found that women often find themselves being silenced or overlooked in social and professional settings, the third question on the survey asked respondents whether they sometimes found themselves in this situation in their business dealings and, if so, how they dealt with or avoided this problem. Although several of the participants responded that they thought many women did experience this situation, and two reported encountering it in other settings, none identified it as a problem in the operation or success of her own business.

Nonetheless, several participants did report ways that they believed they and their businesses had been discriminated against for gender reasons, though most seemed to have found ways to cope that did not negatively affect their confidence or bottom line. For instance, one woman replied, 'I feel like I've had to work twice as hard to prove myself when a man would have been assumed to be competent'. In the most overt case of discrimination reported by the participants, one woman said, 'I've also had customers ask for a male salesperson to come out, because they just couldn't buy equipment from a woman. In that case, I just laughed because I'd be the one cashing their check anyway'. Another respondent noted that her 'friends who run construction companies have a much harder time' than many other women business owners, though she believed that 'there are still situations where we women are simply at a disadvantage'. For instance, she complained, 'golf tournaments drive me nuts'.

A few of the women addressed this issue in terms of gaining outside recognition as the leader of a successful firm. One woman, a self-described introvert, credited her male partner for pushing her to the front even when she found it uncomfortable. In contrast, another respondent reported, 'I'm not the kind of person who allows others not to recognize me. I always step up to leadership positions or take advantage of opportunities for visibility. My company and I have, as a result, received many awards and accolades'. Another woman noted that she had gained more visibility 'since being certified as a WBE [Woman Business Enterprise] and joining WPO'.

A few of the women reported ways in which they had avoided being silenced or overlooked. One replied simply, 'I left corporate America', while another answered, 'For the most part I stay out of the limelight, build on relationships, and rely on recommendations and results'. Another participant noted that her clients came to her for her expertise and that 'those who discriminated against me because I am a woman never contacted me, so I didn't have to deal with them'.

Question 4: Processing Mistakes

Because research on women's achievement has found that women are more likely than men to blame their failures and setbacks on their own abilities, the next question asked respondents if they found it difficult to let go of past mistakes – what Schenkel (1984) terms 'chewing on a mistake forever' – and, if so, if they had found effective ways to break the cycle of self-recrimination. This issue appeared to have more resonance for the respondents than the issues raised in earlier questions. Three of the women business owners answered yes to this question; one wrote 'yes, definitely, to the point where my stomach hurts and I can't sleep'. A second participant replied, 'a resounding YES!', while the third indicated, 'Sure. I thought all women did that'. The first of these respondents added that one way she had learned to manage this cycle was 'to use a mental image of my errors as a lump of dough that is scraped off the counter into a basket and carried away. Because I am a practising Christian, I let God carry the basket'. Another individual mentioned that, on the advice of a business coach, she had taken the StrengthsFinder® assessment and learned that one of her chief strengths is what it terms 'empathy'. She thought being empathetic might actually contribute to her difficulty in making decisions that might displease her sales team; however, she was working with her coach to overcome such 'limiting beliefs'.[2]

The other respondents – even those who answered 'no' to the first part of the question – offered what appeared to be a 'yes, but' answer. This group implied this was a problem they had struggled with in the past, or struggle with occasionally, but had found effective ways to manage it. For instance, one individual said,

> I've learned over the years to let go and to forgive myself . . . We are the kind of business where we cannot recreate or change the result. We have one opportunity to have a successful event . . . In handling mistakes, we take responsibility and make it as right as possible. Then we move on, knowing we are better for the experience and then not look back.

The importance of taking responsibility for one's mistakes in order to move beyond them was, in fact, a theme that emerged in several of the women's responses to this question. It was evident in the following excerpt:

> I have found the best way to deal with mistakes is to swiftly own up to them and to do what you can to make things right. I believe that no one expects us to be perfect (we are, after all, imperfect beings) but what they do expect is authenticity. When I, or my firm, have made mistakes in the past, we immediately came clean and got about to making things right. I have to tell you that we had one of the lowest claims histories in the business, and this wasn't because we never made mistakes. We just made things right when we did make mistakes.

A willingness to learn from one's mistakes was another coping strategy mentioned by several of the participants. One individual noted, 'I generally don't dwell on mistakes. The message I was raised with was "you can't change the past, learn from your mistakes." This has served me well in business and in life'. Another respondent answered,

> The big errors remain burned in my brain, but mostly just make me work harder to compensate and never make them again. In recent years, I've learned to accept that I did the best I knew how, in the timeframe and with the tools I had. If it didn't work, I keep learning, or pull in others who have the wisdom and the skills to handle those situations.

Yet another individual replied, 'Sometimes I do this big time, but for the past nine months I've been very present and on track' as a result of 'lots of spiritual work' and using 'the power of the unconscious mind to attract things to me'.

One participant also made an important distinction between her responses to different kinds of risks and errors:

> I am very good at accepting the consequences of my own behaviour . . . When money is involved, I can assess the risk of loss and my willingness to accept it, and live with it afterward. When emotions are involved, I can and sometimes do kick myself for what seems like eternity. I tell myself that I did the best I could at the time and try to be forgiving.

The following comment seemed to encapsulate the attitudes of a significant group of participants: 'mistakes used to linger a lot longer than they do now. I think women are just conditioned by nature not to let things go so easily and quickly. As I've grown in business, I've learned how to gauge big and small issues'.

Question 5: Relationships

Question 5 of the survey examined whether researchers' claims that women's socialization systematically discourages achievement, and trains them to value relationships over accomplishment, had proven true in the respondents' own lives. Although some participants acknowledged some truth to this statement, especially as it pertains to other women or events in their past, none of the women perceived it to be a current problem for themselves. Several indicated that they had escaped the negative impacts of women's socialization through a strong and early orientation toward achievement or a highly competitive personality. For example, one woman responded, 'I am an achievement-motivated person, motivated by doing a good job as its own reward, rather than being motivated by power or social relationships'.

Perhaps more unexpected in light of previous research was that none of the participants seemed to perceive an inherent conflict between accomplishment and relationships; this indicates that while achievement was important to them, they also had satisfying personal relations with family and friends. One individual, for instance, offered: 'I love competition and winning . . . most of my relationships are rewarding.' Most respondents seemed to believe that a satisfactory balance between achievement and personal relationships was indeed possible, as indicated in the following:

> I've always been oriented toward both. I was always an 'A student.' When I competed, I tried to be the best. Relationships are important, but not trumping the need to achieve. For instance, if a child, family member, or friend needs help, attention, etc., the work can wait, or if it can't, the other is taken care of as promptly as possible. The women I work with are driven by achievement with a strong sense of purpose, mission, and pretty balanced relationships.

Another unanticipated finding in the responses to this question regarding relationships and accomplishment is that many of these successful women appeared to have escaped the supposed conflict between work and relationships by reframing the latter to include their business relationships. For example, one woman initially responded that she was not sure she quite understood the question, then added: 'In my business, relationships trump everything . . . There is no question: you must be able to deliver. But when given the choice, wouldn't you rather work with someone you enjoy working with and whom you trust will take care of your needs, regardless of what the contract states?' Similarly, another participant answered, 'I do value relationships over accomplishments, but I think this makes for a stronger company'.

Question 6: Conflict

Given the centrality of relationships in women's lives, the next question asked respondents if they tended to avoid conflict in their relationships with others and, if they have experienced conflict, how they have avoided, overcome or managed their response to it. This question elicited the largest number of comments that would seem to support Schenkel and others' argument about the socialization of women. Only one of the respondents answered 'No, I don't avoid conflict. I'm very direct', while more than half reported this had been or was an ongoing problem for them as business owners. One woman admitted, 'I could win the conflict-avoidance Olympics. Avoid, avoid, avoid. I really don't feel that I know how to deal effectively with conflict with others.' Similar replies included the following:

- Yes, definitely. Not a good business trait.
- Conflict isn't fun, and I try to avoid it . . . If I'm not vested in the relationship, I still vote with my feet.
- I really dislike conflict and try to avoid it at all possible cost. If I have a client who seems to always operate in a conflict-based way, I get rid of them.
- Yes, I avoid conflict. It is still something I still struggle with as an employer and I am still working on being more forthright.
- I hate conflict. I have struggled with conflict in business for years.
- Yes, I have a tendency to avoid conflict and continually work on that.

Despite their stated discomfort with conflict, most of the women indicated that, in the words of one participant, 'conflict management has come with time and maturity as a business owner'. Further, respondents indicated that through conscious effort they had developed successful strategies for dealing with conflict. As one individual reported, 'My normal instinct is to curl up in a ball and hide. But I don't'. Instead, through training in negotiation skills she had learned to reframe conflict 'as a contest rather than a battle. I've also learned to be very sure of my facts and to always be prepared'. Another participant had adopted a similar empathy-based approach: 'I typically try to understand all aspects of a situation and . . . what is motivating people to behave a certain way or what causes them to think a certain way about an issue before confronting them.' Another woman replied, 'I do find I react too personally sometimes to conflict and have to carefully step back before I respond so that I can thoughtfully work through my feelings'. Even a respondent who had the opposite problem with conflict reported having to learn the same lesson:

I have little tolerance for complacency, and that fire in the belly mentality has then gotten me in trouble for how I handle situations. Now I work at being critical about a situation without attacking the person. Something I've really had to learn by losing a relationship I valued and that I now work on every day.

The most common strategy for dealing effectively with conflict mentioned by these successful business owners involved addressing conflict immediately, rather than avoiding it or letting it fester. Respondents said:

- I understand at this point in my life where the desire to avoid it comes from, but I do try to overcome it by addressing conflict immediately.
- I have long realized that simply ignoring a problem will not resolve the problem. Oftentimes, it comes back manifested into something bigger.
- When a conflict arises, I usually react quickly and deal with it immediately so that the problem doesn't grow before it is resolved.
- Once I learned how to deal with conflict or discord I cannot wait to address it and move through the misunderstanding to understanding and the next steps.

Another strategy described by a participant has to do with knowing her limits and being able to delegate:

Recently I brought on a CEO and have moved to the 'founder' position. I am so happy! My CEO deals with conflict head on, and really negotiates successfully on behalf of the business. My policy is to know what I know and know what I don't know. For the stuff I don't know, hire the best person I can afford to do it.

Question 7: Other Factors in Success

Question 7 gave respondents an opportunity to identify other major factors that have contributed to, or interfered with, their success as women business owners. Of the nine individuals who offered additional comments to this question, one mentioned the recent economic downturn while the others addressed the internal and interpersonal factors that have contributed to their success. For instance, one individual raised the issue of courage: 'What contributed to my success was stepping into the unknown. What interfered was my fear.' Another suggested that her desire for autonomy, and perhaps a fear of asking for help, had kept her from gaining the benefit of others' input and skills for too long. Another reported, 'I care too much about what other people think, and that has interfered greatly, but I am working on trying to address this issue'. Two respondents re-addressed the work–relationship issue, with one reporting:

> I believe that to be truly successful in life, as well as business, you must be passionate about what you do . . . I think that a person who loves their work learns how to make it a part of their lives and blends the work into the personal life in such a way that choices are not severe for either your co-workers who depend on you or your family that depends on you also.

The second individual to return to the work-relationship issue found that creating a balance more difficult; she argued that earlier in her career she had become an 'achievement junkie, working harder and harder to be the best', but failing to take time 'to revel in each success before worrying about how I was going to top that success and move on to the next'. She continued:

> The result was a lack of personal balance in my life. I missed out on time with my kids, and I didn't take care of myself. I became obese, and if I'm honest, I have to acknowledge that my weight was a detriment to me in business dealings. Now that I've lost the weight, I don't feel like I have to try nearly so hard.

DISCUSSION AND IMPLICATIONS

In summary, the behaviours and attitudes described by this sample of successful women entrepreneurs appear to differ in some significant ways from those described in much of the literature about American women, in general, and about women in business and professions, more specifically. In large part, these differences may be explained by the earlier finding that the personality traits of female business owners are more similar to those of male business owners than to women in the rest of the working population (Brush, 1992). This suggests that among women entrepreneurs, personality may trump some aspects of gender-role socialization. As Duffy et al. (2006: 11) note in their study of successful professional and business women in the Americas, 'Being successful in the face of substantial barriers to success implies that these women have personal characteristics, belief systems, and backgrounds that set them apart within their own environments'. In terms of personality traits and motivation, the responses of the women in this sample are consistent with earlier findings that women entrepreneurs possess a high desire for autonomy and achievement, and a strong internal locus of control (Birley, 1989; Bowen and Hisrich, 1986; Duffy et al., 2006; Littunen, 2000; Orhan and Scott, 2001; Sarri and Trihopoulou, 2005; Scott 1986; Sexton and Bowman-Upton, 1990).

However, the traits and motivations of these participants may differ from those of the larger population of women studied by the researchers discussed earlier.

In fact, the findings from these highly successful women business owners also differ from many research findings regarding women entrepreneurs in general. For instance, they do not support earlier findings that women entrepreneurs express lower levels of self-confidence than their male counterparts (Birley, 1989; Chaganti, 1986), greater concern for meeting their combined responsibilities at work and home (Kepler and Shane, 2007; Merrill-Sands et al., 2005), or lower self-assessments of their ability and readiness to run a business than outside evaluators (Jones and Tullous, 2002). Rather, the responses discussed here are consistent with Morris et al.'s (2006: 240) description of the characteristics that distinguished high-growth from moderate-growth women business owners in their extensive study:

> High Growth entrepreneurs demonstrated a more visceral identification with their business, and conceptualized it as an investment whose value needed to be continually enhanced. They perceived fewer conflicts between the venture and other life responsibilities, and viewed the external environment more in terms of challenges and opportunities than as obstacles. They strongly believed in their own abilities to surmount whatever challenges arose.

Certainly, growth is not the only way to measure the success of a woman-owned business, as limiting growth can be a legitimate and effective strategy for maintaining control and autonomy (Cliff, 1998; Mitra, 2002; Still and Timms, 2000). Nonetheless, the positive impact of growth on employment and the economy, and the high job satisfaction demonstrated by this sub-set of women entrepreneurs would seem to merit more research on the behaviours and attitudes that women have developed to deal with the challenges related to business growth and gender socialization.

That the women who responded to the survey headed their own companies apparently obviated the silencing and lack of recognition discussed in much of the research on women in business and professions. Accordingly, a number of researchers have argued that entrepreneurship can offer women several advantages over management positions, where they have less control over their work environment (Fels, 2005; Fletcher, 2002; Greene et al., 2003; Hewlett and Buck, 2005; Riebe, 2001). However, just as women business owners can learn a good deal from the literature on women in management (that can help them become more effective in running their businesses), further research on the coping strategies developed by successful women entrepreneurs would undoubtedly offer useful insights not only for other entrepreneurs, but for business and professional women more generally.

Although only one of the survey questions directly addressed the role of relationships in these successful women's lives, their responses as a whole appear to support earlier findings that the people-oriented management style shared by many women entrepreneurs reflects the centrality of relational connections in women's lives (Allen and Langowitz, 2003; Brush, 1992; Dafna, 2008; Eagly and Johannesen-Schmidt, 2001). Responses also imply that successful women business owners fulfil much of their need for connection in the relationships they maintain with coworkers and customers (Dyke and Murphy, 2006; Riebe, 2001). This may suggest that previous research on the supposed conflict between accomplishment and relationships has focused too narrowly on personal relationships outside of work; the nature of these professional and work relationships, and their relation to women's success, is therefore another promising area for additional research.

While the survey also did not directly address the role of education in these women's success, their responses appear consistent with findings that women entrepreneurs have a stronger belief in the importance of entrepreneurship education than their male counterparts (Scherer et al., 1990). Women are more likely to consult outside sources of information and to seek help from interpersonal networks, including informal mentors such as other business owners (Center for Women's Business Research 2001). Our findings suggest that membership in an association or network of other women business owners, such as the WPO, is associated with increased profitability (Greene et al., 2003). Future research might address whether the belief in the importance and efficacy of professional training results from fewer women entrepreneurs having business-specific training before starting their businesses (Clifford, 1996; Scott, 1986; Stevenson, 1986). Or, do women seek training because they perceive themselves as having to overcome such environmental barriers as gender discrimination and a difficulty in obtaining funding. Learning more about this issue could help educational institutions and organizations better design their courses and effectively shorten women entrepreneurs' learning curve to success.

Finally, the responses reported here – especially those regarding being true to one's ethics, dealing with mistakes and managing conflict – may suggest another promising direction for future research. Specifically, research should interrogate whether women's struggles with these issues are necessarily problems to overcome, or if they reflect a distinctly female and successful style of leadership (Fletcher, 2002; Greene et al., 2003; Hewlett and Buck, 2005; Riebe, 2001; Robinson and Lipman-Blumen, 2003). Perhaps such an exploration will find that the tendency toward reflection and the sensitivity to other people's needs that emerge from these women's responses are important factors in how women entrepreneurs actually acquire, rather than give away, their success.

NOTES

1. The WPO is a membership organization of presidents and CEOs of privately held, multimillion-dollar businesses. According to its 2011 fact sheet, the WPO comprises 90 chapters in North America, the UK, Peru and South Africa, and the revenues of its more than 1400 members average US$13 million. More information is available at their website, www.wpo.org.
2. The Clifton StrengthsFinder® is an online assessment created by Donald O. Clifton and researchers at the Gallup corporation that identifies the takers' major strengths, as part of Gallup's strengths-based personal and organizational development programmes. An explanation of the assessment and developmental approach, as well as access to the assessment itself, can be found in Rath (2007).

REFERENCES

Abramson, L., M. Seligman and J. Teasdale (1978), 'Learned helplessness in humans: Critique and reformulation', *Journal of Abnormal Psychology*, **87**, 49–74.

Allen, I.E. and N.S. Langowitz (2003), *Women in Family-owned Businesses: Gender Does Make a Difference*, Babson Park, MA: Center for Women's Leadership, Babson College.

Babcock, L. and S. Laschever (2007), *Women Don't Ask: The High Cost of Avoiding Negotiation and Positive Change*, New York: Bantam.

Bandura, A. (1986), *Social Foundations of Thought and Action*, Englewood Cliffs, NJ: Prentice Hall.

Betz, N.E. and G. Hackett (1981), 'The relationship of career-related self-efficacy expectations to perceived career options in college women and men', *Journal of Counseling Psychology*, **28**, 399–410.

Birley, S. (1989), 'Female entrepreneurs: are they really any different?', *Journal of Small Business Management*, **27** (1), 32–7.

Bowen, D.D. and R.D. Hisrich (1986), 'The female entrepreneur: a career development perspective', *Academy of Management Review*, **11** (2), 393–407.

Brush, C. (1992), 'Research on women business owners: past trends, new perspectives, and future directions', *Entrepreneurship Theory and Practice*, **16** (4), 5–30.

Center for Women's Business Research (2001), 'Fast growth women and men entrepreneurs take different paths toward business success', available at: http://www.womensbusinessresearch.org/pressreleases/7-10-2001/7-10-2001.htm (accessed 3 February 2005).

Chaganti, R. (1986), 'Management in women-owned enterprises', *Journal of Small Business Management*, **24** (4), 18–29.

Chodorow, N. (1978), *The Reproduction of Mothering*, Berkeley, CA: University of California Press.

Clance, P.R. and S.A. Imes (1978), 'The imposter phenomenon among high-achieving women: dynamics and therapeutic intervention', *Psychology Theory, Research, and Practice*, **15** (3), 241–47.

Cliff, J.E. (1998), 'Does one size fit all? Exploring relationships between attitudes towards growth, gender, and business size', *Journal of Business Venturing*, **13** (6), 523–42.

Clifford, V. (1996), 'A case study of a feminist small business: theory into practice', *International Review of Women and Leadership*, **2** (2), 98–111.

Dafna, K. (2008), 'Managerial performance and business success: gender difference in Canadian and Israeli entrepreneurs', *Journal of Enterprising Communities*, **2** (4), 300–31.

Duffy, J.A., S. Fox, B.J. Punnett and A. Gregory (2006), 'Successful women of the Americas: the same or different?', *Management Research News*, **29** (9), 552–70.

Dyke, L.S. and S.A. Murphy (2006), 'How we define success: a qualitative study of what matters most to women and men', *Sex Roles*, **55**, 357–71.

Eagly, A.H. and M.C. Johannesen-Schmidt (2001), 'The leadership styles of women and men', *Journal of Social Issues*, **57** (4), 781–97.

Fels, A. (2004), 'Do women lack ambition?', *Harvard Business Review*, **82** (4), 50–60.

Fels, A. (2005), *Necessary Dreams: Ambition in Women's Changing Lives*, New York: Random House.

Fletcher, J.K. (2002), 'The greatly exaggerated demise of heroic leadership: gender, power, and the myth of the female advantage', *CGO Insights*, Center for Gender in Organizations, Simmons School of Management, **13**, 1–4.

Försterling, F., S. Preikschas and M. Agathe (2007), 'Ability, luck, and looks: an evolutionary look at achievement ascriptions and the sexual attribution bias', *Journal of Personality & Social Psychology*, **92**, 775–88.

Gilligan, C. (1982). *In a Different Voice: Psychological Theory and Women's Development*, Cambridge, MA: Harvard University Press.

Gilligan, C. (1990), *Meeting at the Crossroads*, New York: Random House.

Gist, M.E. and T.R. Mitchell (1992), 'Self-efficacy: a theoretical analysis of its determinants and malleability', *Academy of Management Review*, **17** (2), 183–211.

Greene, P.G., M.M. Hart, E.J. Gatewood, C.G. Brush and N.M. Carter (2003), 'Women entrepreneurs moving front and center: an overview of research and theory', available at: http://www.usasbe.org/knowledge/whitepapers/greene2003.pdf (accessed 12 January 2010).

Hewlett, S.A. and C.B. Buck (2005), 'Off-ramps and on-ramps: keeping talented women on the road to success', *Harvard Business Review*, R0503B, 1–10.

Hirschy, A.J. and J.R. Morris (2002), 'Individual differences in attributional style: the relational influence of self-efficacy, self-esteem, and sex role identity', *Personality and Individual Differences*, **32**, 183–96.

Horner, M.S. (1972), 'Toward an understanding of achievement-related conflicts in women', *Journal of Social Issues*, **28**, 157–75.

Jones, K. and R. Tullous (2002), 'Behaviors of pre-venture entrepreneurs and perceptions of their financial needs', *Journal of Small Business Management*, **40** (3), 33–50.

Kepler, E. and S. Shane (2007), 'Are male and female entrepreneurs really that different?', *Small Business Research Summary*, available at: http://www.sba.gov/content/archived-economic-research-working papers (accessed 5 March 2010).

Kumar, S. and C.M. Jagacinski (2006), 'Imposters have goals too: the imposter phenomenon and its relationship to achievement goal theory', *Personality and Individual Differences*, **40**, 147–57.

Littunen, H. (2000), 'Entrepreneurship and the characteristics of the entrepreneurial personality', *International Journal of Entrepreneurial Behavior and Research*, **6** (6), 295–310.

Merrill-Sands, D., J. Kickul and C. Ingols (2005), 'Women pursuing leadership and power: Challenging the myth of the "opt-out revolution"', *CGO Insights*, Center for Gender in Organizations, Simmons School of Management, **20**, 1–4.

Mitra, R. (2002), 'The growth pattern of women-run enterprises: an empirical study in India', *Journal of Developmental Entrepreneurship*, **7** (2), 217–37.

Morris, M.H., N.N. Miyasaki, C.E. Watters and S.M. Coombes (2006), 'The dilemma of growth: understanding venture size choices of women entrepreneurs', *Journal of Small Business Management*, **44** (2), 221–44.

Orhan, M. and D. Scott (2001), 'Why women enter into entrepreneurship: an explanatory model', *Women in Management Review*, **16** (5), 232–43.

Rath, T. (2007), *StrengthsFinder 2.0*, New York: Gallup Press.

Riebe, M. (2001), 'The growth-oriented female entrepreneur: an international, qualitative, comparative study', doctoral dissertation, University College, Cork.

Robinson, J.L. and J. Lipman-Blumen (2003), 'Leadership behavior of male and female managers, 1984–2002', *Journal of Education for Business*, **79** (1), 28–33.

Russo, N.F., R.M. Kelly and M. Deacon (1991), 'Gender and success-related attributions: Beyond individualistic conceptions of achievement', *Sex Roles*, **25**, 331–50.

Sarri, K. and A. Trihopoulou (2005), 'Female entrepreneurs' personal characteristics and motivation', *Women in Management Review*, **20** (1), 24–36.

Schenkel, S. (1984), *Giving Away Success: Why Women Get Stuck and What to Do About It*, New York: Random House.

Scherer, R.F., J.D. Brodzinski and F.A. Wiebe (1990), 'Entrepreneur career selection and gender: a socialization approach', *Journal of Small Business Management*, **28** (2), 37–44.

Scott, C.E. (1986), 'Why more women are becoming entrepreneurs', *Journal of Small Business Management*, **24** (4), 37–45.

Sexton, D.L. and N. Bowman-Upton (1990), 'Female and male entrepreneurs: Psychological characteristics and their role in gender-related discrimination', *Journal of Business Venturing*, **51**, 29–36.

Still, L.V. and V. Timms (2000), 'Women's business: the flexible alternative work style for women', *Women in Management Review*, **15** (5/6), 272–82.

Stevenson, L. (1986), 'Against all odds: the entrepreneurship of women', *Journal of Small Business Management*, **24** (4), 30–36.

Swim, J.K. and L.J. Sanna (1996), 'He's skilled, she's lucky: a meta-analysis of observers' attributions for women's and men's successes and failures', Personality and Social Psychology Bulletin, **22** (5), 507–19.

Weiner, B. (1985), 'An attributional theory of achievement motivation and emotion', *Psychological Review*, **92**, 548–73.

Zeldin, A.L. and F. Pajares (2000), 'Against the odds: self-efficacy beliefs of women in mathematical, scientific, and technological careers', *American Educational Research Journal*, **37** (1), 215–46.

PART III

Diverse Approaches

9. More gender equality, less women's self-employment: a multi-country investigation

Kim Klyver, Suna Løwe Nielsen and Majbritt Rostgaard Evald

INTRODUCTION

In this chapter we investigate the link between gender equality at an institutional level and gender differences in employment choice at an individual level. Previous research on this topic is limited. However, qualitative research indicates that countries which focus on gender equality tend to tailor labour market policies to support women in employment, and leave little attention to minority groups such as self-employed women (for example, Kreide, 2003; Neergaard and Thrane, 2009). Women have a relative advantage in choosing employment over self-employment in these countries. Policies that encourage women to participate in the labour force may decrease the likelihood of women participating in self-employment. The purpose of this chapter is to test the qualitative findings on this topic. Based on a statistical analysis that merges two comprehensive datasets dealing with multiple countries, we find support for previous qualitative findings. The more prevalence of institutional gender equality in countries, the less entrepreneurial activity prevails among women (when compared relatively to men). This argument has been validated by the findings that once women are no longer at a childrearing age, the effect of institutional equality disappears. This happens since labour market equality policies are primarily directed to childrearing women.

Women are generally faced with two alternative employment options: to become employed or self-employed. Minniti and Lévesque (2008) claim that the decision to pursue employment is made by rationally evaluating the costs and opportunities of each option in order to maximize the utility of the individual woman. However, women's employment choice is indeed a complex construct (Langowitz and Minniti, 2007) and it has to be understood within a context (De Bruin et al., 2007). The central topic addressed in this chapter is therefore the impact of institutional gender equality on women's employment choice across countries. We define employment as a wage-or-salary career, whereas self-employment is the career of individuals running a business or profession as a sole owner, partner or consultant. Following Gartner's (1993) emergence perspective, we study the nascent career-making processes in which women have to make an occupational decision regarding whether to become employed or self-employed. Institutional gender equality is defined using the definition put forth by the World Economic Forum, which refers to a gap between women's and men's access to resources and opportunities in various countries (Hausmann et al. 2006).

Although it is generally understood that institutional gender equality is an important factor in women's career choice, the topic has been insufficiently investigated. There is significant validation for the argument that a high level of institutional gender equality increases women's participation in employment in both Scandinavian countries and European Union (EU) member states (Borchorts and Siim, 2002, 2008; Cousins, 2000; Guerrina, 2002). In particular, initiatives in the areas of employment legislation and legal rights have proven effective to lowering barriers women face with regard to pregnancy, children, family and work (Kautto et al., 2001). Although it is evident that institutional gender equality provides women with more equal opportunities to participate in the labour market as employees, we still know very little about how institutional gender equality influences women's opportunity to participate equally as self-employed individuals.

PURPOSE AND CONTRIBUTIONS

The purpose of this chapter is to advance our knowledge and test and develop an explanation regarding the impact of institutional gender equality on women's career choice. We examine how institutional gender equality potentially pushes women towards employment and away from self-employment. The literature on women's entrepreneurship has offered some valuable qualitative insights into this question. However, the question as to whether these qualitative patterns are generalizable and valid across countries persists. Moreover, we expect that as women exceed the childrearing age the effect of institutional equality will decline, since they no longer form a target group for most gender equality policies. A test of this theory can shed some light on 'the important interplay between women's childrearing decisions and their choice between employment and self-employment' (Minniti, 2009: 532).

The value-adding contributions of this research can be perceived from a theoretical, methodological and practical perspective. Theoretically, the study fills important gaps of knowledge in the literature of women entrepreneurship that typically relies on individual and social demographic variables in explaining the career choice of women, and pays less attention to influential institutional factors. The methodological contribution of this study is to move the analysis from unique qualitative cases to a more generalizable and sophisticated analysis. Within women's entrepreneurship literature, researchers have expressed a need for this type of study (Arenius and Kovalainen, 2006; De Bruin et al., 2007). From a practical perspective, the study provides policy-makers with significant knowledge which they can use to develop more effective and adequate institutional gender equality policies that support women in being employed as well as self-employed.

WOMEN'S EMPLOYMENT CHOICE

There is a long tradition within mainstream entrepreneurship research that focuses on individual employment choice (for example, Katz, 1992; Kolvereid, 1996). The employment choice concerns 'the individual's decision to enter an occupation as a wage-or-salaried individual or a self-employed one' (Katz, 1992: 30). While this literature has identified many interesting causal relationships, it is generic and focused on male-gendered measuring instruments (Mirchandani, 1999). This creates limitations with regard to explaining the employment choice of women. Previous research has also been preoccupied with comparing already employed and already self-employed people, and less focused on the pre-career decisions of entering employment or self-employment (Georgellis and Wall, 2005).

Literature on female entrepreneurship suggests that many influential factors tend to be unique for women's employment choice (Buttner and Moore, 1997; Marlow, 2006). As mentioned, most of the research on women's entrepreneurship typically points to personal or socio-demographic factors to explain gender asymmetries in employment choice. It reveals how men and women are socialized differently and experience diverse structural barriers. In this way, Bowen and Hisrich's (1986) comprehensive women's career model emphasizes factors such as individual personality, childhood and family issues, education, work status and history as being essential to explain the career choice of women. In particular, 'motherhood' is often highlighted as a decisive influential factor in the employment choice of women (Brush et al., 2009); it is further suggested that the dissimilarities among men and women entrepreneurs are more extensive if the entrepreneur is married and has dependent children (DeMartino and Barbato, 2003). In many societies, women still hold the main responsibility for the family (Haas, 2003), a situation that has para-doxically been argued to both lead women into and prevent women from self-employment. Women are drawn into self-employment by a desire to become independent and flexible, enabling them to create room for synergy and harmony between family and work (Georgellis and Wall, 2005). In contrast, it is argued that motherhood pushes women away from self-employment, as the world of the mother and the world of the self-employed are each demanding in terms of time, effort and commitment, and repre-sent different obligations, constraints and opportunities (Taniguchi, 2002). 'Therefore, the entrance of women into self-employment is at least delayed until children are adult' (Delmar and Davidsson, 2000: 4).

Two distinctive personal factors identified to influence the employment choice of women are self-image and self-efficacy. Women are less likely to perceive themselves as entrepreneurs compared to men (Verheul et al., 2005); they feel a lack of the required skills and competences (Wilson et al., 2007). Further, women often fail to see themselves as entrepreneurs and view the entrepreneurial environment in a less favourable light compared to men (Langowitz and Minniti, 2007). Taken together the self-image and self-efficacy of women will prevent women from consider-ing self-employment. In addition, a range of other personal and socio-demographic factors have been identified as having various impacts on the self-employment choice of men and women (Minniti, 2009).

However, it is interesting that the literature on the employment choice of women tends to disregard institutional factors. Although research on women's entrepreneurship widely accepts that employment decisions are made in a context, and recent research is beginning to address how the institutional context influences the employment choice of women (for example, Arenius and Kovalainen, 2006; Baughn et al., 2006; Verheul et al., 2006), the institutional perspective still remains rather unexplored in research on women's entrepreneurship (Brush et al., 2009). The relation-ship between the institutional environment and the employment choice of women has seldom been approached theoretically or empirically; as a result, we are left with insufficient and superficial understandings of women's employment choice.

INSTITUTIONS AND EMPLOYMENT CHOICE

The employment decisions of women are made within an institutional, economic, cultural and political context. The context influences the decision-making process, as it affects the cost and opportunities related to employment and self-employment respectively. In general, entrepreneurship research points to a link between a weak supportive institutional environment and low entrepreneurial activity (Aldrich and Fiol, 1994). An individual who does not understand that the institutional context legitimizes her choice of employment will identify herself as a displaced person (Shapero and Sokol, 1982). As a result, she may not pursue a career.

Prior research on the impact of the institutional dimension of women's self-employment is nevertheless limited in terms of methodological advancement and focus. Country is often applied as the unit of analysis (for example, Baughn et al., 2006; Verheul et al., 2006). This causes at least two weaknesses. First, using country as the unit of analysis restricts the number of observations possible and thereby decreases the odds of significant results. Secondly, this approach overlooks the possibility that the effects of institutions are best explored by examining cross-country variation in individual decision-making.

In terms of focus, Scott (1995) suggests that institutions can be seen as compositions of different cultural-cognitive, normative and structural regulative dimensions that, together with a wealth of resources and activities, influence human life (including the employment choice). When women's entrepreneurship researchers bring in the institutional context as an explanatory factor to women's employment choice, the normative dimension tends to be in focus. Emphasis is often on the ways that institutional norms, in the form of contextual guidelines regarding what women ought to do, actually regulate women's employment choice (for example, Baughn et al., 2006).

Apart from the previously mentioned qualitative studies collected from various unique contexts, the impact of institutional gender equality on women employment choice is a limited story in entrepreneurship (Arenius and Kovalainen, 2006). The general picture from these studies is that a high level of institutional gender equality in a given country does not necessarily equal more self-employment among women, as gender equality policies tend to be tailored to employment and not self-employment. Neergaard and Thrane (2009) find that self-employed women in Denmark are prevented from working during their maternity leaves. They also note that 30 per cent of Danish women perceive the child care system as a barrier to self-employment (Neergaard and Thrane, 2009). Kreide's qualitative analysis shows that women in self-employment face structural hurdles because welfare state regulations are mainly oriented towards the model of the male breadwinner and 'towards a standardized employee-employer relationship' (2003: 216). Based on a historical analysis of the development of the Swedish welfare state, Anderson-Skog (2007: 469) concludes: 'women have become their own breadwinners, [and are] less dependent on their husbands; at the same time, welfare policy has strengthened the gender divisions of the labour market. Together, these features have created a strong initiative for women to become employees rather than entrepreneurs'. In their analysis of women entrepreneurs in Denmark, Nielsen, Klyver and Evald (2010) argue that the welfare system itself is a main barrier to women's entrepreneurship. One of the aims of the welfare system is to create gender equality by promoting social support activities that replace traditional responsibilities of women. However, these state initiatives often monopolize the areas and industries in which many women are trained and skilled. In this way, the welfare state, on one hand, provides women with opportunities to participate in the labour market as employees; alternatively though, it also negates many of the opportunities women may pursue through self-employment.

In political science there is a strong interest to estimate the impact of institutional gender equality on women's employment opportunities, with the aim of investigating whether or not women have the opportunity to enter employment in contrast to staying at home as wife/mother (Mandel, 2009). In this regard, the 'women friendly' policies associated with the Scandinavian welfare state model have received attention (Esping-Andersen, 2002). Interestingly this literature has less focus on the fact that women may choose to become self-employed for various reasons. Studies only indirectly point out that labour market gender equality policies are directed towards facilitating conventional employer–employee relationships (for example, Borchorst and Siim, 2002; Mandel, 2009; Morgan and Zippel 2003). Seemingly, even progressive countries, which actively seek to provide institutional equality through 'women friendly' policy regulations, tend to disregard minority groups such as self-employed women.

In this light, we propose a negative link between high levels of institutional gender equality and self-employment among women. In terms of gender equality, women living in countries with a focus on employment, as opposed to self-employment, simply have to give up too much when choosing self-employment over employment. In contrast, women living in countries with a low level of institutional gender equality experience a lower level of opportunity costs connected to choosing self-employment instead of employment. The trade-offs between employment and self-employment are not as high for this group of women as compared to the previous group. We therefore hypothesize:

Hypothesis: The gap between men and women in choosing self-employment will be higher in countries with higher gender equality.

METHODOLOGY

To predict women's employment choice as a function of institutional equality we use two datasets. The first dataset, the Global Entrepreneurship Monitor survey, contains detailed occupational data on employment choice at an individual level. The second dataset, World Economic Forum's Global Gender Gap index, contains data on gender equality at the institutional level. The two datasets were merged and integrated in order to complete the analysis.

Global Entrepreneurship Monitor was initially launched in 1999 and has developed into a well-known global project on entrepreneurship. The underlying method of the Global Entrepreneurship Monitor is to collect yearly information from a representative sample of adults about their engagement in self-employment (Minniti et al., 2006; Reynolds et al., 2005). In 2003 the countries involved in the survey counted for 90 per cent of the world's GDP and covered 60 per cent of the world's population (Klyver, 2008).

In 2006 the World Economic Forum introduced the Global Gender Gap index as a reaction to the worldwide persistent gap between women's and men's access to resources and opportunities. In 2009 the index covered 134 countries and over 90 per cent of the world's population, and included all countries involved in Global Entrepreneurship Monitor except Hong Kong. Global Gender Gap creates benchmarks for all the various countries involved and aims to provide useful guidance for policy formation aimed at promoting gender equality. It identifies gender gaps within four critical areas: economy, education, politics and health. Taken together, these categories constitute an overall gender gap index. In recent years, different gender equality measures have been developed, including Gender-Related Development Index (GDI) and Gender Empowerment Measure (GEM). Each of these measures has previously been criticized (Klasen, 2006a). Klasen (2006b), for instance, argues that both GDI and GEM suffer from serious conceptual and empirical challenges that hinder their usefulness. Schüler (2006) reviews previous research that adapts the GDI and GEM measures and concludes that both measures have been frequently used. However, the use or misuse involves problems of interpreting the meaning of the measures and their implications. Although the Global Gender Gap does contain weaknesses, this index was developed to fulfil, or at least improve, some of the limitations of previous measures. In particular, improvements include a change from levels to gaps, from means to outcomes, and from women's empowerment to gender equality (Hausmann et al., 2006).[1]

Data was selected for countries that were included in both datasets; as a result, the study includes 50 countries. The pooled data across six survey years in the Global Entrepreneurship Monitor (GEM) equalled 638 824 usable respondents. Although wealthy and industrialized countries are overrepresented, the sample is gender equality heterogeneous. The sample includes countries from all six continents: North America (2 countries), South America (9 countries), Europe (23 countries), Africa (2 countries), Asia (12 countries) and Australia (2 countries). Of the 638 824 respondents, 23 976 (4 per cent) are actually in the process of starting a new business. In this chapter these individuals are identified as in the process of becoming self-employed. Table 9.1 describes the variables used.

FINDINGS

Table 9.2 shows descriptive statistics. The dependent variable, entry to self-employment, is negatively correlated with age, female, GDP per capita and gender equality, and positively correlated with education and national start-up rate. The highest correlation ($r = 0.35$) is between GDP per capita and gender equality. This indicates that gender equality is more likely in countries with a high GDP per capita. As 0.35 is the highest correlation among the variables, no multi-collinearity exists.

In order to test our hypothesis, hierarchical logistic regressions are used. In the baseline model (Model 1) we included all individual level variables (age, education and female). Previous research clearly indicates that age and education have significant influence on the vocational decision to become self-employed (Shane, 2003). We also added three society-level control variables: GDP per capita, GDP-squared and national start-up rate. Previous studies reveal that individuals' entry to self-employment depends on the economic development of the country in which they live (for example, Wennekers et al., 2005). In Model 2 we added the main effect of gender equality. Finally, in Model 3 we added the interaction effect of female by gender equality (Table 9.3).

In Model 3 the hypothesis is tested. The added interaction effect of female (at the individual level) by gender equality (at the society level) has a significant negative association with individuals considering entry to self-employment ($p < 0.001$). Supporting our hypothesis, this means that women are less likely to consider entry to self-employment in societies with high gender equality compared to women in societies with low gender equality. Thus the gender gap in the odds of entry to self-employment increases as the gender equality increases.

In order to better understand the main effects and the interaction effect, we calculated the likelihood of considering entry to self-employment

Table 9.1   Description of variables

Variables	Question/Source	Coding
Dependent variable:		
Entry to self-employment	'Are you, alone or with others, currently trying to start a new business, including any self-employment or selling any goods or services to others?'	0 No 1 Yes
Independent variables:		
Female		1 Male 2 Female
Gender equality	Index adapted from World Economic Forum's Global Gender Gap Report 2009 (Hausmann et al., 2009) ranging from 0.58 to 0.82. It captures the scope of gender-based disparity within four areas: economy, education, politics and health. The variable is a society level variable	
Control variables:		
Age	Categorical variable computed from respondent's exact age	
Education	Respondents' level of education coded as: 111 for none or some secondary education, 1212 for secondary education, 1316 for post-secondary education, and 1720 for graduate experience. The figures represent the years of education (1–11 years; 12 years; 13–16 years; 17–20 years). In the regression analysis dummies with none or some secondary education are used as reference category	
GDP per capita	Gross domestic product per capita in US$. The data were adapted from the United Nations Development Program's Human Development Index 2007	
National start-up rate	Country-level scale variable measuring the proportion of the adult population within each country that is in the process of entering self-employment. The used variable is an average of the national start-up rate from 2003–06	
Year of survey	A dummy variable for year of GEM survey	

Table 9.2   Means, standard deviation and Pearson correlations

	Mean	SD	1	2	3	4	5	6	7
1. Entry to self-employment	.04	.19	1						
2. Age	2.13	.75	−.05**	1					
3. Education	920.24	612.91	.03**	−.09**	1				
4. Female	1.53	.50	−.06**	.03**	−.01**	1			
5. GDP per capita (US$)	37.51	29.31	−.01**	.04**	.06**	.01**	1		
6. National start-up rate	4.20	3.08	.16**	−.07**	−.04**	.00	.02**	1	
7. Gender equality	0.73	.05	−.04**	.06**	.02**	.01**	.35**	−.14**	1

*Note: * $p < 0.05$; ** $p < 0.01$.*

depending on both gender equality and female as 0.855 (female) + 3.291 (gender equality) − 2.042 (female gender equality). We then calculated the ratio between men and women for different levels of gender equality. The results are shown in Table 9.4.

Table 9.4 confirms previous observations. First, for men higher gender equality results in a higher likelihood of entering self-employment, whereas higher gender equality results in a lower likelihood of entering self-employment for women. Secondly, being a woman decreases the likelihood of entering self-employment, regardless of gender equality. In the fourth column of Table 9.4 it is reported that women's and men's likelihood of considering entering self-employment depends on gender equality. We see that the ratio decreases as gender equality increases, indicating a dampening effect.

Initially, Table 9.3 provides a sufficient test of the hypothesis. Meanwhile an additional test might provide further realiability to our results. We argued that challenges to self-employment as a career choice for women are more prevalent in societies with a high level of gender equality because gender equality initiatives are often aimed at employment, and biased towards self-employment. This means that factors often associated with 'women friendly' policies, such as maternity leave, parentel leave and childcare services, are implemented to a satisfactory degree for employment but not for self-employment. When we associate 'women friendly' policies regarding the labour market with the just mentioned factors, we implicitly narrow down the age group of the women that we are dealing with (namely-women in the childrearing age). Therefore, if we ran similar

*Table 9.3   Hierarchical logistic regression predicting entry to
self-employment*

	Model 1 Base model	Model 2 Main effect model	Model 3 Interaction effect model
	B	B	B
Individual level			
Age (ref 15–29 years old)			
Age – 30–49 years old	.184***	.186***	.187***
Age – >50 years old	−.573***	−.573***	−.572***
Education (ref is no higher education)			
Education – secondary degree	.197***	.201***	.202***
Education – post-secondary degree	.496***	.502***	.504***
Education – graduate experience	.578***	.581***	.584***
Female	−.624***	−.624***	.855*
Society level			
GDP per capita	−.011***	−.012***	−.012***
GDP per capita * GDP per capita	.000***	.000***	.000***
National start-up rate	.105***	.105***	.105***
Gender equality		.517**	3.291***
Interaction			
Female by gender equality			−2.042***
Constant	−2.568***	−2.917***	−4.929***
Pseudo R^2 (Nagelkerke)	0.084	0.084	0.084
N respondents	638.824		
N societies	50		

*Note: * $p < 0.05$; ** $p < 0.01$; *** $p < 0.001$.*

tests for a split sample of different age groups we expect that the interaction effect of gender equality will decrease; we anticipate that as women grow older the disadvantages of being women, in respect of self-employment, will disappear. For instance, a woman over a certain age may not experience any disadvantages in relation to her employment choice (owing to initiatives such as maternity leave) because she is no longer able to become pregnant. In order to increase the realibility of our results we therefore ran similar tests on a split sample for seven age groups. Table 9.5 presents the results.

Table 9.5 confirms our previous results, namely, that the coefficient for the interaction effect decreases as women grow older. Even more

Table 9.4   *Likelihood of entry to self-employment depending on gender and gender equality*

Gender equality	Gender		Female/male ratio
	Male	Female	
0.55	4.7	3.6	0.8
0.60	5.0	3.4	0.7
0.65	5.3	3.3	0.6
0.70	5.6	3.2	0.6
0.75	6.0	3.1	0.5
0.80	6.4	2.9	0.5
0.85	6.8	2.8	0.4

Table 9.5   *Logistic regressions predicting entry to self-employment on split samples of age groups*

Age	Main	Interaction	N
15–17	3.308	−9.008*	8 273
18–24	3.394***	−3.286***	77 386
25–34	2.964***	−2.468***	122 607
35–44	4.509***	−2.174***	141 694
45–54	3.225**	−1.235*	124 626
55–64	2.317	−0.23	104 064
65–98	−3.244	2.61	57 823

Note: $* p < 0.05$; $** p < 0.01$; $*** p < 0.001$.

interesting, the interaction effects become insignificant for women older than 55 years of age. This confirms our expectation that the disadvantages experienced by women, with regard to self-employment in societies with a high level of gender equality, disappear as women reach a certain age.

DISCUSSIONS AND CONCLUSION

In this study we have investigated the link between gender equality at an institutional level and gender differences in employment choice at an individual level. Following previous anecdotal evidence from qualitative research (for example, Kreide, 2003; Neergaard and Thrane, 2009) we argued that the disadvantages associated with self-employment compared to employment are higher for women in societies with high gender equality. This is because these societies tend to tailor policies and initiatives towards the conventional job market (that is, women's employment) and not towards minorities (such as women entrepreneurs). Consequently, initiatives associated with women-friendly policies such as maternity leave, parental leave and childcare services are only implemented to a satisfactory degree for employment, and are not implemented (or implemented only to an unsatisfactory degree) for self-employment. Women, therefore, experience a relative disadvantage of being self-employed in societies with higher gender equality.

This argument was statistically tested using two datasets: the national population surveys from Global Entrepreneurship Monitor (2001 to 2006) and the Global Gender Gap Index (2009) from World Economic Forum. Ironically, our statistical test showed that compared with men, women are less likely to choose self-employment in societies with high gender equality. This reveals that the gender gap in the odds of self-employment (compared to employment) increases as gender equality increases at an institutional level.

These results were further validated after similar tests were conducted with split samples for different age groups. Initially, we tested women's likelihood to choose self-employment over employment depending on the level of gender equality in the society they live in. We argued that a high level of gender equality at a societal level is primarily characterized by a range of initiatives aimed at promoting women's participation as employees in the conventional job market. Initiatives associated with gender equality include a range of services but are primarily tailored towards women in the childrearing age. Our first statistical test is therefore reinforced, as we demonstrated that the gender gap decreases as women grow older, and is non-existent for women older than 55 years of age.

Although the current study benefits from the use of representative sampling at the individual level and the inclusion of participants from 50 countries, we acknowledge at least three limitations. First, with regard to measurement, we initially argued that gender equality influences the gender gap in self-employment across countries. Behind this argument lies the assumption that gender equality is linked to a number of initiatives associated with promoting women's participation in the job market. This is not necessarily true. Logically there is not a strong link (although there is probably an empirical link) between gender equality and political initiatives which promote women's participation as employees in the conventional job market. Further, the causality between gender equality and initiatives promoting women's participation in the labour market is more blurred and complex than anticipated.

Secondly, as we are living in an increasingly globalized world, using a country as a unit of analysis diminishes this study's explanatory power. This has been emphasized in studies on national culture (Bandura, 2002) and may also be the case with regard to gender equality. Different groups of individuals might approach gender equality issues differently depending on, for instance, their geographical, political, religious or professional affiliation.

The completion of any research endeavour raises a 'so what' question; thus, we turn to the theoretical, methodological and practical implications of our findings. Although previous research mainly focuses on personal and socio-demographic factors, it has validated the importance of recognizing institutional factors that affect the employment choice of women. The employment choice of women is a result of a complex set of factors and relationships. By taking the institutional aspect into account, our understanding of the trade-off between employment and self-employment in women's entrepreneurship will increase. Therefore, future research should further examine the institutional level as a central element of women's employment choice. Brush et al. (2009) have suggested a general conceptual framework on women entrepreneurship that takes institutional factors into account. However, there is a need to further test the links between costs and opportunities related to self-employment over employment at an individual level. Understanding how the institutional context reinforces these costs and opportunities will help build a more advanced academic theory on the topic.

Above we have already discussed the central methodological limitations of our research. Since the relationship between 'more gender equality, less women self-employment' has primarily been addressed by a small number of qualitative studies in women's entrepreneurship research, an implication of this study is that it challenges future research to move beyond a carefully selected number of unique qualitative approaches. Although qualitative studies can be valuable, they do not identify the institutional effects on women's employment choice in a broader context; therefore, it is hard to apply qualitative findings to other situations. The drawbacks are that we develop only fragmented insights into unique employment choice situations and cannot confirm or come up with any general conclusions which future researchers can use to build hypotheses.

Finally, as outlined in the beginning of the chapter, our findings have practical implications. First and foremost, they provide policy-makers with a platform of knowledge from which they can ratify and design gender equality policies. Women's self-employment is important for wealth-creation (Wilson et al., 2007). However, as long as the relationship between institutional gender equality and women's employment choice is shrouded with mystery, a strategy for facilitating more women's self-employment may also remain a mystery. Conceptual and empirical research (Baumol, 1990; Bowen and De Clercq, 2008) shows that political instruments, such as gender equality policies, can have an impact on the allocation of entrepreneurship in society. This makes policy-makers an important target group for women entrepreneurship research. Our findings highlight that some types of gender equality policies can in fact hinder women's self-employment. To prevent this from happening our findings point to one central guideline to consider in formulating labour market policies. Specifically, countries with a high level of gender equality (with policies designed to facilitate women in employment) need to minimize the relative costs or improve the positive aspects for women entering self-employment. There are many ways in which policy-makers can efficiently address this issue. Crucially, they should bear in mind two alternative career routes for women, employment *and* self-employment, when developing 'women friendly' policies and programmes.

NOTE

1. As a validation of the results obtained in this study by using the Global Gender Gap Index, we conducted similar analyses using Gender-Related Development Index and Gender Empowerment Measure as measures of gender equality. Using these two alternative measures of equality we reached the same conclusion as to how gender equality in a society increases the gender gap in self-employment. Thus the results seem to be reliable across different measures of gender equality.

REFERENCES

Aldrich, H. and M. Fiol (1994), 'Fools rush in? The institutional context of industry creation', *Academy of Management Review*, **19** (4), 645–70.

Anderson-Skog, L. (2007), 'In the shadow of the Swedish welfare state: women and the service sector', *Business History Review*, **81** (3), 451–70.

Arenius, P. and A. Kovalainen (2006), 'Similarities and differences across the factors associated with women's self-employment preference in the Nordic countries', *International Small Business Journal*, **24** (1), 31–59.

Bandura, A. (2002), 'Social cognitive theory in cultural context', *Applied Psychology: An International Review*, **151**, 269–90.

Baughn, C.C., B. Chua and K.E. Neupert (2006), 'The normative context for women's participation in entrepreneurship: a multicountry study', *Entrepreneurship Theory and Practice*, **30** (5), 687–708.

Baumol, W.J. (1990), 'Entrepreneurship: productive, unproductive and destructive', *Journal of Political Economy*, **98** (5), 893–921.

Borchorst, A. and B. Siim (2002), 'The women-friendly welfare states revisited', *Nordic Journal of Feminist and Gender Research*, **10** (2), 90–98.

Borchorst, A. and B. Siim (2008), 'Woman-friendly policies and state feminism: theorizing Scandinavian gender equality', *Feminist Theory*, **9** (2), 207–24.

Bowen, D.D. and R.D. Hisrich (1986), 'The female entrepreneur: a career development perspective', *Academy of Management Review*, **11** (2), 393–407.

Bowen, H.P. and D. De Clercq (2008), 'Institutional context and the allocation of entrepreneurial effort', *Journal of International Business Studies*, **39** (4), 747–67.

Brush, C.G., D.A. Bruin and F. Welter (2009), 'A gender-aware framework for women's entrepreneurship', *International Journal of Gender and Entrepreneurship*, **1** (1), 8–24.

Buttner, E.H. and D. Moore (1997), 'Women's organizational exodus to entrepreneurship: Self reported motivations and correlates with success', *Journal of Small Business Management*, **35** (1), 34–46.

Cousins, C. (2000), 'Women and Employment in Southern Europe: the implications of recent policy and labor market directions', *South European Society & Politics*, **5** (1), 97–122.

De Bruin, A., C.G. Brush and F. Welter (2007), 'Advancing a framework for coherent research on women's entrepreneurship', *Entrepreneurship Theory and Practice*, **31** (3), 323–40.

Delmar, F. and P. Davidsson (2000), 'Where do they come from? Prevalence and characteristics of nascent entrepreneurs', *Entrepreneurship and Regional Development*, **12** (1), 1–23.

DeMartino, R. and R. Barbato (2003), 'Differences between women and men MBA entrepreneurs: exploring family flexibility and wealth creation as career motives', *Journal of Business Venturing*, **18** (6), 815–32.

Esping-Andersen, G. (2002), *Why We Need a New Welfare State*, Oxford: Oxford University Press.

Gartner, W.B. (1993), 'Words lead to deeds: towards an organizational emergence vocabulary', *Journal of Business Venturing*, **8** (3), 231–9.

Georgellis, Y. and H. Wall (2005), 'Gender differences in self-employment', *International Review of Applied Economics*, **19** (3), 321–42.

Guerrina, R. (2002), 'Feminist critique of European policies on motherhood and employment', *The European Journal of Women's Studies*, **9** (1), 49–68.

Haas, L. (2003), 'Parental leave and gender equality: lessons from the European Union', *Review of Policy Research*, **20** (1), 89–126.

Hausmann, R., L.D. Tyson and S. Zahidi (2006), *The Global Gender Gap Report 2006*, Geneva: World Economic Forum.

Katz, J.A. (1992), 'A psychological cognitive model of employment status choice', *Entrepreneurship Theory and Practice*, **17** (1), 29–37.

Kautto, M., J. Fritzell, B. Hvinden, J. Kvist and H. Uusitalo (2001), 'Introduction: how distinct are the Nordic welfare states?', in J. Fritzell, B. Hvinden, M. Kauto, J. Kvist and H. Uusitalo (eds), *Nordic Welfare States in the European Context*, London: Routledge, pp. 1–13.

Klasen, S. (2006a), 'Guest editor's introduction', *Journal of Human Development*, **7** (2), 145–59.

Klasen, S. (2006b), 'UNDP's gender related measures: some conceptual problems and possible solutions', *Journal of Human Development*, **7** (2), 243–74.

Klyver, K. (2008), 'An analytical framework for micro-level analysis of GEM data', *International Journal of Entrepreneurship and Small Business*, **6** (4), 583–603.

Kolvereid, L. (1996), 'Prediction of employment status choice intentions', *Entrepreneurship Theory and Practice*, **21** (1), 47–57.

Kreide, R. (2003), 'Self-employment of women and welfare-state policies', *International Review of Sociology*, **13** (1), 205–18.

Langowitz, N. and M. Minniti (2007), 'The entrepreneurial propensity of women', *Entrepreneurship Theory and Practice*, **31** (3), 341–64.

Mandel, H. (2009), 'Configurations of gender inequality: the consequences of ideology and public policy', *The British Journal of Sociology*, **60** (4), 693–719.

Marlow, S. (2006), 'A safety net or ties that bind? Women, welfare and self-employment', *International Journal of Sociology and Social Policy*, **26** (9/10), 397–410.

Minniti, M. (2009), 'Gender issues in entrepreneurship', *Foundations and Trends in Entrepreneurship*, **5** (7/8), 497–621.

Minniti, M. and M. Lévesque (2008), 'Recent developments in the economics of entrepreneurship', *Journal of Business Venturing*, **23** (6), 603–12.

Minniti, M., W.D. Bygrave and E. Autio (2006), *Global Entrepreneurship Monitor: 2005 Executive Report*, Boston, MA: Babson College and London Business School.

Mirchandani, K. (1999), 'Feminist insight on gendered work: new directions in research on women and entrepreneurship', *Gender, Work and Organization*, **6** (4), 224–35.

Morgan, K. J. and K. Zippel (2003), 'Paid to care: the origins and effects of care leave policies in Western Europe', *Social Politics*, **10** (1), 49–85.

Neergaard, H. and C. Thrane (2009), 'The Nordic welfare model: barrier or facilitator of women's entrepreneurship in Denmark' *International Journal of Gender and Entrepreneurship*, **10** (2), 88–104.

Nielsen, S.L., K. Klyver and M.R. Evald (2010), 'Denmark', in S.L. Fielden and M.J. Davidson (eds), *International Research Handbook on Successful Women Entrepreneurs*, Cheltenham, UK and Northampton, MA, USA: Edward Elgar Publishing, pp. 60–72.

Reynolds, P.D., N. Bosma, E. Aution, S. Hunt, N. De Bono, I. Servais, P. Lopez-Garcia and N. Chin (2005), 'Global entrepreneurship monitor: data collection design and implementation 1998–2003', *Small Business Economics*, **24** (3), 205–31.

Schüler, D. (2006), 'The uses and misuses of the Gender-related Development Index and Gender Empowerment Index: a review of the literature', *Journal of Human Development*, **7** (2), 161–81.

Scott, R.W. (1995), *Institutions and Organizations*, Thousand Oaks, CA: Sage.

Shane, S. (2003), *A General Theory of Entrepreneurship: The Individual-Opportunity Nexus*, Cheltenham, UK and Northampton, MA, USA: Edward Elgar Publishing.

Shapero, A. and L. Sokol (1992), 'The social dimension of entrepreneurship', in C.A. Kent, D.L. Sexton and K.H. Vesper (eds), *Encyclopedia of Entrepreneurship*, Englewood Cliffs, NJ: Prentice-Hall, pp. 72–90.

Taniguchi, H. (2002), 'Determinants of women's entry into self-employment', *Social Science Quarterly*, **83** (3), 875–93.

Verheul, I., L. Uhlaner and R. Thurik (2005), 'Business accomplishment, gender and entrepreneurial self-image', *Journal of Business Venturing*, **20** (4), 483–518.

Verheul, I., A. Van Stel and R. Thurik (2006), 'Explaining female and male entrepreneurship at the country level', *Entrepreneurship Theory and Practice*, **18** (2), 151–83.
Wennekers, S., A. Van Stel, R. Thurik and P. Reynolds (2005), 'Nascent entrepreneurship and the level of economic development', *Small Business Economics*, **24** (3), 293–309.
Wilson, F., J. Kickul and D. Marlino (2007), 'Gender, entrepreneurial self-efficacy, and entrepreneurial career intentions: implications for entrepreneurship education', *Entrepreneurship Theory and Practice*, **31** (3), 387–406.

10. Sectoral segregation or gendered practices? A case study of roles and identities in a copreneurial venture

Maura McAdam and Susan Marlow

INTRODUCTION

Dyadic couples that share emotional ties within a domestic context and also a business relationship through entrepreneurial venturing are described as 'copreneurs' (Marshack, 1994, 1998). This form of business ownership is relatively common, representing at least 30 percent of all family businesses in the USA (Fitzgerald and Muske, 2002). The copreneur phenomenon is not surprising given the necessity for spousal or partner engagement and support, particularly during the period start-up phase of a new business. At this stage, the business is likely to draw heavily upon joint financial resources (savings) and require time and labour commitments from both partners to establish the venture. As such, a spouse or partner becomes a critical stakeholder within the business (Aldrich and Cliff, 2003; Ruef et al., 2003; Steier and Greenwood, 2000). Evidence indicates, however, that in the majority of cases where partners operate copreneurially, men undertake the leadership position, with the critical contribution of their female partners afforded little recognition or value. In effect, women become 'invisible' within these partnerships (Hamilton, 2006; Mulholland, 1996).

Increasing numbers of women are now undertaking the role of entrepreneurial leader (Danes & Olsen, 2003; Seymour, 2002). However, little is known about the dynamics of these copreneurial relationships which represent a reversal of the normative gendered binary (with women taking the lead). Accordingly, Hamilton (2006) argues that the current debate 'commonly reflects and reinforces the relative silence and invisibility of women in entrepreneurial discourse. Embedded in that discourse is the assumption that the leadership involved in founding and running a business is most naturally male' (Hamilton, 2006: 256). Consequently, in this chapter we aim to explore how gendered roles are managed, challenged or changed when the normative binary relationship is reversed (that is, when the female partner is positioned as the visible entrepreneur). To achieve this aim, we first undertake a critical analysis of gender subordination and examine how this notion is articulated within prevailing entrepreneurial narratives. After surveying the literature we then comment on how women are represented within this discourse. Next, having created our theoretical framework, we draw on an inductive methodology and present in-depth empirical evidence that describes the functional division of labour and partnership roles in a successful, jointly owned au pair agency based in New Zealand (a peripheral diverse region). Finally, the implications of this research for theory and practice are critically evaluated.

Entrepreneurship is a gendered activity within a masculinized domain. The concept of gender emerged into mainstream debate in the 1970s (Oakley, 1973) as a critique of the idea that biological categorizations of humans into males and females imbues them with specific and fixed social characteristics (Holmes, 2007). Thus, gender is a *social* construction of sex; this analysis has been critical in demonstrating that assumed behavioural differences ascribed to men and women arise from ingrained social training, habits, expectations and pressures to conform to contextualized displays of masculinity and femininity. Consequently, while genetic differences underpin the labels 'male' and 'female', performing associated masculinities and femininities is 'not something innate or unchangeable, but rather something that is created by historical forces' (Gilbert, 2001:41). While the notion of gendered identities is critical to understanding the ontology of the constructed subject positions ascribed to men and women (through ascribed masculinities and femininities), it is also fundamental to revealing the valorization process embedded within gendered orders (Bowden and Mummery, 2009). As such, masculinity and femininity are contextualized, dynamic characterizations, but they exist within a hierarchical duality. This duality orders social relations between men and women, with women and femininity subordinated (Hirdman, 2001; Holmes, 2007). Thus, gendered ascriptions map socialized behavioural expectations onto the biological categories of male and female while subtly producing and reproducing the devaluation of females and femininity (Harding, 1987; Knights and Kerfoot, 2004). This valuation process is reproduced and, consequently, embedded within critical social and economic institutions (such as the labour market, welfare systems, education and organized politics) in contemporary developed economies (Daly and Rake, 2003). Thus, the association between stereotypical femininity and weakness or powerlessness is self-reinforcing and endures across time and space (Holmes, 2007).

That is not to say, however, that gendered identities are fixed. As Linstead and Pullen (2006) argue, they are shifting, fragmented and sensitive to context; they exist as 'multiplicities'. Accordingly, individuals perform their gender according to particular situations and circumstances. However, such performances generally reflect a range of responses around broad notions of masculinity and femininity, rather than overt challenges to gender stereotypes. A refusal to perform gender can lead to suspicion, distrust and, in some cases, outright violence (McRobbie, 2009). Therefore, women, as a biological category, are subordinated by gendered ascriptions (Holmes, 2007). Their femininity is constructed and reconstructed in relation to, and in reflection of, particular socio-economic environments and contexts.

Given the assumed autonomy associated with independent business venturing, it could be argued that the entrepreneurial context might offer women more opportunities to challenge the stereotypical, institutional impacts of gendered subordination. As such, drawing upon individual agency in combination with entrepreneurial autonomy may offer the potential to enhance status and power (Allen and Trueman, 1993; Rouse, 2005). However, it is persuasively argued that entrepreneurship theory, policy and practice reflects the normative gendered order and is, in fact, embedded within masculinity (Ahl, 2006; Ogbor, 2000). Thus, the stereotypical entrepreneur is defined in terms of aggression, competitiveness, risk taking and trying to maximize wealth. All of these characteristics are typically associated with masculinity (Ahl, 2004). While few entrepreneurs are likely to articulate this stereotypical identity, the dominating social characterization of entrepreneurial behaviour effectively marginalizes 'feminine' traits. As a result, women become interlopers within the field (Lewis, 2009). This analysis suggests that women do not easily 'fit' into the accepted model of entrepreneurship – as those who are associated with femininity stand in opposition to entrepreneurship's masculinized characterization. Building on this analysis, we investigate how gender is performed within copreneurial relationships. However, rather than exploring how gender is articulated within partnerships that reflect the normative binary ordering (where the male dominates), our analysis explores partnerships where the hierarchy is reversed (and a women adopts the primary and visible entrepreneurial leader role).

HUSBANDS AND WIVES

Despite popular and romantic notions of the entrepreneur as a lone hero, the management of new ventures is generally a shared effort (Gartner et al., 1994; Hamilton, 2006). Indeed, Marshack (1998) and Firkin et al. (2003) found that within copreneurship, female partners tacitly support the business effort by taking sole responsibility for domestic labour and related caring tasks. Thus, women often absolve the male business owner from such activities. While this gendered division of labour is common-place in most households (Holmes, 2007), it is noted that where men are business owners, women are tasked to take care of domestic labour and, additionally, participate as invisible, unpaid business partners (Hamilton, 2006; Marshack, 1994; Mulholland, 1996). Consequently, entrepreneurial couples that work closely together 'are often trapped by a gender-based division of responsibilities and authority' that typically results 'in the wife acquiescing to (the husband's) benevolent authority' (Marshack, 1998: 169). This serves to reinforce and perpetuate entrepreneurship as a male construct and limit our understanding of entrepreneurship and entrepreneurial endeavours.[1]

However, a traditional gendered ordering within copreneurial businesses is not uniform; there is evidence that women are increasingly assuming the role of lead entrepreneur within copreneurial ventures (Koss-Feder, 2001; Poza and Messer, 2001). Lucaccini and Muscat (2001: 9) attribute this growth to 'corporate down-sizing, a return to pre-industrial values regard-ing family life, a belief in the equality of the sexes and a desire for greater control of one's own life'. To explore this proposition, we investigate how gendered and entrepreneurial identities are managed and overlap in a copreneurial venture where a woman represents the public and visible 'face' of the business owner.

METHODOLOGY

To explore and analyse the manner in which copreneurs manage their overlapping business and domestic lives, we draw upon an in-depth case study method. Our approach reflects an interpretist ontology founded upon the notion of constructed, multiple realities (Leitch et al., 2009). Such insight is critical given our ambition to explore how situated realities are collectively constructed and articulated. Where the research question focuses upon the exploration of meaning as an outcome of lan-guage, interpretation and significance, an interpretist approach is useful (Case, 2003; Weick, 2007). By drawing upon contextualized accounts, however, we do not claim to present a complete picture. Inevitably, what we describe are partial, fragmented accounts of the entrepreneurial and domestic roles of these copreneurs. Analysing this interplay offers an opportunity to reflect upon how it reproduces, challenges and contradicts theoretical articulations of the gendered ordering within a copreneurial partnership where a woman undertakes the role of entrepreneurial business leader. Through this approach, we distance this study from any ambition to create a 'grand narrative' that suggests universal dimensions of order. Rather, our aim is to explore the multiplicity of the complexities and contradictions that shape situated experience and activity (Boyce, 1996).

This study was part of a wider research project that resulted in the lead author spending time in New Zealand in order to explore the pattern and evolution of entrepreneurship in a peripheral, diverse region. Thus, an au pair business operating within the early childhood sector that matches New Zealand families with Swedish au pairs was deemed an appropriate case site. This au pair business is owned by Rosie and Jim, a copreneurial couple. Rosie works full-time in the business. Jim has alternative employment, but is a partner in the firm and takes a full active decision-making role in this capacity. At the time of the study the company had 80 client families on their books, with an expected year-on-year growth of 25 per cent.

The case data was collected in 2008–09. The interaction with the respondents (Rosie and Jim) consisted of four semi-structured interviews. Each interview lasted between one and four hours and was tape-recorded and, subsequently, transcribed. In addition to these interviews, ongoing conversations and observations were undertaken with the copreneurs at their home and at their place of business in order to generate a detailed and dynamic picture of their entrepreneurial endeavour. Thus, we were able to gain insight into their domestic and business activities, contextualized within particular frames of reference. Subsequent telephone conversations (three in total) were undertaken to clarify and expand upon specific issues where meanings were unclear. We also sought feedback regarding our reflective interpretations of the data.

The data analysis commenced with open coding that reflected key concepts relating to the couple's experiences of managing a business and personal relationship concurrently. After initial coding, it was possible to identify the following key themes: functional divisions of labour, partnership roles, human capital (general and specific), mentors, structural barriers, normative barriers, work–life balance and gender issues. These areas were informed by the extant literature and used to structure our analysis of the results (which are discussed in the following sections of this chapter). Table 10.1 provides descriptive detail regarding Rosie and Jim's personal profiles and the characteristics of their business.

Table 10.1   Dimensions of the copreneurial partnership

The idea	The partnership	Implementation of idea
Originator of idea: the wife – Rosie Being a former au pair inspired the venture Encouraged and supported by her husband Jim	Rosie is 24 years and lead entrepreneur Husband, Jim, is 28 years, employed as a marketing manager for an IT company; Chief Operating Officer in venture Both are directors and owners of the business, with Rosie having the majority share Family situation: currently no children	Founded in 2006 Currently 12 employees and 18 months in operation Second office opened in December 2009 Responsibilities: Rosie: Full-time; day-to-day responsibilities including dealing with clients and customers Jim: Part-time: strategic planning; managing finances and negotiations Eventually plan to adopt a franchising business model

FINDINGS

The Au Pair Business: Women's Work?

Our findings suggest that an au pair business is a useful example of how market choices carry implicit gendered connotations arising from a specific market sector. This was evident as both copreneurs repeatedly stressed the importance of having 'caring' female employees in order to reassure and convince mothers that their loved ones were in safe hands. Jim noted, 'People probably respond better to women in the childcare industry. It is bit of a shame that if you are man and you are involved in early childhood education, there are some creepy connotations.' Sargent (2005) highlights the dilemma that males who want to be early childhood educators experience. In Sargent's (2005) findings, men who nurtured, and failed to adapt more distant and masculine ways of being with children, experienced suspicion of paedophilia. Indeed, this reinforces the dominant patriarchal ideology that childcare is women's work (Calás et al., 2009; Williams, 1992). Consequently, there exists an underexplored and unarticulated gendered set of processes and behaviours that influence new venture creation (Marlow, 2002). When asked to discuss to what extent the viability of the business rested upon having a visible female owner, Rosie was adamant that 'clients in this type of business feel more comfortable when dealing with a woman'. These illustrative conversational fragments are useful indicators of the interstices between entrepreneurial activities, broader social norms and embedded gendered social expectations. In this instance, we see how the social identity of a child-carer is firmly embedded within the female domain (given the 'natural' associations between caring, femininity and maternal sentiments and feelings) (Bowden and Mummery, 2009). Thus, it is 'normal' for women to be associated with childcare but not for men; consequently, those men who might attempt to challenge such norms risk not only being seen as defying their gender identity, but risk being viewed with outright suspicion and hostility (Simpson, 2004). This hostility is strengthened where men engage professionally with childcare; not only does this disrupt gender roles, it also raises questions of deviant sexual intentions, since men providing childcare is deemed 'unnatural' (Mac an ghail and Haywood, 2007). In this case, we can see the interaction between entrepreneurial intentions and embedded social norms. Both Rosie and Jim felt that the viability of this business rested upon the appropriate articulation of normative gendered roles. Therefore, it was critical to present a woman as the visible element of the partnership.

Doing Business and Doing Gender: Division of Labour

According to Fitzgerald and Muske (2002: 5), the dominant partner in the copreneurial couple is 'the person most involved in the day-to-day management of the business'. Within our case, the explanation for the entrepreneurial roles taken was discursively linked to a division of labour that ostensibly exploited individual competences. Yet, upon closer examination, we see Rosie contextualizing her leadership role through her gendered identity. Female clients were, in effect, handing part of their maternal identity over to another woman to act as a proxy mother. The deeply gendered nature of this transaction needed to be enacted within a feminized interchange in order to satisfy client concerns and ease their comfort. Thus, Rosie was not just the visible face of the business. Her gender was indicative of empathy and understanding, and played a central part in nature and value of transactions. Crucially however, although Rosie was the visible face of the business, from ensuing conversations Jim emerged as the 'power behind the throne'. For instance, Jim made the key entrepreneurial decisions around business management, strategy and finance.

As such, Rosie managed client interaction but Jim took the role of key entrepreneurial actor when engaging with formal business contacts and stakeholders. As Rosie observed, 'when we are negotiating with banks,

I let hubby lead as he comes across better to business people. However, I always meet the families, as they feel more comfortable dealing with a woman'. Commenting on working as a partnership, Rosie remarked, 'it's a two way street – acknowledging each other's strengths and weaknesses, and then playing to our strengths'. However, the resources that each partner brought to the business did not simply reflect competences and skills; they actually reproduced normative gendered orders and expectations. Therefore, although this business venture did not reflect traditional sex-role orientation, where wives do 'women's work' (Marshack, 1994:62), Rosie's role did require her to personify a gendered enactment of both woman and business owner.

Playing to Strengths

The literature suggests that copreneurial couples usually have a division of tasks that reflect gendered norms. In turn, this division elevates the male in terms of status and visibility (Loscocco and Robinson, 1991; Ponthieu and Caudill, 1993; Fitzgerald and Muske, 2002; Fairlie and Robb, 2008). Our copreneurial couple felt that their contributions to the business reflected individual competences. For example, regarding business finance, Rosie reflected, 'I feel more comfortable when he handles the bank negotiating, even if I'm the one that does the paper work behind the scenes. I usually let him lead the discussions, because you see there is a boy's culture, and they find it easier to relate to him. So if [Jim] leads it, it usually goes really well.' This sentiment reflects arguments put forth by Gherardi and Poggio (2001) and Bruni et al., (2005). These authors note that women business owners encounter ambiguous and contradictory circumstances with regard to the construction of their professional and gender identities. Indeed, Rosie felt that Jim offered a much better representation of a 'stereotypical entrepreneur'. She says, 'my husband comes across very well. He's a suit and tie guy, so he comes across very well when he presents things. So it's about putting your best foot forward'. Dressing as an entrepreneur (wearing a jacket, shirt and tie) was a tactic adopted to forestall any conflict with the (male) gendered business world. In their choice of clothing the copreneurial partnership aimed to blend in with the world in which they are situated. Rosie notes, 'you have to present yourself in a way that people take you seriously; so when we go to meetings we get dressed up in our best gear'. Yet, while both individuals may have dressed in their 'best gear', the masculine presence and dress afforded the greatest credibility to the venture. This men's clothing reflects the norms and expectations most strongly associated with a competent businessperson and successful entrepreneur.

Sharing of the Strategic Vision

Collaborative decision-making as copreneurs is essential for the success of a venture (Folker, 2008). There is some evidence to indicate that the 'copreneurial husband tends to be the primary business decision maker although the wife is an equal partner in sharing the activities and responsibilities of the firm' (Lucaccini and Muscat, 2001:6). In this case, Jim stressed that 'we make most important business decisions together and definitely share the same ambitions'. One key strategy that Jim was keen to pursue was business growth. He felt the business had considerable potential for expansion, and possibly franchising. However, when discussing future ambitions, Rosie offered a more nuanced view. She says: 'I probably want to grow, but he doesn't see the business every day, doesn't see the day-to-day grind that I go through. So for me it's really important that we're realistic and not overambitious.' Rosie was essentially apologetic for this stance; she felt she was not sharing Jim's truly entrepreneurial ambitions. Rosie identified herself as more 'conservative and realistic', but did not consider this to be a rational response to the essentially vulnerable position of a fragile young business. Rather, this was a problem she had to overcome to reproduce what she considered Jim's more legitimate aspirations and ambitions. In the way that Rosie's perspective conflicts with the growth-oriented social identity of the idealized entrepreneur, her comments reflect arguments put forth by Ogbor (2000), Smith and Anderson (2004) and Ahl (2006). These authors discuss how masculine characteristics (risk, aggression and competitiveness) have been seamlessly transferred onto the identity of a 'real' entrepreneur.

DISCUSSION

In recognizing the need to analytically explore why and how femininity is reproduced as the subordinated element of the gender binary within the entrepreneurial discourse, we have focused on a copreneurial husband and wife partnership operating within the childcare sector. Our findings suggest that the gendered expectations associated with childcare work intersect with and shape the entrepreneurial roles undertaken by copreneurs. Consequently, the entrepreneurial leadership role undertaken by Rosie is not only a reflection of her primary role in identifying a market opportunity and developing the business idea, but it also corresponds to gendered stereotypes regarding men, women and childcare. Thus, in this case it was felt that for the business to be considered credible and trustworthy, it was essential that at least one of the owner-managers should be female. This would reflect gendered expectations pertaining to childcare responsibilities.

Within this case study, Rosie was the visible face of the business. She was able to utilize her previous experience working within the au pair industry to inform the venture. Her femininity offered legitimacy and reassurance to the clientele, who were, essentially, subcontracting their parenting role to her. Jim remained behind the scenes in what initially appeared to be a secondary role. However, he did in fact take a highly influential role in terms of strategic management, funding issues and growth planning (tasks normally associated with the lead entrepreneur). Rosie fully acknowledged Jim's contribution in these areas, agreeing that while she was a visible presence, she was also a 'reassuring' presence given the sector in which this firm operated. Indeed, in many respects Rosie often acted as a vicarious 'lead entrepreneur'. For instance, she dealt with the daily administration and point of client contact while Jim pursued entrepreneurial growth plans and gained financial backing. Jim was instrumental in encouraging Rosie to act upon the outcomes of these ambitions. While Rosie did not perceive herself as coerced, in terms of the manner in which the business was developing, she frequently expressed disquiet regarding the pace of change and the difficulties this caused her (in terms of daily management). These problems Jim, as a salaried employee working elsewhere, never had to deal with. Consequently, Jim's presence was invaluable primarily when negotiating business deals and helping to project a credible business image.

While Rosie is undoubtedly recognized as the primary entrepreneurial actor, we see a more subtle reproduction of normative gendered ordering. Rosie defers to her husband's growth plans for the firm and acknowledges that being female constrains her legitimacy and influence with external stakeholders (such as investors). Furthermore, Rosie unquestionably affords Jim the role of strategic decision-maker. As such, assuming a position and identity as a lead entrepreneur is not sufficient to effectively challenge gendered roles and expectations. It may be suggested that these findings are fairly predictable given the sectoral influences intervening here. Gendered occupational segregation is a critical influence upon the valuation of work; it is well established that regardless of the substantive skill or ability levels required, work undertaken by women is persistently devalued when compared with that of male counterparts (Halford and Leonard, 2001; Holmes, 2007). This effect is reproduced in the entrepreneurial arena where women dominate as owners of firms within feminized sectors, such as lower order services (Marlow et al., 2008). Therefore, this case is not an exception but, rather, a reflection of a general rule. Thus, it can be argued that this case merely illustrates that sectoral influences will ensure the reproduction of gendered norms despite the roles undertaken by the individual entrepreneurial actors. While the importance of sector is not disputed, we would strongly argue that this intersection merely confirms the extent to which gendered norms are embedded and, consequently, reproduced within copreneurial partnerships. Indeed, by focusing upon a feminized segment of the market, it would be expected that Rosie's position within the business partnership might be strengthened. In effect, she occupied the symbolic role of visible leader within a firm which itself exploited the gendered expectations surrounding the service it offered. It may be expected, therefore, that this combination of factors would reverse and challenge the assumed hierarchical gendered binary that permeates most mixed sex entrepreneurial partnerships. However, this was not evident in this particular case.

CONCLUSION

In conclusion, the aim of this chapter was to explore potential tensions and contradictions arising from the transposition of the normative gender binary within the context of copreneurship. As has been well revealed within the literature, gendered ascriptions are socially constructed and mapped onto biological sex categories; therefore, gender itself has no reality (Butler, 1990, 2004; Harding, 1987). However, while it is agreed that there is no essential femininity or masculinity that is mapped onto the biological categories of males and females, gender makes things culturally intelligible. As social actors, we make sense of others in terms of their ascribed gender. Moreover, challenging gender conformity and creating 'gender trouble,' (Butler, 1993; Jagose, 1996; Roseneil, 2000) by disputing the alleged 'natural order,' creates uncertainty and suspicion (Fiske, 1989; Keltner, 1995). Indeed, gender contravention is met with considerable hostility. This hostility is particularly evident when biological sex contradicts with assumed gender performances (for example, homophobic reactions towards gay men and women) (Fine, 2010). Accordingly, exploring gender presents a paradox, as it comprises of a constructed binary that fundamentally shapes human interaction but has no fixed or essential basis. Thus, we engage with one strand of this paradox through our consideration of how gender is reconfigured or reproduced within a situated context where the binary is contested. Drawing on the example of copreneurship is particularly useful for this task. As has been established, the practice of entrepreneuring is, in itself, embedded within a masculine discourse. Therefore, a male persona is embedded in the identity of an entrepreneur (Ahl, 2004; Marlow, 2002). Discoursal representations are confirmed by data that suggests that men form the majority of business owners (Marlow, et al. 2008) and are the visible, dominant partner in spousal entrepreneurial ventures (Hamilton, 2006). Consequently, the hierarchal gender binary is reproduced both discursively and contextually within the entrepreneurial field. Examples where this binary is transposed – such as when a women undertakes the visible role of lead entrepreneur – offer a fruitful opportunity to explore how any associated tensions and contradictions are managed.

As our work here focuses upon one in-depth case study we cannot make any empirical generalizations. Nonetheless, we can offer theoretical observations. Accordingly, while the actual leadership roles were reversed in this case, such that Rosie was the visible business owner, the hierarchal gender binary remained in tact. Rosie deferred to the allegedly superior business acumen of her male partner, even though she had founded and grown the business. This was evident through her self-criticism regarding her concerns over business growth. Moreover, when seeking business finance, Rosie defined this as a role for Jim. This was primarily because Jim was male and, therefore, would be deemed more professional and credible. In essence, within almost every element of the business process, there is evidence of gender deference. This deference arises from the notion that entrepreneuring is a male driven activity within which women are interlopers. Only in terms of customer management did Rosie claim a primary role. However, this was related to the possession of her softer, feminine skills (so again, this serves to confirm normative expectations). Thus, in this case, the normative gender binary was unconsciously reconstituted despite the symbolic exchange of entrepreneurial roles. From this analysis, we see a subtle but pervasive re-enactment of normative gendered performances. Not surprisingly, contextual challenges are not sufficient to erode these expectations. Finally, this chapter has explored how the construct of gender is enacted within the context of copreneurship where male and female roles are transposed. What has been revealed is the subtle pervasiveness of the normative gender binary. This normative binary persists in constraining the possibilities that entrepreneuring may offer to challenge such hierarchical ordering.

NOTE

1. For a critical analysis of gendered copreneurial assumptions see Ahl (2007).

REFERENCES

Ahl, H. (2004), *The Making of the Female Entrepreneur*, Jonkoping International Business School Dissertation Series, 15, Sweden: Jonkoping University.

Ahl, H. (2006), 'Why research on women entrepreneurs needs new directions', *Entrepreneurship Theory and Practice*, **30** (5), 595–621.

Ahl, H. (2007), 'Sex business in the toy store: a narrative analysis of a teaching case', *Journal of Business Venturing*, **22**, 673–93.

Aldrich, J. and J. Cliff (2003), 'The pervasive effects of family on entrepreneurship: toward a family embeddedness perspective', *Journal of Business Venturing*, **18**, 573–96.

Allen, S. and C. Truman (1993), *Women in Business: Perspectives on Women Entrepreneurs*, London: Routledge.

Bowden, P and Mummery, J. (2009). *Understanding Feminism*, New York: Acumen.

Boyce, M. (1996), 'Organisational story and storytelling', *Journal of Organisational Change Management*, **9** (5), 5–26.

Bruni, A., S. Gherardi and B. Poggio (2005), *Gender and Entrepreneurship: An Ethnographical Approach*, London: Routledge.

Butler, J. (1990), *Gender Trouble: Feminism and the Subversion of Identity*, London: Routledge.

Butler, J. (1993), *Bodies that Matter: On the Discursive Limits of Sex*, New York: Routledge.

Butler, J. (2004), *Undoing Gender*, New York: Routledge.

Calás, M.B., L. Smirich and K.A. Bourne (2009), 'Extending the boundaries: reframing "entrepreneurship as social change" through feminist perspectives', *Academy of Management Review*, **34**, 511–32.

Case, P. (2003), 'From objectivity to subjectivity: pursuing subjective authenticity in organizational research', in R. Westwood and S. Clegg (eds), *Debating Organization: Point-Counterpoint in Organization Studies*, Oxford: Blackwell, pp. 35–49.

Daly, M. and K. Rake (2003), *Gender and the Welfare State*, London: Polity Press.

Danes, S.M. and P.D. Olson (2003), 'Women's role involvement in family businesses, business tensions, and business success', *Family Business Review*, **16** (1), 53–64.

Fairlie, R.W. and A.M. Robb (2008), 'Gender differences in business performance: evidence from the characteristics of Business Owners Survey', available at: http//ssrn.com/abstract=1260987 (accessed 1 June 2010).

Fine, C. (2010), *Delusions of Gender*, London: Icon Books.

Firkin, P., A. Dupuis and A. De Bruin (2003), 'Familial entrepreneurship', in A. de Bruin and A. Dupuis (eds), *Entrepreneurship: New Perspectives in a Global Age*, Ashgate: Aldershot, pp. 92–108.

Fiske, J. (1989), *Reading the Popular*, Boston, MA: Unwin Hyman.

Fitzgerald, M.A. and G. Muske (2002), 'Coprenuers: an exploration and comparison to other family businesses', *Family Business Review*, **15** (1), 1–16.

Folker, C. (2008), 'Women in family firms: characteristics, roles and contribution', *Small Business Institute Research Review*, **35**, 157–68.

Gartner, W.B., K.G. Shaver, E. Gatewood and J.A. Katz (1994), 'Finding the entrepreneur in entrepreneurship', *Entrepreneurship Theory and Practice*, **18** (3), 5–10.

Gherardi, S. and B. Poggio (2001), 'Creating and recreating gender order in organizations', *Journal of World Business*, **36** (3), 245–59.

Gilbert, M. (2001), 'A sometime woman: gendered choice and cross socialisation', in F. Haynes and T. McKenna (eds), *Unseen Genders: Beyond the Boundaries*, New York: Peter Lang, pp. 41–50.

Halford, S. and P. Leonard (2001), *Gender, Power and Organisations*, London: Palgrave.

Hamilton, E. (2006), 'Whose story is it anyway? Narrative accounts of the role of women in founding and establishing family businesses', *International Small Business Journal*, **24** (3), 253–72.

Harding, S. (1987), *Feminism and Methodology*, Bloomington, IN: Indiana University Press.

Hirdman, Y. (2001), *Genus – om det stabilas foranderliga (Gender – Changes of the Stable)*, Stockholm: Liber AB.

Holmes, M. (2007), *What is Gender?* London: Sage.

Jagose, A. (1996), *Queer Theory: An Introduction*, New York: New York University Books.

Keltner, D. (1995), 'Signs of appeasement: evidence for the distinct displays of embarrassment, amusement and shame', *Journal of Personality and Social Psychology*, **68**, 441–54.

Knights, D. and D. Kerfoot (2004), 'Between representations and subjectivity: gender binaries and the politics of organisational transformation', *Gender, Work and Organisation*, **11** (4), 430–54.

Koss-Feder, L. (2001), 'Wife is boss in new business model for couples, *Women's eNews*, available at: www.womensenews.org/article.cfm/dyn/aid/573/context/archive (c2002123) (accessed 15 November 2009).

Leitch, C., R. Harrison and F. Hill (2009), 'The philosophy and practice of interpretist research in entrepreneurship: quality, validation and trust', *Organisational Research Methods*, **13** (1), 67–84.

Lewis, P. (2009), 'The female entrepreneur: a new entrepreneurial identity and a new gendered challenge for women business owners', paper presented at the 26th EURAM Conference, Liverpool, May.

Linstead, J. and S. Pullen (2006), 'Gender as multiplicity: desire, displacement, difference and dispersion', *Human Relations*, **59** (90), 1287–310.

Loscocco, K.A. and J. Robinson (1991), 'Barriers to women's small business success in the United States', *Gender and Society*, **5**, 511–32.

Lucaccini, L.F. and E.J. Muscat (2001), 'Family Business and careers: classic and contemporary issues', *Career Planning and Adult Development Journal*, **17** (2), 84–105.

Mac an ghaill, M. and C. Haywood (2007), *Gender, Culture and Society*, London: Palgrave.

Marlow, S. (2002), 'Women in self employment – a part of, or apart from, theoretical construct?', *The International Journal of Entrepreneurship and Innovation*, **3** (2), 83–91.

Marlow, S., E. Shaw and S. Carter (2008), 'Constructing female entrepreneurship policy in the UK: is the USA a relevant role model?', *Environmental Planning C*, **26** (1), 335–51.

Marshack, K. (1994), 'Copreneurs and dual-career couples: are they different?', *Entrepreneurship Theory and Practice*, **19** (1), 49–69.

Marshack, K. (1998), *Entrepreneurial Couples: Making It Work at Work and at Home*, Palo Alto, CA: Davies-Black.

McRobbie, A. (2009), *The Aftermath of Feminism*, London: Sage.

Mulholland, K. (1996), 'Gender and property relations within entrepreneurial wealthy families', *Gender, Work and Organisation*, **3** (2), 78–102.

Oakley, A. (1973), 'Interviewing women: a contradiction in terms', in H. Roberts (ed.), *Doing Feminist Research*, London: Routledge and Kegan Paul, pp. 36–43.

Ogbor, J. (2000), 'Mythicizing and reification in entrepreneurial discourse: ideology-critique of entrepreneurship studies', *Journal of Management Studies*, **37** (5), 605–35.

Ponthieu, L.D. and H.L. Caudill (1993), 'Who's the boss? Responsibility and decision making in copreneurial ventures', *Family Business Review*, **6** (10), 3–17.

Poza, E and T. Messer (2001), 'Spousal leadership and continuity in the family firm', *Family Business Review*, **14** (1), 25–36.

Roseneil, S. (2000), 'Queer frameworks and queer tendencies: towards an understanding of post modern transformations of sexuality', *Sociological Research Online*, **5**, 3, available at: www.socresonline.org.uk (accessed 7 May 2008).

Rouse J. (2005), 'Pregnancy and maternity in self-employment: individualised social reproduction?', paper presented at the 28th Institute for Small Business Entrepreneurship National Conference, Blackpool, November.

Ruef, M., H.E. Aldrich and N.M. Carter (2003), 'The structure of founding partnerships: homophily, strong ties, and isolation among U.S. entrepreneurs', *American Sociological Review*, **68** (2), 195–222.

Sargent, P. (2005), 'The gendering of men in early childhood education', *Sex Roles*, **52** (3/4), 251–9.

Seymour, N. (2002), 'Copreneurs, center of entrepreneurial leadership', DIGEST Number 02–03, available at: www.celcee.edu (accessed 27 October 2010).

Simpson, R. (2004), 'Masculinity at work: the experiences of men in female-dominated occupations', *Work, Employment and Society*, **18** (2), 349–68.

Smith, R and A.R. Anderson (2004), 'The Devil is in the e-tail: forms and structures in the entrepreneurial narratives', in D. Hjorth and C. Steyaert (eds), *Narrative and Discursive Approaches in Entrepreneurship*, Cheltenham, UK and Northampton, MA, USA: Edward Elgar Publishing, pp. 125–43.

Steier, L. and R. Greenwood (2000), 'Entrepreneurship and the evolution of angel financial networks', *Organization Studies*, **21** (1), 163–92.

Weick, K. (2007), 'The generative properties of richness', *Academy of Management Journal*, **50** (1), 14–19.

Williams, C. (1992), 'The glass escalator: hidden advantages for men in the female professions', *Social Problems*, **39** (3), 253–67.

11. Gender and the multidimensional nature of entrepreneurial self-efficacy: factor-analytic findings

Cristina Díaz García*

INTRODUCTION

Over the past few decades, women have significantly advanced in new venture creation and contributed more to the economy. However, these developments have only been in absolute terms, since women's participation in entrepreneurship is still considerably lower than men's (Allen ct al., 2008). This can be explained by personal attributes, background and disposition. However, 'a lack of confidence is perhaps the greatest barrier to women's progression into micro and small business ownership' (Fielden et al., 2003: 162). This lack of confidence is rooted in social, cultural and institutional arrangements that frame how women perceive opportunities and make strategic choices; a lack of confidence also impacts how women view their businesses (De Bruin et al., 2007).

Entrepreneurial self-efficacy (ESE), or the subjective self-assessment of having adequate skills and knowledge, is positively related to women's propensity to start new businesses (Langowitz and Minniti, 2007; Wilson et al., 2007). In this regard, the majority of studies concentrate on the relation between self-efficacy and entrepreneurial intentions (Kickul et al., 2008; Kourilsky and Walstad, 1998; Wilson et al., 2007), with many studies concluding that men tend to have higher self-efficacy than women (Kirkwood, 2009; Kourilsky and Walstad, 1998; Wilson et al., 2007). However, self-efficacy also affects men's actions in their ongoing businesses (Kirkwood, 2009). Furthermore, much of the preceding empirical research has relied on an 'overall entrepreneurship self-efficacy measure' (Kickul et al., 2008: 325). Recently, several articles have questioned this approach, calling for research on the multidimensionality of the ESE construct (McGee et al., 2009; Drnovšek et al., 2010). They have called for further refinement of the construct since its multidimensionality has yet to be fully established. As McGee et al. (2009: 983) argue 'a number of entrepreneurship researchers and scholars have proposed and tested the use of an education (or training) "intervention" to raise an individual's level of ESE . . . for such important applications, the availability of a refined, consistent, and robust measure of ESE is essential'. It is also important to know what self-efficacy encompasses in order to better understand its relationship to important entrepreneurial outcomes, such as start-up intentions, new venture growth and personal success of entrepreneurs (Drnovšek et al., 2010).

Therefore, the aim of this study is to observe potential gender differences in self-efficacy and make a fourfold contribution to cumulative knowledge in this area. First, I focus on the gender–ESE relation in business activity, instead of entrepreneurial intention. Self-efficacy is not a static trait (Mau, 2003) and can be modified by education and experience, which women normally acquire when they manage their own firm. Second, I take into account that ESE is a multidimensional construct with a gender component to it. Third, I examine if certain personal (education, age) or contextual (sector) variables might affect these differences. The potential differences in ESE dimensions might not be constant across educational levels (Wilson et al., 2007) and across traditionally and non-traditionally female-dominated sectors (Anna et al., 2000). Finally, this chapter questions if there is any difference in the dimensions of ESE between individuals according to their intention to grow the business.

RESEARCH FRAMEWORK

Self-efficacy is based on an individual's perceptions of his or her own abilities and capacities to successfully develop a specific task (Bandura, 1977). Boyd and Vozikis (1994) propose a broader definition of self-efficacy as a task-specific construct that includes not only an assessment of the beliefs an individual maintains about internal (personality) constraints and possibilities, but also takes into account external factors (environment). The individual's actual abilities only matter if he or she has confidence in those abilities (Bandura, 1989, 1997). In this way, it is more about what people believe they are capable of doing than on what is objectively true (Markman et al., 2002). Therefore, it will be more probable that those individuals who perceive themselves with a high self-efficacy in a specific task will carry it out and persevere with the task (Bandura, 1997).

Rauch and Frese (2007) performed a meta-analysis and demonstrated that entrepreneurial self-efficacy for starting a new business is a crucial factor in increasing the likelihood of business start-up activity. Therefore, it can be also argued that some individuals do not create their own firm, or do not aim for growth, because they do not believe they can (Wilson et al., 2007).

Previous studies present self-efficacy as a multidimensional construct (Anna et al., 2000; Chen et al., 1998; De Noble et al., 1999; Krueger and Kickul, 2006) composed of risk taking, coping with unexpected challenges, initiating investor relationships and economic management. However, the majority of these studies ignore the multidimensional character of the construct when using an 'overall entrepreneurship self-efficacy measure' (Kickul et al., 2008: 325). Recently, several articles have questioned this approach and called for research on the multidimensionality of the ESE construct (Drnovšek et al, 2010; McGee et al., 2009). Taking the above arguments into consideration, I establish the following hypothesis:

Hypothesis 1: Entrepreneurial self-efficacy is multidimensional rather than unidimensional in nature.

Within the literature on ESE and gender, no study has examined the potential gender differences within the dimensions of self-efficacy. However, some studies within the gender literature have put forth results that suggest we should expect differences in the dimensions of self-efficacy in ongoing business activity. For example, with regard to risk taking, Cliff (1998) observes that women business owners establish lower growth thresholds than their male counterparts, and aim for a slower and more controlled growth path. Similarly, Carter (2002) proposes that women have a higher risk aversion in comparison to their male counterparts; this leads women to refrain from borrowing financial capital or risking their personal assets. Essentially, women place more emphasis on the financial risk associated with a business opportunity, even when perceiving it as an attractive option for growth (Baker et al., 2003).

Finding financing has been highlighted as a principal barrier to the formation, survival and growth rate of businesses (Brush et al., 2004). This systemic barrier can be a greater hurdle for women, since 'women business owners when searching for finance are confronted by prejudices about their capability to manage large quantities of money' (Bruni et al., 2004: 262). However, this occurrence might encourage women to increase their network activity in order to reach key sources of finance for their firms (Baron and Markman, 2003). Shaw et al. (2008) observed that when asked if they experienced problems being 'taken seriously as a business person', significantly more women (30 per cent) than men (none) expressed that this was something they had encountered. These authors also suggest that female entrepreneurs recognize that their social capital has a lower value than that of male entrepreneurs and, therefore, they seek to compensate and legitimize their position as business owners by actively engaging in networking. Baron and Markman (2003) observe that women business owners use their social competences in interacting with others in order to obtain better financial performance. Social competences include social perception (degree of precision in order to 'read' the motivations of others) and social adaptability (ability to adapt and be comfortable in any social situation).

However, postulating that there can be gender differences in ESE without relating them to other personal (education, age) or contextual (type of industry) factors is problematic; a naive interpretation might be that differences in ESE are due simply to differences between men and women. This is much contested in current feminist literature, which argues that thinking in terms of difference is understood as legitimizing the segregation of women and men and thus risks underpinning gender inequality (Blomqvist and Frennberg, 2010).

In this chapter I propose that social, cultural and institutional arrangements will have different impacts on the self-perception of women in distinct circumstances. Therefore, the claim that there might be gender differences in ESE in certain groups of business owners, and not others, does not necessarily reflect essentialist thinking. In this line, Kirkwood (2009) proposes that self-efficacy can be improved through certain actions and situations. Although, she observes that women business owners perceive themselves with less self-efficacy than men, both in start-up and ongoing business activity.

Accordingly, previous literature demonstrates that the different expectations imposed by society in relation to gender can mould individuals' perception of self-efficacy in different areas. For example, young women perceive themselves with less self-efficacy in areas that are stereotypically masculine – such as entrepreneurship. This has lead to a gender gap in entrepreneurial intention (Kourilsky and Walstad, 1998). The persistence of lower entrepreneurial self-efficacy for women, in comparison to men, is even evidenced among highly qualified women who hold an MBA degree and have previous work experience (Wilson et al., 2007). Furthermore, in traditionally male-dominated industries, women business owners perceive themselves with less self-efficacy in opportunity recognition (Anna et al., 2000). Therefore, I propose the following:

Hypothesis 2a: The extent of gender differences in ESE dimensions will depend upon the nature of the industry; more specifically, there will be gender differences in male-dominated industries but not in traditionally female-dominated industries.

Hypothesis 2b: Female entrepreneurs will be especially likely to report lower ESE than their male counterparts in male-dominated industries.

Recent research suggests that an individual's ESE may be elevated through training and education, thus potentially improving the rate of entrepreneurial activities (Florin et al., 2007; Mueller and Goic, 2003; Zhao et al., 2005). Bandura (1997) notes that the sources that individuals draw on to develop confidence in their abilities and increase their level of self-efficacy are: practice, moderated levels of failure and acquired experience from observing how other individuals develop a task. Hence, self-efficacy increases as the time that the business owners are operating their business extends (Kirkwood, 2009; Koellinger et al., 2006); it also increases as individuals gain specific training in entrepreneurship (Cooper and Lucas, 2007). This is especially important for women (Wilson et al., 2007). Furthermore, many men tend to have overconfidence in their performance (Barber and Odean, 2001; Niederle and Vesterlund, 2005). Fletcher (1999) also finds evidence that women tend to underestimate their skills or performance in comparison to men. However, since 'veteran entrepreneurs might be more aware of the role of luck and favourable timing in their achievements and therefore more humble about their own ability to control the destinies of their ventures', the gender gap in self-efficacy perception, if any, might decrease with time (McGee et al., 2009: 984). Besides this, gender works as a status category only when the women involved are young and less experienced (Hopcroft, 2006). Therefore, the following hypotheses are proposed:

Hypothesis 3a: The extent of gender differences in ESE dimensions will depend upon business owners' education; more specifically, among those individuals with lower levels of education (primary and secondary), female entrepreneurs will be more likely to report lower ESE than their male counterparts.

Hypothesis 3b: The extent of gender differences in ESE dimensions will depend upon business owners' age; more specifically, among younger individuals, female entrepreneurs will be more likely to report lower ESE than their male counterparts.

Finally, Baron and Markman (2003) propose that a business owner's intention to grow his or her business is anchored in individual factors such as self-efficacy. Other research finds evidence that ESE enhances firm performance (Chandler and Jansen, 1992; Forbes, 2005). Furthermore, Trevelyan (2008) observes a positive effect of confidence on entrepreneurial tasks (entrepreneurial self-efficacy) in both action and judgement tasks. This suggests that the motivational impact of confidence outweighs the decision-making bias of overconfidence in new venture development. Therefore, it can be argued that business owners intending to grow their firms have greater degrees of confidence in having the necessary competence (for example, the ability to successfully acquire external funding). In addition, McGee et al. (2009) call for research on how the different dimensions of ESE relate to venture growth expectations. Hence, the following hypothesis is proposed:

Hypothesis 4a: The extent of differences in ESE dimensions will depend upon business owners' growth intentions; more specifically, business owners with growth intentions will be more likely to report higher ESE than their counterparts without growth intentions.

As stated earlier, Cliff (1998) observes that women business owners establish lower growth thresholds than their male counterparts, aiming for a slower and more controlled path of growth. Other studies have found that women have consistently been shown to have lower growth expectations and intentions (Marlow and Carter, 2004; Orser and Hogarth-Scott, 2002). However, research also shows that women own businesses of all sizes, in every sector and in many different stages of development; further, some women-owned businesses do achieve high growth (Gundry and Welsch, 2001; Morris et al., 2006). Therefore, the following hypothesis is proposed:

Hypothesis 4b: The extent of gender differences in ESE dimensions will depend upon business owners' growth intentions; more specifically, among business owners with growth intentions female entrepreneurs will report similar ESE than their male counterparts and the same will occur for those groups without growth intentions.

METHODOLOGY

The empirical data for this study comes from a survey of Spanish firms administered from June 2008 until April 2009. Several criteria were used to select the sample. First, the firms were in knowledge-intensive industries. According to the Economic Activities National Classification (CNAE), this group encompasses the following activities: mailing and telecommunications; financial brokerage; assurances and pensions; auxiliary activities of financial brokerage; property developers and real estate agencies;

computing activities; research and development; education; health and veterinary activities, and social services. A breakdown of the knowledge-intensive industries was performed in order to better understand the industry context and control for exogenous factors, as previous research recommends (Jennings et al., 2009). Second, the firms were of small size (less than 50 employees) and founded from 2002 onwards. Therefore, each firm was at least six years old and can be considered in the critical operational phase (Littunen, 2000).

The Analysis System of Iberian Balances (SABI) database was used in order to obtain a population of 32 684 firms. All the firms were contacted in those sectors in which there were less than 1000 firms operating. In the rest of the sectors, I selected 1000 firms that had updated information. Further, in order to over sample the number of women-led firms, 250 firms that had a man listed as lead business owner were replaced by firms that listed a woman as lead business owner. From this sample of 7068, some firms were eliminated due to incorrect addresses, leaving a sampling frame of 5842 firms. The reception of 1030 questionnaires yields a response rate of 17.63 per cent. A response bias test revealed no significant differences between respondents and non-respondents with respect to number of employees, gross revenues, firm age and the age and education of the business owners.

The survey consisted of a number of questions that were designed to measure business characteristics, characteristics of the lead entrepreneur, the team (where a team existed), the networks and social capital, time distribution and performance. The questionnaire was developed using questions and scales validated in previous research; the questions were pilot-tested on six men and women business owners.

To measure *entrepreneurial self-efficacy*, Krueger and Kickul (2006), and Barbosa et al. (2007) use factors obtained by previous studies that intended to establish specific scales for entrepreneurial self-efficacy. Following their procedure, the subscales of *risk taking* by Chen et al. (1998), of *coping with unexpected challenges* and *initiating investors' relationships* by De Noble et al. (1999), and *economic management* by Anna et al. (2000) were used in this study. The items that comprise these subscales are shown in Table 11.1. The items were measured with a 7-points Likert scale. There were 941 usable responses to the self-efficacy question. In their analysis, Barbosa et al. (2007: 92) obtained four factors or task-specific types of entrepreneurs' self-efficacy: (1) relationship self-efficacy (the individual's perceived self-efficacy concerning his or her capacities to build relationships with people connected to sources of capital); (2) managerial self-efficacy (the individual's perceived self-efficacy concerning his or her managerial capacities, especially concerning economic and financial management); (3) tolerance

Table 11.1   Subscales of ESE dimensions obtained in previous research and used in this study

---

De Noble et al. (1999) 'Coping with unexpected challenges'
  I can work productively under continuous stress, pressure and conflict
  I can tolerate unexpected changes in business conditions
  I can persist in the face of adversity

De Noble et al. (1999) 'Initiating investors relationships'
  I can develop and maintain favourable relationships with potential investors
  Develop relationships with key persons to access capital sources
  Identify potential sources of funding to invest in the firm

Anna et al. (2000) 'Economic management'
  Manage cash flow
  Control business costs
  Manage expenses

Chen et al. (1998) 'Risk taking'
  Take decisions under uncertainty and risk
  Take risks in a calculated way
  Assume the responsibility of ideas and decisions

---

self-efficacy (the individual's perceived self-efficacy concerning his or her capacities to work productively under conditions of stress, uncertainty and change); and (4) opportunity-identification self-efficacy.

In this study, *sex* was operationalized as one for women and zero for men. Regarding the variable *traditionally female-dominated sector*, the criteria for classifying the sectors was the same one used by Sappleton (2009). Industries that are comprised of at least 70 per cent women are considered to be female-dominated; those comprised of between 31 and 69 per cent women are considered 'balanced,' and those with 30 per cent or fewer women are considered male-dominated (Sappleton, 2009). In this study, the sectors that have been classified as female-dominated are education and health-veterinary. In Spain,women represent 63 per cent and 97.54 per cent of the total occupied population in the former industries (INE, 2008). The rest of the industries were classified as male-dominated. *Education* was operationalized as one for primary education, two for secondary education, three for graduate education and four for postgraduate education. Alternatively, *age* was operationalized with an open variable in which the individuals reported how old they are. *Intention to grow* was measured using the following question: what are your expectations of growth in number of employees for the following three years? The variable was coded zero if the individual stated that there would be a decrease or equilibrium in the number of employees and coded one if the individual stated that there would be an increase in the number of employees. Growth intentions are used as a proxy for growth, since entrepreneurs with high growth intentions are more likely to realize growth (Wiklund and Shepherd, 2003).

RESULTS

Sample Characteristics

The sample is composed of 632 (61.4 per cent) men business owners and 398 (38.6 per cent) women business owners. This is a proportion that is similar to the distribution of self-employment by gender in Spain. From those who responded to the question regarding the type of industry the firm operated in, 651 of the cases can be classified as non-traditionally female-dominated industries and 284 as cases within traditionally female-dominated industries. The firms had been operating, on average, for 7.38 years; 70.45 per cent of the firms were less than six years old. The average number of full-time employees was 9.26, but 84 per cent of the firms had fewer employees than the average. This lead to a sample in which 99.5 per cent of the firms had less than 200 employees.

With regard to the business owners' characteristics, 11.4 per cent were under 30 years of age; 42.9 per cent were between 31 and 40 years of age, while 40.6 per cent were between 41 and 50 years of age. The individuals in the sample are highly educated, with 60.8 per cent having degrees and 10.7 per cent having post-graduate degrees. This is related with their concern for lifelong learning, since the individuals reported having attended courses before (76 per cent) and after (79.4 per cent) their firm's creation. Although 88.4 per cent of the sample had previous work experience (average of 8.27 years), only 24.3 per cent of the individuals had managerial experience (average of 5.36 years) and only 17.7 per cent had entrepreneurial experience (average of 1.56 years). In this sample, 73 per cent of the individuals have been managing their current firm for less than six years. Additionally, 42.3 per cent of the participants are co-owners of other firms.

Table 11.2 shows t-tests and Chi-squared tests that were performed comparing demographic characteristics. The t-tests were used to observe differences in means between men and women business owners for continuous variables, and the Chi-squared tests were used to study categorical variables. As can be observed, there are significant gender differences with regard to the industry activity. As identified, 44.05 per cent of the women

Table 11.2   *Significant differences in means with regard to firm characteristics and human capital for men and women business owners*

	Men	Women	Test-t	Significance
Traditionally female-dominated sectors	0.2385	0.4405	−6.959	0.000 (W+)
Firm age	7.4010	7.3503	0.158	0.875
Firm size (number of full-time employees)	10.143	7.8763	0.709	0.479
Age	41.927	39.489	4.247	0.000 (M+)
Years of previous managerial experience	6.2061	3.0187	4.567	0.000 (M+)
Years of previous entrepreneurial experience	1.9731	0.9146	3.750	0.000 (M+)
Number of other firms created	1.2265	0.7143	2.894	0.004 (M+)
Years in the management of the current firm	6.6402	5.9288	2.191	0.029 (M+)
Growth in the previous three years	0.35	0.28	2.404	0.016 (M+)
Growth in the following three years	0.34	0.26	2.745	0.006 (M+)
			Chi-squared	Significance
Education	2.7968	2.7955	1.297	0.730
Unemployed before creating the firm	0.2436	0.3636	16.985	0.000 (W+)
Previous work experience	0.8782	0.7990	11.848	0.000 (M+)
Experience as employee	0.7266	0.8540	18.895	0.000 (W+)
Experience as manager	0.3034	0.1366	31.029	0.000 (M+)
Experience as business owner	0.2046	0.1273	8.429	0.004 (M+)
Co-owner of other firms	0.4591	0.3660	8.487	0.004 (M+)

business owners developed their activity within traditionally female-dominated industries in comparison to only 23.85 per cent of their male counterparts.

With regard to human capital, women business owners were significantly younger than their male counterparts and, although equally educated, their profiles differed in terms of experience. First, more women were unemployed before creating their firm than men. Women less frequently had either previous work experience or managerial and entrepreneurial experience. Further, when they had this experience, they typically had less than their male counterparts. They also had created fewer firms, with less frequency and they had been managing their current firms for less time. With regards to growth, 33 per cent of the firms had grown in the last three years, while 31 per cent aimed to grow in the following three years. Male business owners reported these plans more frequently than female business owners.

From this analysis it can be observed that men and women business owners were relatively dissimilar across the industries where they developed their entrepreneurial activity. They were also dissimilar with regard to human capital variables. Therefore, in the comparison of their ESE dimensions, these variables have to be taken into account in order to preclude that the potential differences depend on variations of these variables.

Analysis of ESE

Data collected on self-efficacy was analysed using factor analysis of principal components with varimax rotation (Table 11.3). To evaluate the validity and viability of carrying out the principal components analysis, Barlett's test of sphericity and Kaiser-Meyer-Olkin (KMO) tests were conducted. The results of these tests reach acceptable levels. The level of significance of Barlett's test is 0.000. Therefore, the null hypothesis that there is no correlation between original variables can be rejected, since the variables are sufficiently correlated. The KMO test is over 0.5, the generally accepted criteria (George and Mallery, 1995); this justifies the use of the principal components analysis. Principal components factor analysis of the items disclosed a three-factor structure with items loading only on one factor, similar to Barbosa et al.'s (2007) findings. All the items had punctuations larger than 0.5 in one of the factors and, therefore, none of them were dropped from the analysis. The corresponding Cronbach alphas derived in reliability analysis are above or near to .80. This indicates a healthy level of reliability for each dimension.

Factor 1, Decisional self-efficacy, explains 23.76 per cent of the variance. The variables that acquire high saturation are those related to *coping with unexpected challenges* (work productively under continuous stress, pressure and conflict, tolerate unexpected changes in business conditions and persist in the face of adversity) and *risk assumption* (take decisions under uncertainty, take risks in a calculated way and assume the responsibility of ideas and decisions).

Factor 2, Financial self-efficacy, explains 20.54 per cent of the variance;

Table 11.3   Factorial analysis of the self-efficacy construct

	Component		
	1	2	3
I can work productively under continuous stress, pressure and conflict	**.782**	.092	−.045
I can tolerate unexpected changes in business conditions	**.748**	.123	.181
I can take decisions under uncertainty and risk	**.693**	.131	.289
I can persist in the face of adversity	**.635**	.189	.274
I can assume the responsibility of ideas and decisions	**.561**	.397	.221
I can take risks in a calculated way	**.515**	.351	.305
I can control business costs	.139	**.885**	.113
I can manage expenses	.234	**.835**	.095
I can manage *cash flow*	.179	**.734**	.293
I can develop relationships with key persons to access capital sources	.153	.149	**.827**
I can develop and maintain favourable relationships with potential investors	.220	.094	**.761**
I can identify potential sources of funding to invest in the firm	.193	.242	**.758**
Eigenvalues	2.851	2.466	2.279
% of explained variance	23.762	20.547	18.994
Alpha of each factor	.810	.821	.771
Kaiser-Meyer-Olkin measure = .869			
Bartlett's test of sphericity: Chi-squared= 4464.692, df= 66; Sig.=0.000			

the variables that acquire high saturation are those related to *economic management* (control of business costs, management of expenses and cash flow).

Factor 3, Relational self-efficacy, explains 18.99 per cent of the variance; the variables that acquire high saturation are those related to *developing relationships with investors* (identify potential sources of funding to invest in the firm, develop relationships with key persons to access capital, and develop and maintain favourable relationships with potential investors).

Principal components factor analysis identified a multi-dimensional structure for ESE, supporting hypothesis 1. Subsequently, a comparison of means between women and men business owners is included in Table 11.4. There are no significant gender differences in means within decisional and relational self-efficacy. However, women perceived themselves to have more financial self-efficacy.

*Table 11.4   Comparison of means between women and men business
                owners in ESE dimensions for the whole sample*

	Mean		T tests for means equality		
	Men	Women	t	df	Sig.
Decisional self-efficacy	.0410202	−.0692656	1.637	939	.102
Financial self-efficacy	−.0476430	.0804486	−1.902	939	.058
Relational self-efficacy	−.0200259	.0338152	−.798	939	.425

A comparison of means between women and men business owners in traditionally female and male-dominated sectors is included in Table 11.5.

Hypotheses 2 proposed that the extent of gender differences in ESE dimensions would depend upon the nature of the industry. More specifically, hypothesis 2a proposed that there would be gender differences in male-dominated industries but not in traditionally female-dominated industries. As is evident in Table 11.5, there are no gender differences in the dimensions of self-efficacy within traditionally female-dominated industries, but there are differences in male-dominated industries. Therefore, the findings support hypothesis 2a.

In traditionally male-dominated industries, men reported having comparatively more decisional self-efficacy (t = 1.986, sig.= .047) and women reported having comparatively more financial self-efficacy (t = −4.018, sig.= .000). Since hypothesis 2b proposed that female entrepreneurs would be especially likely to report lower ESE than their male counterparts in male-dominated industries, support was found for both this hypothesis and its opposite.

In Table 11.6, the comparison of means between highly educated women and men business owners is included. As proposed in hypothesis 3a, there are no gender differences in the dimensions of self-efficacy within higher educated business owners (graduate and postgraduate). Therefore, hypothesis 3a is supported. However, within business owners with primary and secondary education, women marginally reported more financial self-efficacy than their male counterparts (t = −1,980; sig. = 0.049).

A comparison of means between women and men business owners in different age intervals is included in Table 11.7. Hypothesis 3b is supported since there are no gender differences in the dimensions of self-efficacy within post-career individuals. In younger age intervals (career building and mid-career), women reported more financial self-efficacy.

Table 11.8 demonstrates that the perception of higher decisional self-efficacy differentiates business owners with growth intentions from those who do not want their business to grow. Therefore, since only one ESE

Table 11.5   Comparison of means between women and men business owners in ESE dimensions in the subsamples of traditionally female- and male-dominated sectors

	Mean		T tests for means equality		
	Men	Women	t	df	Sig.
Female dominated sectors (137 men vs 147 women)					
Decisional self-efficacy	.0747295	.0167516	.497	282	.620
Financial self-efficacy	−.1129322	−.1360349	.166	282	.868
Relational self-efficacy	−.0087242	.0366130	−.374	282	.709
Male dominated sectors (451 men vs 200 women)					
Decisional self-efficacy	.0383173	−.1311766	1.986	649	.047
Financial self-efficacy	−.0269658	.2471228	−4.018	510.81	.000
Relational self-efficacy	−.0287165	.0579472	−1.036	649	.300

Table 11.6   Comparison of means between women and men business owners in ESE dimensions in the subsamples of more and less educated business-owners

	Mean		T tests for means equality		
	Men	Women	t	df	Sig.
Graduate and postgraduate business owners (424 men vs 251 women)					
Decisional self-efficacy	.1107895	−.0293309	1.915	673	.056
Financial self-efficacy	−.0097689	.0659528	−.974	673	.330
Relational self-efficacy	.0149331	.0425756	−.349	673	.727
Business-owners with primary and secondary education (166 men vs 97 women)					
Decisional self-efficacy	−.1446883	−.1958776	.343	261	.732
Financial self-efficacy	−.1266461	.1257408	−1.980	227.62	.049
Relational self-efficacy	−.1105098	.0306296	−1.087	261	.278

dimension seems to impact individuals for growing their firms, hypothesis 4a is only partially supported.

Analysing both subsamples for gender differences, it is clear that within the group with growth intentions women reported more financial self-efficacy (t = −2.261, sig. = 0.025); however, no gender differences were found within the group that did not have growth expectations. Therefore, hypothesis 4b is only partially supported, as no gender differences were expected once individuals were split according to their growth intentions. Nonetheless, it seems that women not only need to perceive themselves

Table 11.7   Comparison of means between women and men business owners in ESE dimensions in the subsamples of career building, mid-career and post-career according to the age of business owners

	Mean		T tests for means equality		
	Men	Women	t	df	Sig.
Career building (under 40 years old) (291 men vs 219 women)					
Decisional self-efficacy	.0499206	−.0292837	.917	508	.360
Financial self-efficacy	−.1633208	.0407489	−2.296	491.62	.022
Relational self-efficacy	−.0871120	−.0092271	−.905	508	.366
Mid-career (40–49 years old) (227 men vs 142 women)					
Decisional self-efficacy	.0937752	.0027837	.891	367	.373
Financial self-efficacy	−.1179267	.1763656	−2.886	336.77	.004
Relational self-efficacy	−.0156435	−.0535462	.344	367	.731
Post-career (50 years old or more) (126 men vs 39 women)					
Decisional self-efficacy	.0083782	−.2755372	1.396	163	.164
Financial self-efficacy	.1324913	.1647070	−.175	163	.861
Relational self-efficacy	.0751904	.1672225	−.493	163	.623

with decisional self-efficacy, but also with financial self-efficacy, in order to grow their businesses.

DISCUSSION

This study contributes to our limited understanding of the multidimensional character of entrepreneurial self-efficacy. Specifically, it identifies the potential gender differences in this construct and examines if certain variables can help better explain these differences. Findings show that there are no gender differences in the following ESE dimensions: decisional, relational and financial. Although, with regards to the latter, women perceive themselves as marginally more self-efficacious. The lack of gender differences in ESE is particularly evident when highly educated and experienced business owners are compared in traditionally female-dominated sectors. In this respect, these findings differ from those of previous studies that conclude that women have lower ESE for entrepreneurial intention (Kickul et al., 2008; Kourilsky and Walstad, 1998; Wilson et al, 2007). This includes when their businesses are nascent (Menzies et al., 2006) or even significantly developed

Table 11.8   Comparison of means between business owners in ESE dimensions according to their growth intention and gender

	Mean		T tests for means equality		
	B-Os without growth intentions (626)	B-Os with growth intentions (287)	t	df	Sig.
Whole sample					
Decisional self-efficacy	−.0461196	.0931310	−2.084	659.3	.038
Financial self-efficacy	.0308498	−.0302828	.867	911	.386
Relational self-efficacy	.0408714	−.0426834	1.184	911	.237
Subsample of business owners with growth intentions (198 men vs 89 women)					
	Men	Women	t	df	Sig.
Decisional self-efficacy	.1133073	.0482443	.580	285	.562
Financial self-efficacy	−.1152357	.1587135	−2.261	285	.025
Relational self-efficacy	−.0678620	.0133318	−.637	285	.525
Subsample of business owners without growth intentions (372 men vs 254 women)					
	Men	Women	t	df	Sig.
Decisional self-efficacy	.0030777	−.1181724	1.411	624	.159
Financial self-efficacy	−.0013655	.0780313	−.971	624	.332
Relational self-efficacy	.0190527	.0728264	−.670	624	.503

(Kirkwood, 2009). An encouraging finding is that young women perceive higher self-efficacy in the financial ESE dimension than their male counterparts. This finding might reflect a generational change, in which women are highly qualified before they decide to create their firm. In addition, it can be observed that those individuals with more decisional self-efficacy are more likely to try to grow their firms. For this group, being financially savvy seems to be more important for women than for men.

Anna et al. (2000) find that when comparing women in non-traditionally female-dominated sectors with those in traditionally female-dominated ones, those women in the former group perceive themselves with higher self-efficacy for planning. Alternatively, those women in the latter group are more self-efficacious in opportunity recognition. Certain similarities can be observed with regard to the findings of this study, since women in non-traditionally female-dominated sectors report less decisional self-efficacy (which is related to opportunity recognition) and perceive more financial self-efficacy in comparison to men.

These findings show that self-efficacy is to some extent situation-dependent; the learning acquired in one situation can be applied to new situations. This could be an explanation for why women in traditionally male-dominated sectors with high education and experience do not differ in ESE from their male counterparts. Therefore, self-efficacy is not a static trait, but can be changed over time. This fact points to the importance of designing training programmes directed to self-efficacy. In the case of women business owners within non-traditionally female-dominated sectors, programmes should focus on increasing risk tolerance and, in turn, decisional self-efficacy. At the same time, they should teach women how to benefit from their financial self-efficacy. Therefore, the findings of this study suggest that a properly designed entrepreneurship education programme should take into account the multidimensional nature of ESE. Although this study does not provide evidence of a positive moderating effect of entrepreneurial education on ESE in the case of women (Wilson et al., 2007), it nonetheless shows that education is a crucial factor and can level the playing field for men and women in business activity.

Furthermore, Mau (2003) suggests that once an individual internalizes self-efficacy, confidence encourages that individual to accept greater challenges. Subsequent success then reinforces the individual's perception of efficacy, thus creating a spiral effect that improves self-efficacy even more. For this reason, the emphasis needs to be on learning. Learning can be an ongoing, active process that can improve both personal development and the development of an individual's firm.

Other variables might moderate the relationship between ESE and gender, such as control beliefs or being part of a team. With regards to the former, Gatewood et al. (2002) point out that negative feedback with regard to entrepreneurial abilities alters women's entrepreneurial intentions significantly more than is the case of their male counterparts. Therefore, a future line of research should, as proposed by Drnovšek et al. (2010), take into account goal beliefs (assessments of one's capabilities to engage in activities that will lead to a successful task or outcome completion), and also control beliefs (an entrepreneur's beliefs about his or her abilities to control negative thoughts and bolster positive thoughts during goal pursuit). This might help explain why apparently efficacious individuals let negative feedback from others inhibit their progress through the business start-up and growth phases. Secondly, Godwin et al. (2006) propose that establishing a mixed-sex entrepreneurial founding team may benefit women entrepreneurs in male-dominated cultures and industries, and provide enhanced legitimacy, access to a larger number of resources, and a stronger and more diverse social network. Also,

Menzies et al. (2006) find that women, despite having a lower degree of self-efficacy, actually stand on an equal footing with men in starting their firms, especially when they are part of a team. They observe that women who are members of a start-up team are six times more likely to achieve an operating business than those who are solo-entrepreneurs. Therefore, it can be proposed that another benefit that being in a team might create, irrespective of the members' gender, is the perception of support. This perception of support increases the individuals' perception of confidence in his or her capacities (a finding that is worth being further investigated in future research).

Another potential line of research is to test if the dimensions of ESE impact the actual growth of a firm. However, researchers have to be aware that it is quite difficult to determine the causal direction of ESE. In other words, does the creation of a new venture (or business growth) increase one's ESE, or does high ESE lead one to start a new company (or grow the business)?

With regards to the potential limitations of this study, it is important to take cultural influences on ESE into account (McGee et al., 2009). Therefore, generalizing from Spanish data to other cultures can be problematic. However, although in Spain women are still defined through roles connected to family and household responsibilities, the empowerment of women is a global phenomenon; it can be assumed that these results will be valid in other contexts. In addition, this study is focused on knowledge-intensive firms and the women business owners within these industries. They have high levels of human capital, in terms of both education and skills, which is similar to their male counterparts (Bates, 1995). This can help explain the lack of differences due to gender found in this study.

Finally, this study should provide a fruitful starting point for future research that further explores the gradual events that influence the development of self-efficacy over time. A combination of both quantitative and qualitative methods is called for in order to advance our understanding of this area.

NOTE

*   This work has benefited from the Project 19/06 by the Spanish Women's Institute. The author is also grateful to the editors for their constructive comments.

REFERENCES

Allen, I.E., A. Elam, N. Langowitz and M. Dean (2008), *Global Entrepreneurship Monitor 2007 Report on Women and Entrepreneurship*, MA: Babson Park.

Anna, A.L., G.N. Chandler, E. Jansen and N.P. Mero (2000), 'Women business owners in traditional and non-traditional industries', *Journal of Business Venturing*, **15**, 279–303.

Baker, T., R. Aldag and E. Blair (2003), 'Gender and entrepreneurial opportunity evaluation', in W.D. Bygrave (ed.), *Frontiers of Entrepreneurship Research: Proceedings of the Babson Kauffman Entrepreneurship Research Conference*, Babson Park, MA: Babson College, pp. 689–703. Available at: http://www.babson.edu/entrep/fer/BABSON2003/XXVI/XXVI-Pl/xxvip6.htm.

Bandura, A. (1977), 'Self-efficacy: toward a unifying theory of behavioural change', *Psychological Review*, **84**, 191–215.

Bandura, A. (1989), 'Human agency in social cognitive theory', *American Psychologist*, **44** (9), 1175–84.

Bandura, A. (1997), *Self-efficacy: The Exercise of Control*, New York: W.H. Freeman.

Barber, B.M. and T. Odean (2001), 'Boys will be boys: gender, overconfidence and common stock investment', *Quarterly Journal of Economics*, **116** (1), 261–92.

Barbosa, S.D., M.W. Gerhardt and J. Kickul (2007), 'The role of cognitive style and risk preference on entrepreneurial self-efficacy and entrepreneurial intentions', *Journal of Leadership and Organizational Studies*, **13** (4), 86–104.

Baron, R.A. and G.D. Markman (2003), 'Beyond social capital: the role of entrepreneurs' social competence in their financial success', *Journal of Business Venturing*, **18** (1), 41–60.

Bates, T. (1995), 'Self-employment entry across industry groups', *Journal of Business Venturing*, **10** (2), 143–56.

Blomqvist, M. and H. Frennberg (2010), 'Changing gendered processes through collaborative action research', paper presented in the Gender, Work and Organization Conference, Keele, June.

Boyd, N.G. and G.S. Vozikis (1994), 'The influence of self-efficacy on the development of entrepreneurial intentions and actions', *Entrepreneurship Theory and Practice*, **18** (4), 63–90.

Bruni, A., S. Gherardi and B. Poggio (2004), 'Entrepreneur-mentality, gender and the study of women entrepreneurs', *Journal of Organizational Change Management*, **17** (3), 256–68.

Brush, C.G., N. Carter, E. Gatewood, P. Greene and M. Hart (2004), *Clearing the Hurdles: Women Building High-Growth Businesses*, Upper Saddle River, NJ: Prentice Hall.

Carter, N. (2002), 'The role of risk orientation on financing expectations in new venture creation: does sex matter?', *Frontiers of Entrepreneurship Research*, Babson-Kauffman Foundation, available at: www.babson.edu/entrep/fer/Babson2002/VI/VI_P2/P2/html/vi-p2.htm (accessed 9 July 2010).

Chandler, G.N. and E. Jansen (1992), 'The founder's self-assessed competence and venture performance', *Journal of Business Venturing*, **7**, 223–36.

Chen, C.C., P.G. Green and A. Crick (1998), 'Does entrepreneurial self-efficacy distinguish entrepreneurs from managers?', *Journal of Business Venturing*, **13** (4), 295–316.

Cliff, J.E. (1998), 'Does one size fit all? Exploring the relationship between attitudes towards growth, gender, and business size', *Journal of Business Venturing*, **13**, 523–42.

Cooper, S. and W. Lucas (2007), 'Building entrepreneurial self-efficacy and intent through education and experience', paper presented at ISBE Conference, Glasgow, November.

De Bruin A., C. Brush and F. Welter (2007), 'Advancing a framework for coherent research on women's entrepreneurship', *Entrepreneurship Theory and Practice*, **31**(3), 323–39.

De Noble, A., D. Jung and S. Ehrlich (1999), 'Entrepreneurial self-efficacy: the development of measure and its relationship to entrepreneurial action', in P.D. Reynolds, W.D. Bygrave, S. Manigart, C.M. Mason, G.D. Meyer, H.J. Sapienza and K.G. Shaver (eds), *Frontiers of Entrepreneurship Research*, Babson College, MA: Babson Park, pp. 73–87.

Drnovšek, M., J. Wincent and M.S. Cardon (2010), 'Entrepreneurial self-efficacy and business start-up: developing a multi-dimensional definition', *International Journal of Entrepreneurial Behaviour & Research*, **16** (4), 329–48.

Fielden, S.L., M.J. Davidson, A.J. Dawe and P.J. Makin (2003), 'Factors inhibiting the economic growth of female owned small businesses in North West England', *Journal of Small Business and Enterprise Development*, **10** (2), 152–66.

Fletcher, C. (1999), 'The implications of research on gender differences in self-assessment and 360 degree appraisal', *Human Resource Management Journal*, **9** (1) 39–46.

Florin, J., R. Karri and N. Rossiter (2007), 'Fostering entrepreneurial drive in business education: an attitudinal approach', *Journal of Management Education*, **31**(1), 17–42.

Forbes, D.P. (2005), 'The effects of strategic decision making on entrepreneurial self-efficacy', *Entrepreneurship Theory and Practice*, **29** (5), 599–626.

Gatewood, E.J., K.G. Shaver, J.B. Powers and W.B. Gartner (2002), 'Entrepreneurial expectancy, task effort and performance', *Entrepreneurship Theory and Practice*, Winter, 95–114.

George, D. and P. Mallery (1995), *SPSS/PC+ Step by Step: A Simple Reference*, Belmont, CA: Wadsworth Publishing Company.

Godwin, L., C. Stevens and N. Brenner (2006), 'Forced to play by the rules? Theorizing how mixed-sex founding teams benefit women entrepreneurs in male-dominated contexts', *Entrepreneurship Theory and Practice*, **30** (5), 623–42.

Gundry, L.K. and H.P. Welsch (2001), 'The ambitious entrepreneur: high growth strategies of women-owned enterprises', *Journal of Business Venturing*, **16** (5), 453–70.

Hopcroft, R.L. (2006), 'Status characteristics among older individuals: the diminished significance of gender', *The Sociological Quarterly*, **47** (2), 361–74.

Instituto Nacional de Estadística (2008),'Encuesta de Población Activa', available at: www.ine.es (accessed 9 July 2010).

Jennings, J.E., P.D. Jennings and R. Greenwood (2009), 'Novelty and new firm performance: the case of employment systems in knowledge-intensive service firms', *Journal of Business Venturing*, **24** (4), 338–59.

Kickul, J, F. Wilson, D. Marlino and S.D. Barbosa (2008), 'Are misalignments of perceptions and self-efficacy causing gender gaps in entrepreneurial intentions among our nation's teens?', *Journal of Small Business and Enterprise Development*, **15** (2), 321–35.

Kirkwood, K. (2009). 'Is a lack of self-confidence hindering women entrepreneurs?', *International Journal of Gender and Entrepreneurship*, **1** (2), 118–33.

Koellinger, P., M. Minniti and C. Schade (2006), '"I think I can, I think I can": overconfidence and entrepreneurial behaviour', *Journal of Economic Psychology*, **28**, 502–27.

Kourilsky, M.L. and W.B. Walstad (1998), 'Entrepreneurship and female youth: knowledge, attitudes, gender differences, and educational practices', *Journal of Business Venturing*, **13** (1), 77–88.

Krueger, N. And J. Kickul (2006), 'So you thought the intentions model was simple? Navigating the complexities and interactions of cognitive style, culture, gender, social norms, and intensity on the pathways to entrepreneurship', paper presented at USASBE conference, Tuscon, AZ, 12–15 January.

Langowitz, N. and M. Minitti (2007), 'The entrepreneurial propensity of women', *Entrepreneurship Theory and Practice*, **30** (1), 341–64.

Littunen, H. (2000), 'Networks and local environmental characteristics in the survival of new firms', *Small Business Economics*, **15**, 59–71.

Markman, G.D., D.B. Balkin and R.A. Baron (2002), 'Inventors and new venture formation: the effects of general self-efficacy and regretful thinking', *Entrepreneurship Theory and Practice*, **27** (2), 149–65.

Marlow, S. and S. Carter (2004), 'Accounting for change: professional status, gender disadvantage and self-employment', *Women in Management Review*, **19** (1), 5–16.

Mau, W.C. (2003), 'Factors that influence persistence in Science and Engineering career aspirations', *The Career Development Quarterly*, **51**, 234–43.

McGee, J.E., M. Peterson, S.L. Mueller and J.M. Sequeira (2009), 'Entrepreneurial self-efficacy: refining the measure', *Entrepreneurship Theory and Practice*, July, 965–88.

Menzies, T.V., M. Diochon, Y. Gasse and S. Elgie (2006), 'A longitudinal study of female vs. male nascent entrepreneurs in Canada: characteristics, process and outcome differences', *International Entrepreneurship and Management Journal*, **2** (4), 441–53.

Morris, M.H., N.N. Miyasaki, C.E. Watters and S.M. Coombes (2006), 'The dilemma of growth: understanding venture size choices of women entrepreneurs', *Journal of Small Business Management*, **44** (2), 221–44.

Mueller, S.L. and S. Goic (2003), 'East-West differences in entrepreneurial self-efficacy: Implications for entrepreneurship education in transition economies', *International Journal of Entrepreneurship Education*, **1** (4), 613–32.

Niederle, M. and L. Vesterlund (2005), *Do Women Shy Away from Competition? Do Men Compete Too Much?* NBER Working Paper, No. 11474.

Orser, B. and B. Hogarth-Scott (2002), 'Opting for growth: gender dimensions of choosing enterprise development', *Canadian Journal of Administrative Sciences*, **19** (3), 284–300.

Rauch, A. and M. Frese (2007), 'Let's put the person back into entrepreneurship research: a meta-analysis on the relationship between business owners' personality traits, business creation, and success', *European Journal of Work and Organizational Psychology*, **16** (4), 353–85.

Sappleton, N. (2009), 'Women non-traditional entrepreneurs and social capital', *International Journal of Gender and Entrepreneurship*, **1** (3), 192–218.

Shaw, E., W. Lam and S. Carter (2008), 'The role of entrepreneurial capital in building service reputation', *Services Industries Journal*, **28** (7), 899–917.

Trevelyan, R. (2008), 'Overconfidence and effort in new venture development', *Frontiers of Entrepreneurship Research*, **28** (5), Article 1, available at: lhttp:// digitalknowledge.babson.edu/fer/vol28/iss5/1.

Wicklund, J. and D. Shepherd (2003), 'Aspiring for and achieving growth: The moderating role of resources and opportunities', *The Journal of Management Studies*, **40** (8), 1919–41.

Wilson, F., J. Kickul and D. Marlino (2007), 'Gender, entrepreneurial self-efficacy, and entrepreneurial career intentions: Implications for entrepreneurship education', *Entrepreneurship Theory and Practice*, **31** (3), 387–406.

Zhao, H., C. Seibert and C. Hills (2005), 'The mediating role of self-efficacy in the development of entrepreneurial intentions', *Journal of Applied Psychology*, **90** (2), 1265–72.

12. Conceptualizing 'woman' as an entrepreneurial advantage: a reflexive approach

Albert James

INTRODUCTION

Scholarly work in social inquiry has a long tradition of approaching phenomenon through the lens of problems (Hammersley and Atkinson, 2007; Harding, 1987). Business scholars have often followed this same approach. Most entrepreneurship and organizational research follows the approach of observing the world, noting problems or issues, and trying to come up with explanations for those problems. This is the approach that has also been applied in much of the ongoing women's entrepreneurship research. An introduction into women's entrepreneurship literature inevitably involves a baptism into the reality of the many problems, challenges and different experiences that women entrepreneurs face. It is a literature in which women entrepreneurs are often 'portrayed as something weaker and in need of special assistance' (Ahl, 2002: 53).

Much of the women's entrepreneurial literature focuses on the comparative differences between women-led and men-led businesses (for example, Boden and Nucci, 2000; Carter et al., 1997; Chrisman et al., 1990; Cliff et al., 2005; Fasci and Valdez, 1998; Gupta et al., 2009; Marlow and Patton, 2005; Watson and Robinson, 2003). In this work, a problem-based focus emphasizes the nature, causes and consequences of why women-led businesses do comparatively worse than men-led businesses. In this chapter I propose that the result of this focus is that there is a significant body of knowledge about the problems of women entrepreneurs, but little understanding of successful women entrepreneurs.

WOMEN'S ENTREPRENEURSHIP RESEARCH: CENTRAL PREMISES

As academics interested in women's entrepreneurship, scholars have been trained and socialized according to the rigours and norms of scientific research. According to our training and socialization, we are taught both implicitly and explicitly that 'research always begins with some problem or set of issues' (Hammersley and Atkinson, 2007: 21). Our approach to the world we live in is to apply accepted forms of rigour, methods and theorization to the problems and issues we identify. These problems and issues Malinowski (2004: 9) refers to as 'foreshadowed problems', which are 'the main endowment of a scientific thinker'. Foreshadowed problems 'arise in the scholar's mind by the interaction of their theoretical studies and our observations of the world around us' (Malinowski, 2004: 9). From our foreshadowed problems we shape our theories 'according to facts and seeing facts in their bearing upon theory' (Malinowski, 2004: 9). Thus, the tradition of our work as academics is rooted in seeking out and understanding problems and issues; as Medawar (1967: 70) suggests, our 'professional business' is to solve the most important problems we think we can solve. Research on entrepreneurship, in general, and women's entrepreneurship, in particular, reflects this tradition of academia.

In the general body of entrepreneurship research our 'professional business' has led us to seek and understand the differences in entrepreneurship between people, entrepreneurs, organizations, populations and environments. Much research has arisen from the foreshadowed problems of observations that do not neatly fit with theoretical expectations. This process has lead to a body of work that revolves around entrepreneurial problems and issues such as opportunity, emergence and discovery (Gaglio, 1997; Van de Ven, 1993), new venture creation (Brush, et al., 2001, 2008), firm performance (Jennings et al. 2009; Lumpkin and Dess, 1996) and organization survival (Gunther McGrath, 1999).

Women's entrepreneurship research begins from similar sets of problems and issues as the general body of entrepreneurship literature, but extends into 'understanding the gendered influences on the experiences and contributions' of women entrepreneurs (Brush et al., 2006: 6). I suspect that in the development of existing women's entrepreneurship literature much is owed to two additional traditions of inquiry: critical theory and feminist theory. By critical theory I do not refer to the narrow Frankfurt School tradition of critical theory that is associated with Western European Marxism. Instead, I refer to critical theory in a broader sense, as being associated with the 'many social movements that identify varied dimensions of the domination of human beings' (Bohman, 2005: 1).

As such, critical theory provides the framework that identifies problems of domination and emancipation. From the tradition of various feminist theories, it is the domination and emancipation of women that the women's entrepreneurship literature seeks to address.

By feminist theory I do not refer to any particular branch of feminist theory, but instead I refer to the many methods, methodologies and epistemologies that 'involve critically analysing how traditional social science conceptualizes women's and men's lives' (Harding, 1987: 2). Although feminist analysis does not constitute a single set of claims, there are a few 'generalities that could be called feminism' (Harding, 1991: 6). Within these generalities, feminist analysis seeks empirical data, theory that is less partial, as well descriptions and explanations that take women and gender into account (Harding, 1991). A feminist approach to women's entrepreneurship research is one that examines women's experiences within the broader discourse of entrepreneurship; by so doing it makes our theorizing and understanding of women entrepreneurs more complete.

This feminist approach to women's entrepreneurship 'generates its problematics from the perspective of women's experiences' and uses these experiences as significant indicators 'of "reality" against which hypotheses are tested' (Harding, 1987: 7). Gender is seen as a social construction that exaggerates differences, fundamentally structures society and creates differences that perpetuate power relations among men and women (Calas et al., 2009; Withers Osmund and Thorne, 1993). Much women's entrepreneurship research seeks to address (implicitly and explicitly) the domination of women entrepreneurs. It does so by seeking to understand the issues and problems relating to differences between men's and women's entrepreneurial experiences. There is an often unstated goal of gaining a 'better understanding of how to promote women's entrepreneurship, eliminate obstacles women may face in business creation, and facilitate the growth process of their businesses' (Brush et al., 2006: 4).

As a result, women's entrepreneurship literature has contributed to our understanding of the empirical realities of women's entrepreneurship and provided important descriptions and explanations of those realities. Entrepreneurship literature benefits from the work that has identified the problems, disadvantages, issues and obstacles that women entrepreneurs face. There are, however, consequences to the uneven focus on certain types of questions and consequences that come at the expense of attention to other types of questions (Calas et al., 2009). Consequently, in this chapter I suggest that women's entrepreneurship research is dominated by a research tradition that focuses on problems and addresses the emancipation of the oppressed (as understood by a general sense of feminism). As such, this body of research has developed from an assumption and categorization of women's entrepreneurship as problematic. This may not, however, be the only way to view this phenomenon.

AN ALTERNATIVE VIEW OF WOMEN'S ENTREPRENEURSHIP RESEARCH

In suggesting the possibility of an alternate view on women's entrepreneurship, I do not mean to discount either the critical theory or feminist theory traditions as described above. Doing so would risk diminishing the valuable contributions both traditions have made to our understanding of the world. What I am suggesting is that there may be value in breaking from the tradition of approaching our theorizing and research through foreshadowed problems. My approach here is not a result of my own musings about gender, women and entrepreneurship, but rather it emerges from my discussions with a former employer of mine, whom I will call 'Sarah'. I was associated with Sarah while working in what might be considered an unfriendly environment for women entrepreneurs. When we first met she was a recent entrant into a decidedly male-dominated industry, in a remote community that prides itself on its frontier mentality. She was new to the industry and also new to her role as business owner. Yet, in the face of these challenges and transitions, Sarah became a successful 'serial entrepreneur' (see Table 12.1) (Westhead and White, 1998). Her business thrived under her leadership and became the anchor from which she launched two other successful, and ongoing, ventures. It was over the course of several discussions with Sarah about the women's entrepreneur literature, and her experiences, that I started to wonder if women's

Table 12.1   Sarah: a successful female entrepreneur[1]

Entrepreneurial activities			
In order	Ownership stake	Partnership	Number of employees
Automotive	51%	Mixed gender	34
Regional airline	25%	Mixed	40
Hotel	42%	All women	30
Total revenue: $30 million (Canadian)			

Recognitions, awards and credentials	
Business Person of the Year	Chamber of Commerce
Selected to attend Quantum Shift for Entrepreneurs 2010	University of Western Ontario, Ivey School of Business
CMA	Graduated 2nd in her provincial category

entrepreneurship could be viewed as something other than problematic. More specifically, my musings grew from her comment that 'focusing on the problems is unhelpful' to her. Instead she stated that she wanted to know about 'our advantages so we can leverage them'.

Sarah seemed to intuitively understand that our academic field has developed knowledge that attempts to identify and explain the causes of the inequalities that women entrepreneurs face, but has neglected what may empower women entrepreneurs. To Sarah, what is more important is to understand the relationships and connections 'that contribute to the flourishing and optimal functioning of people, groups and institutions' (Gable and Haidt, 2005: 104).

There are strong and useful theories in women's entrepreneurship literature that delve 'into underlying processes so as to understand the systematic reasons for particular occurrence or non-occurrence' (Sutton and Staw, 1995: 378). In a study on the relationship between trust and the perception of the psychological contract breach, Robinson (1996) demonstrated that people tend to find what they are looking for.[2] This suggests that when we engage in research from a problem- and issue-based framework, our analysis is more likely to result in our finding problems and issues (at the expense of uncovering causes for flourishing and optimal functioning enterprises). One might argue the non-occurrence of problems and issues is flourishing and optimal functioning. This is not the case, however, as both flourishing and optimal functioning are concepts that signify something far more substantial than simply the absence of problems and issues. Consequently, it is that neither our problem-based framework nor our theories provide much insight into Sarah's entrepreneurial successes.

Alternative View: Within Existing Frameworks

As described above, Sarah is a woman in a male-dominated industry, community and environment. In Sarah's entrepreneurial activities she acknowledges having been the sole woman (a token) in most of her business dealings. Her self-description fits well with the notions of 'tokenism' (Kanter, 1977, 1980). According to Sarah (and as tokenism predicts), she was given extra attention from her male peers and resource holders, her actions were scrutinized and she was expected to live up to both male and female standards. Tokenism also predicts negative consequences for Sarah, both with her male peers and with other females (subordinates). Tokenism has a problem-focused framework which leaves little space to understand how Sarah's status might have been advantageous to her entrepreneurial activities. This approach would fail to take into account the conditions that contribute to her flourishing and optimal functioning.

Further, in focusing on problems, the relationships and connections that led to her flourishing as a woman entrepreneur could easily be overlooked. In Sarah's analysis, she constructed her success in terms of the advantages of being a token; the advantage was her 'uniqueness'. She was more noticeable. She says, 'I was memorable to them.' Her male peers paid attention to her competencies. From Sarah's perspective, it was her uniqueness that highlighted her competencies and, in turn, offered her access to peers and gave her legitimacy in negotiating for needed resources. This understanding of tokenism runs contrary to the problem-based focus on token status that predicts backlash and jealous reactions from the high-status group. In this case the high-status group is Sarah's male peers, while Sarah is the token (Yoder, 1991). Instead, Sarah understands her uniqueness as an advantage she holds to be leveraged in certain environments, she says, 'much as I would my CMA designation in other environments'. This is a simple example of theorizing about the possible advantages women entrepreneurs may possess; nonetheless, it is also an example of an advantage that may not be specific to either men or women. This would be the case if we consider the role of uniqueness, but fail to consider the role of gender.

Women's entrepreneurship literature takes into account much more than biological sex differences. As tokenism and much of feminist thought suggests, gender is a central principle of social organization that exaggerates differences between men and women (Withers Osmund and Thorne, 1993; Yoder, 1991). Sarah's uniqueness, gender and its influences on how sex is perceived, is useful in theorizing how her uniqueness as a female entrepreneur worked to her advantage. More specifically, it is the gendered nature of entrepreneurship that is helpful.

As Ahl (2006) demonstrates, many aspects of entrepreneurship are gendered to be masculine. Because entrepreneurship is thought to be a masculine field, women are expected to be weaker entrepreneurs, have their legitimacy questioned, have more trouble securing financial resources and be lower-status entrepreneurs (Godwin et al., 2006; Yoder, 1991). Yet, Sarah was able to access resources from within her group of male peers. According to Sarah, she was able to do so because her uniqueness drew attention to her and allowed her to demonstrate her competency to her peers. For a man entering the industry, his competency is measured only against industry norms. Alternatively, Sarah's competency was measured against both industry expectations and gender norms. She met and exceeded both, thereby gaining legitimacy. Instead of gender being an additional burden for Sarah, her entrepreneurial abilities were highlighted by her uniqueness in a way that a man's entrepreneurial abilities could not have been.

What I have described is one example of an alternative view of women's entrepreneurship as advantageous instead of problematic. It is also an example of how changing focus from problems to optimal functioning can provide us with useful theoretical insights into the world of work. By shifting focus from problems to success, it is doubtless that other theoretical frameworks can add additional insights into women's entrepreneurship. Instead of seeking to explain and understand the problem of lower performance for women entrepreneurs from a network theory perspective, I use this framework to explain how women-led firms optimize their performance. The difference may be subtle, but, as the above example demonstrates, when one theorizes with an eye towards flourishing, new understandings and predictions can emerge from existing theories. Thus far I have suggested, and attempted to identify, how shifting the focus away from problems can be an instrumental approach to Sarah's call for useful knowledge. In the next section, I further suggest an additional direction of research that might help to identify and understand the advantages of women entrepreneurs.

Alternative View: Moderated Model of Women's Entrepreneurship

Models of women entrepreneurship are typically models which seek to explain women entrepreneurship by identifying the 'x' factors that mediate their entrepreneurial outcomes (see Figure 12.1). An alternative approach would be to think of moderated models of women entrepreneurship (see Figure 12.2). This would involve research on factors associated with positive women entrepreneurial outcomes. This approach would require

Figure 12.1   Traditional mediated model of women's entrepreneurship

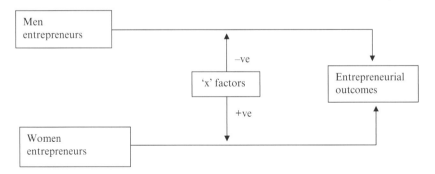

Figure 12.2   Alternative moderated model of women's entrepreneurship

not beginning with a problem-centric focus. Here, the first step involves observing the empirical world of women entrepreneurs and applying academic training to the conditions of the flourishing and optimal functioning that we identify. As factors associated with women entrepreneurial success are identified, the next step would be to examine if the factors' effects are different for men and women. Here, too, Sarah has suggested some possible factors.

In our conversations, one factor Sarah suggested is parenthood (as the combination of motherhood expectations versus fatherhood expectations). Sex role theory suggests expressive gender roles for women and instrumental roles for men (Withers Osmund and Thorne, 1993). Men are expected (and socialized) to value rational non-emotional behaviours while women are socialized towards emotionally driven behaviours. These gendered role norms and expectations also apply to parenthood. In explaining and reflecting on her success, Sarah suggested that the role expectations that come with parenthood for women (behaving with fairness and equity) are actually an entrepreneurial advantage.

Consider the critical entrepreneurial activity of resource acquisition (Brush et al., 2001). Access to resources requires the decisions by resource holders to engage in some sort of exchange with the entrepreneur. Entrepreneurship is dominated by a masculine-gendered discourse (Ahl, 2006). This masculine discourse values reciprocal exchange relationships between the focal individual and the target, at the expense of affective relationships. Following Sarah's line of reasoning, parenthood has different behavioural effects on men and women. Parenthood influences men toward reciprocal exchanges. For women, parenthood (and the expressive role women take on) influences them towards balanced and fair exchanges. In entrepreneurial environments, especially those with masculine-gendered discourse, exchanges where the target is influenced by decision rules of fairness and balance may result in a focal individual experiencing unexpected exchange results. Unexpected exchange outcomes can result in affective responses towards the exchange target and anchoring events in the relationship between the target and focal individual (Ballinger and Rockman, 2010). Anchored relationships are theorized to provoke affective, non-reciprocal, relationships between the focal individual and target. Non-reciprocal relationships are those relationships where decision rules are influenced by feelings of obligation, gratitude and trust. Anchored relationships that develop from parenthood's gendered effect on women entrepreneurs' (targets) exchanges with resource holders (focal individuals) may result in resource acquisition advantages for women entrepreneurs. This is not to say that men are not also capable of provoking affective responses and anchoring events. Instead, it is meant to serve as an example of how, because of the pervasiveness of the effect of gender roles, behaviours, reactions to behaviours and the consequences of behaviours might be different for women and men. It is also meant as an example of an 'x' factor that may have very different moderating effects on the entrepreneurial actions of women and men.

Sarah suggested two other possible 'x' factors in her success: career path and gendered role expectations. According to Sarah, the typical general manager career path requires a person to move through the sales department into general management. As a result, most senior managers in this segment of the industry are salesoriented. In this segment there is also a gendered career path – one that places most of the women who enter the segment in back office and in administrative roles. Consequently, women's career paths typically do not lead towards senior management positions. It was Sarah's observation that the result of the nature of the two career paths is that, although the businesses are all multi-divisional, senior management's understanding of the business is based on only one of the divisions (sales). Alternatively, women who become senior managers typically have a career path that exposes them to all of the divisions; this gives them a more complete view of the nature, contribution and opportunities of each division.

The other additional advantage Sarah described can be conceptualized as another positive effect of gendered expectations and norms. In describing her experiences as an entrepreneur, Sarah attributed a portion of her success to an outcome arising from expectations placed on women by gendered notions of parenthood. In Sarah's words, 'we are built to have babies' and are expected to raise, nurture, care for and meet each child's specific needs. As a result, women develop skills and are accustomed to 'multitasking between many needs and demands'. As described above, this industry segment is one of multi-divisional businesses, 'multiple businesses under one roof'. Each division has its own set of practices and industry norms for performance, and its own set of performance factors. The practices and norms of one division are often in opposition to those of other divisions. For Sarah, the skills developed by 'doing' parenthood give her an advantage over men because she is better able to multitask and manage the needs of the various divisions.

In the above discussion of possible 'x' factors there is one, as yet, unmentioned 'x' factor: context. For all the advantages Sarah identified, context is important. It is essential to take context into account when considering how uniqueness and gendered performance expectations were advantageous for Sarah. Uniqueness and gender expectations are contextual. For example, from work on tokenism it has been shown that in any social situation where there are inequalities in proportional representation and power of people there are token effects (Ely, 1994, 1995; Yoder, 1991). I have described Sarah's context as masculine, in industry and community. By virtue of her sex, Sarah represents an under-represented category. A comparison of the websites of seven similar sized firms in the same industry segment as Sarah's first business confirmed this. In total 75 employees were listed on the websites. Of the 75 only 10 were women. None of the women were in leadership positions; eight were employed in administrative support roles and two in non-managerial sales roles. With regard to anchoring events, context is instrumental in determining how reliant the focal individual is on the target. Through precedent and organizational climate, context determines if an exchange outcome is unexpected or not. Arguably, for any of Sarah's entrepreneurial advantages the effect and degree of affect of the advantages may vary greatly depending on context.

A Cautionary Word on a Possible Omitted 'X' Factor

Before concluding this chapter there is a variable that I have disregarded up to this point. I have avoided this variable for two reasons: (1) I agree with Sarah when she said that this variable is not an advantage; and (2) I believe its inclusion serves to perpetuate the historic power relationship between men and women. This variable is sexuality.

In our conversations regarding women entrepreneurship as an advantage, Sarah began with the idea that her uniqueness as a woman has been advantageous to her achieving her entrepreneurial outcomes. As Sarah developed the idea of uniqueness as an advantage, she described several occasions where her uniqueness had seemed an obvious advantage, as well as times where she had leveraged it to become an advantage. It was at this point in the conversation, when she was describing the need and usefulness of leveraging advantages that she brought up sexuality. Sarah did so by stating quite forcefully, 'and I don't mean sexuality, it is not an advantage'. Sarah is careful to minimize perceptions of her sexuality. When at work, or otherwise representing her businesses, it is Sarah's practice to purposely choose her attire and mannerisms so as to minimize any hint of sexuality. It seems that for Sarah to do otherwise would delegitimize her as well as call her credibility into question.

Sexuality is 'defined by desire and whatever practices a given culture regards as sexual' and is closely related to gender (Withers Osmund and Thorne, 1993: 605). The close relationship between sexuality and gender seems to be born out in how often negative connotations of sexuality are associated with females. For example, in romantic relationships in the workplace the sexuality of males is perceived as seeking 'excitement, ego satisfaction, and sexual experience, while the female is viewed as in search of organizational rewards' (Quinn, 1977: 36). Another example of female sexuality being constructed as negative comes from organizational leadership. In leadership literature, leadership is most often constructed as masculine; using sexuality is thought of as the opposite of leadership. The continued association of sexuality with female sexuality is a tool that strengthens male dominated leadership patterns (Hearn and Parkin, 1986). This negative association of female sexuality extends beyond organizations and into wider society. For instance, Foucault's identification of the 'hysterical woman' as one of the four prime targets of control in society (Foucault, 1990) relates well here.

It seems counterproductive to continue to inject a variable so entwined with the perpetuation of the gendered power structure into our academic conversations about women entrepreneurs, especially when the goal of our conversations is to correct the inequalities women entrepreneurs face. However, based on feedback received while developing this project it became obvious that the conceptualization of women entrepreneurial advantages continues to evoke various negative notions of female sexuality. This suggested to me the need to address sexuality in this chapter.

CONCLUSION

The genesis of this chapter was a seminar on women entrepreneurs and the ensuing conversations with Sarah that the seminar prompted. From that seminar experience it was my impression that the literature seemed to have much to say about why women entrepreneurs may experience difficulties in their entrepreneurial activities, but less to say about women entrepreneurs excelling (for an example see Fielden and Davidson, 2010). Prompted by this perception of the literature, I contacted Sarah, someone I respect and who seemed to be an example of a woman entrepreneur who excels. It was Sarah who first suggested that being a woman entrepreneur is an advantage; further, it was also Sarah who suggested that knowledge about women entrepreneur advantages would be useful.

It is in the spirit of Sarah's insights that this chapter has been written. Past focus on problems has resulted in many powerful insights on the disadvantages and challenges that our gendered societies impose on women entrepreneurs. But, as Calas et al. (2009) highlight, this focus has emerged at the expense of alternative views of women's entrepreneurship and the insights these perspectives might offer. In this chapter I have attempted to argue for the value of building theories that suggest relationships and connections that contribute to the flourishing and optimal functioning of women entrepreneurs. I have also attempted to provide examples of such relationships and connections, as well as suggesting two general approaches to such theory-building.

What I have not done is take up the many issues that will need to be addressed in order to better understand what flourishing and optimal functioning might mean. I have left to others the task of teasing out if women entrepreneurial advantages are associated with outcomes considered important in a male-gendered field of research (Ahl, 2002), or if the advantages are associated with other (less male-gendered) outcomes. I have also left to others the work of identifying many of the 'x' factors from which we can build the body of useful knowledge that Sarah has asked for.

I am aware of my position as a man attempting to insert himself into a conversation that is concerned with correcting the historic and ongoing inequalities faced by women. As a man, and as a person socialized as part of the privileged gender, I am sensitive to the fact that I am unlikely to recognize gender as an issue. Furthermore, I am also unlikely to recognize the full extent to which gender might be an issue (Withers Osmund and Thorne, 1993). This discussion of women entrepreneur as advantageous is in no way meant to distract attention from, or make light of, the negative effects that gender biases have on women (Farrington and Chertok, 1993). Sarah recently reminded me that she continues to feel that there are advantages to being a woman entrepreneur. However, Sarah also feels the gendered effects of society:

> Although I am widely respected I know a great number of men resent my success and are confused by it. The whole 'how is it that a pretty young gal has reached that level of success and I have not?' So although my physical appearance and minority position have differentiated me in a way that makes me memorable and helps me progress in my aspirations, it has also created some challenges. I envy the men in society that achieve success and are respected for it with very little jealousy or resentment. I seem to draw as much jealousy as I do respect.

Despite the challenges Sarah and other women entrepreneurs continue to face, Calas et al., (2009: 554) illuminates the need to examine what a 'scholar is doing, for whom, and for what'. I echo Sarah's assertion that focusing on advantages, not problems, in research and theory-building will serve to add to and enhance the usefulness of the body of knowledge about women entrepreneurs. If we fail to adequately study women's advantages, then women entrepreneurship will remain 'yet another arena for the ongoing reproduction of women's secondary position in society' (Ahl, 2002: 53).

NOTES

1. The nature of the context of Sarah's case and the need to maintain anonymity limits my ability to demonstrate many details that are normally associated with entrepreneurial success. Describing in any great detail the elements of her entrepreneurial success may expose her identity. As such I present in Table 12.1 a brief picture of Sarah as a successful entrepreneur.
2. In this work Robinson (1996) studied 125 newly hired managers over a 30-month period. She found a negative relationship between initial trust and the perception of psychological contract breach. Those employees with lower initial trust of their supervisor were more likely to perceive a contract breach by their supervisor (beta $-.19$ p $<.05$).

REFERENCES

Ahl, H. (2002), 'The construction of the female entrepreneur as the other', in B. Czarniawska and H. Hopfl (eds), *Casting the Other: The Production and Maintenance of Inequalities in Work Organizations*, New York: Routledge, pp. 52–66.

Ahl, H. (2006), 'Why research on women entrepreneurs needs new directions', *Entrepreneurship Theory and Practice*, **30**, 595–621.

Ballinger, G. and K. Rockman (2010), 'Chutes versus ladders: anchoring events and a punctuated-equalibrium perspective on social exchange relationships', *Academy of Management Review*, **35** (3), 373–91.

Boden, R. and A. Nucci (2000), 'On the survival prospects of men's and women's new business ventures', *Journal of Business Venturing*, **15** (4), 347–62.

Bohman, J. (2005), 'Critical Theory', available at: http://plato.stanford.edu/entries/critical-theory (accessed 20 August 2009).

Brush, C., N. Carter, E. Gatewood, P. Greene and M. Hart (2006), 'Introduction: the Diana Project International', in C. Brush, N. Carter, E. Gatewood and P. Greene (eds), *Growth-oriented Women Entrepreneurs and their Businesses: A Global Research Perspective*, Cheltenham, UK and Northampton, MA, USA: Edward Elgar Publishing, pp. 3–22.

Brush, C., P. Green and M. Hart (2001), 'From initial idea to unique advantage: the entrepreneurial challenge of constructing a resource base', *Academy of Management Executive*, **15** (1), 64–80.

Brush, C., T. Manolova and L. Edelman (2008), 'Properties of emerging organizations: an empirical test', *Journal of Business Venturing*, **23**, 547–66.

Calas, M., L. Smircich and K. Bourne (2009), 'Extending the boundaries: reframing "entrepreneurship as social change" through feminist perspectives', *Academy of Management Review*, **34** (3), 552–69.

Carter, N., M. Williams and P. Reynolds (1997), 'Discontinuance among new firms in retail: the influence of initial resources, strategy, and gender', *Journal of Business Venturing*, **12** (2), 125–45.

Chrisman, J., A. Carsrud, J. DeCastro and L. Herron (1990), 'A comparison of assistance needs of males and female preventure entrepreneurs', *Journal of Business Venturing*, **5** (4), 235–48.

Cliff, J., N. Langton and H. Aldrich (2005), 'Walking the talk? Gendered rhetoric vs. action in small firms', *Organization Studies*, **26** (1), 63–91.

Ely, R. (1994), 'The effects of organisational demographics and social identity on relationships among professional women', *Administrative Science Quarterly*, **39** (2), 203–38.

Ely, R. (1995), 'The power in demography: women's social constructions of gender identity at work', *Academy of Management Journal*, **38** (3), 589–634.

Farrington, K. and E. Chertok (1993), 'Social conflict theories', in P. Boss, W. Doherty, R. LaRossa, W. Schumm and S. Steinmetz (eds), *Sourcebook of Family Theories and Methods: A Contextual Approach*, New York: Plenum Press, pp. 357–81.

Fasci, M. and J. Valdez (1998), 'A performance contrast of male- and female-owned accounting practices', *Journal of Small Business Management*, **36** (3), 1–7.

Fielden, S. and M. Davidson (eds), (2010), *International Research Handbook on Successful Women Entrepreneurs*, Cheltenham, UK and Northampton, MA, USA: Edward Elgar Publishing.

Foucault, M. (1990), *The History of Sexuality Volume 1: An Introduction*, New York: Vintage Books.

Gable, S. and J. Haidt (2005), 'What (and why) is positive psychology?', *Review of General Psychology*, **9** (2), 103–10.

Gaglio, C. (1997), 'Opportunity identification: Review, critique, and suggested research directions', *Advances in Entrepreneurship, Firm Emergence and Growth*, **3**, 139–202.

Godwin, L., C. Stevens and N. Brenner (2006), 'Forced to play by the rules? Theorising how mixed-sex founding teams benefit women entrepreneurs in male-dominated contexts', *Entrepreneurship Theory and Practice*, **30** (5), 623–42.

Gunther McGrath, R. (1999), 'Falling forward: real options reasoning and entrepreneurial failure', *Academy of Management Review*, **24** (1), 13–30.

Gupta, V., D. Turban, S. Wasti and A. Sikda (2009), 'The role of gender stereotypes in perception of entrepreneurs and intentions to become an entrepreneur', *Entrepreneurship Theory and Practice*, **33** (2), 397–417.

Hammersley, M. and P. Atkinson (2007), *Ethnography, Principles in Practice,* (3rd edn), London: Routledge.

Harding, S. (1987), 'Preface & Introduction', in S. Harding (ed.), *Feminism and Methodology: Social Science Issues*, Bloomington, IN: Indiana University Press, pp. vii–14.

Harding, S. (1991), *Whose Science? Whose Knowledge? Thinking from Women's Lives*, Ithaca, NY: Cornell University Press.

Hearn, J. and P. Parkin (1986), 'Women, men, and leadership: a critical review of assumptions, practices, and change in the industrialized nations', *International Studies of Management & Organization*, **16** (3/4), 33–60.

Jennings, J., P. Jennings and R. Greenwood (2009), 'Novelty in new firm performance: the case of employment systems in knowledge-intensive service firms', *Journal of Business Venturing*, **24** (4), 338–59.

Kanter, R. (1977), *Men and Women of the Corporation*, New York: Basic Books.

Kanter, R. (1980), *A Tale of O: On Being Different in an Organization*, New York: Harper and Row.

Lumpkin, G. and G. Dess (1996), 'Clarifying the entrepreneurial orientation construct and linking it to performance', *Academy of Management Review*, **21** (1), 135–72.

Malinowski, B. (2004), *Argonauts of the Western Pacific*, London: Routledge.

Marlow, S. and D. Patton (2005), 'All credit to men? Entrepreneurship, finance, and gender', *Entrepreneurship Theory and Practice*, **29** (6), 717–35.

Medawar, P. (1967), *The Art of the Soluble*, London: Methuen.

Quinn, R. (1977), 'Coping with cupid: the formation, impact, and managment of romantic relationships in organizations', *Administrative Science Quarterly*, **22** (1), 20–45.

Robinson, S. (1996), 'Trust and breach of the psychological contract', *Administrative Science Quarterly*, **41**, 574–99.

Sutton, R. and B. Staw (1995), 'What theory is not', *Administrative Science Quarterly*, **40** (2), 371–84.

Van de Ven, A. (1993), 'The development of an infrastructure for entrepreneurs', *Journal of Business Venturing*, **8**, 139–202.

Watson, J. and S. Robinson (2003), 'Adjusting for risk in comparing the performances of male- and female-controlled SME's', *Journal of Business Venturing*, **18**, 773–88.

Westhead, P. and M. White (1998), 'Novice, portfolio and serial founders: Are they different?', *Journal of Business Venturing*, **13** (3), 173–204.

Withers Osmund, M. and B. Thorne (1993), 'Feminist theories: the social construction of gender in families and society', in P. Boss, W. Doherty, R. LaRossa and W.S. Schumm (eds), *Sourcebook of Family Theories and Methods: A Contextual Approach*, New York: Plenum Press, pp. 591–623.

Yoder, J. (1991), 'Rethinking tokenism: looking beyond numbers', *Gender and Society*, **5** (2), 178–92.

Conclusion: reflecting on the diversity of women's entrepreneurship research

Karen D. Hughes and Jennifer E. Jennings

Our goal in this book has been to illuminate the breadth and variety of women's entrepreneurship research around the world. Exploring *diverse settings*, *diverse questions* and *diverse approaches*, the chapters in this volume help to build a more comprehensive picture of female enterprise, offering new insights that enrich the collective 'tapestry' (de Bruin et al., 2007) or 'quilt' (Campbell, 2005) that is being assembled by scholars across the globe. In this concluding chapter, we reflect upon the patterns and common threads evident not only within the diverse work included in this volume but also within that envisioned for the future.

COMMON THREADS WITHIN THIS COLLECTION

Without doubt one of the strongest cross-cutting themes to emerge from this volume concerns the important and ongoing task of developing a 'contextualized' body of knowledge – one that attends to the wide array of settings in which female entrepreneurs operate (Ahl, 2006; Brush et al., 2009, 2010). As the chapters in Part I demonstrate, national contexts play a particularly critical role in influencing women's experiences and approaches to entrepreneurship – shaping their entrepreneurial identities and practices, their access to finance and networks, and their entrée into emerging sectors of the knowledge economy. Notably, a number of other chapters in this volume speak to this theme as well. For instance, both Klyver et al. (Chapter 9) and Fairclough (Chapter 5) highlight how national policy regimes may encourage, or discourage, women as nascent and active entrepreneurs. Industry settings, especially those that are non-traditional for women, also emerge as an important contextual feature, as the work of Fuentes et al. (Chapter 3), McAdam and Marlow (Chapter 10) and James (Chapter 12) all show.

A second theme that emerges concerns the importance of understanding the 'family embeddedness' of women-led business (Aldrich and Cliff, 2003;

Brush et al., 2009; Jennings and McDougald, 2007). Indeed, there are very few chapters in this collection that do not at some point note the impact of family responsibilities and expectations on women's business aspirations. In some cases the focus is explicit. Both the studies by Sharifian et al. (Chapter 6) and McAdam and Marlow (Chapter 10), for example, offer intriguing insights into copreneurship, addressing important but less explored questions about the gender dynamics within such businesses and their consequences for business performance, as well as for work and family satisfaction. Women's family roles also factor into discussions on Turkish migrant women's entrepreneurship in the UK and Netherlands (Humbert and Essers's Chapter 1) and the experience of women business owners in Bangladesh (Zohir and Greene's Chapter 2).

Some intriguing connections exist between family embeddedness and a final theme that emerges in this collection, which concerns the motivations and orientations of women entrepreneurs. For instance, in examining the performance of female-led firms, Coleman and Robb (Chapter 4) note the potential importance of women's motivations and the desire for controlled growth in understanding the financial performance gap. Taking a related but somewhat different tack, Hechavarria et al. (Chapter 7) show that women are more likely to emphasize social and environmental value creation as part of their entrepreneurial goals, rather than purely traditional economic outcomes. Work by Riebe (Chapter 8) and Díaz García (Chapter 11) also contribute towards an enriched understanding of the orientations and dispositions of female entrepreneurs, painting a more complex picture than research has suggested to date.

DIRECTIONS FOR FUTURE RESEARCH

Going forward, more 'threads' are definitely needed to complete the tapestry of global women's entrepreneurship research. In terms of *diverse settings*, for instance, the field would benefit from more studies set in South-East Asia and Latin America, where rates of women's entrepreneurship are often much higher than those within Europe and North America – and sometimes even higher than the rates for men (Allen et al., 2007; Minniti et al., 2005). Likewise, China and India certainly merit attention given their high rates of economic growth, vast populations, and growing significance to the global economy. We also need more studies set in the Middle East and Africa. Although such investigations might not reveal that rates of women's entrepreneurship are particularly high within such regions, they are likely to reveal that the institutional regimes within these countries exert influences that challenge the field's prevailing conception of the 'typical' challenges (and opportunities) facing female entrepreneurs. In addition to calling for more research set in these specific macro contexts, we echo Brush et al. (2009) in encouraging greater attention to the different meso contexts in which women engage in entrepreneurial activity. Given the 'common thread' of family embeddedness cutting across so many of the chapters within this volume, we especially encourage more systematic investigation of how women's relationships with business venturing evolve across the life course.

There are also so many more *diverse questions* worthy of further exploration. While concurring with the compelling arguments that have been made to explore questions that have gone 'unasked' within mainstream entrepreneurship research (Ahl 2006; Calás et al., 2009), we also agree with de Bruin et al. (2007) that it is important to continue taking up questions that are currently central within the dominant discourse. In doing so, we do not wish to signal that we believe such questions are more important. Rather, we believe that examining core questions from the standpoint of female entrepreneurs may help to highlight where limitations, shortcomings or exceptions exist with respect to widely accepted perspectives. Consider, for example, such currently in vogue topics as opportunity recognition, effectuation and entrepreneurial passion. Would it not be interesting and important to know whether the insights derived from mainstream work in these areas apply to all (or some) groups of female entrepreneurs – and if not (or if so), why that is the case? More specifically, we envision and encourage future research that links these mainstream process-oriented topics with the 'common thread' of women's motivations and orientations cutting across the micro-oriented chapters in this volume. In other words, as Bird and Brush (2002) previously noted, the field could still benefit from additional research on how these motivations and orientations influence the processes by which women launch and build new ventures.

As more and more scholars around the globe join in contributing to the rich quilt of knowledge that is being pieced together about women entrepreneurs, we have no doubt that increasingly *diverse approaches* will be brought to the project. Like others (for example, Ahl, 2006; Brush et al., 2009; de Bruin et al., 2007), we encourage gatekeepers in the field to be open to these less orthodox approaches. At the same time, however, we also encourage future researchers to be both creative and rigorous in their efforts to build upon existing knowledge and generate new insights. Typically research that is 'done differently' faces even more exacting standards in order to enter into scholarly debate in the field. Studies that are well designed and executed – regardless of the specific theoretical or methodological approach adopted – are therefore much more likely to make it past the field's gatekeepers. Successfully carrying out such work may require that we further extend our collaborative networks, reaching out to experts in other fields – such as those in institutional theory, family studies or psychology if one is picking up on the common threads of contextual determinism, family embeddedness or gendered orientations, respectively. But would not fostering an ever-expanding circle of collaboration, expertise and creative exchange be an especially powerful way to further showcase and extend the diversity of women's entrepreneurship research?

REFERENCES

Ahl, H. (2006), 'Why research on women entrepreneurs needs new directions', *Entrepreneurship Theory and Practice*, **30** (5), 595–621.

Aldrich, H.E. and J.E. Cliff (2003), 'The pervasive effects of family on entrepreneurship: toward a family embeddedness perspective', *Journal of Business Venturing*, **18** (5), 573–96.

Allen, I.E., A. Elam, N. Langowitz and M. Dean (2007), '2007 report on women and entrepreneurship', *Global Entrepreneurship Monitor*, Babson Park, MA: Babson College and The Center for Women's Leadership at Babson College.

Bird, B. and C. Brush (2002), 'A gendered perspective on organizational creation', *Entrepreneurship Theory and Practice*, **26** (3), 41–65.

Brush, C.G., A. de Bruin, and F. Welter (2009), 'A gender-aware framework for women's entrepreneurship', *International Journal of Gender and Entrepreneurship*, **1** (1), 8–24.

Brush, C.G., A. de Bruin, E.J. Gatewood and C. Henry (2010), 'Introduction: women entrepreneurs and growth', in C.G. Brush, A. de Bruin, E.J. Gatewood and C. Henry (eds), *Women Entrepreneurs and the Global Environment for Growth*, Cheltenham, UK and Northampton, MA USA: Edward Elgar Publishing, pp. 1–18.

Calás, M.B., L. Smircich and K.A. Bourne (2009), 'Extending the boundaries: reframing "entrepreneurship as social change" through feminist perspectives', *Academy of Management Review*, **34** (3), 552–69.

Campbell, K. (2005), 'Quilting a feminist map to guide the study of women entrepreneurs' in D. Hjorth and C. Steyaert (eds), *Narrative and Discursive Approaches in Entrepreneurship*. Cheltenham, UK and Northampton, MA, USA: Edward Elgar Publishing, pp. 194–209.

De Bruin, A., C.G. Brush and F. Welter (2007), 'Advancing a framework for coherent research on women's entrepreneurship', *Entrepreneurship Theory and Practice*, **31** (3), 323–39.

Jennings, J.E. and M.S. McDougald (2007), 'Work–family interface experiences and coping strategies: implications for entrepreneurship research and practice', *Academy of Management Review*, **32** (3): 747–60.

Minniti, M., I.E. Allen and N. Langowitz (2005), '2005 report on women and entrepreneurship', *Global Entrepreneurship Monitor*, Babson Park, MA and London: Babson College and London Business School.

Index

academic entrepreneurs 56–71
  entrepreneurial inhibitors 56–7
    institutional theory and 58–60
    maternity/work–family balance
      58–9, 62, 63, 65
  recommendations for change 71
  spin-off companies' characteristics
    64
  study contexts
    case selection 61–2
    data collection 62–3
    institutional approach 57–60,
      70–71
    macro-environment 58–9
      findings 63–5, 69–70
    meso-environment 59, 62
      findings 65–6, 70
    research design 60–61
accomplished entrepreneurs 152–65
  imposter phenomenon behaviour
    152–3
  relationships and 159, 164
  study findings (questionnaires)
    dealing with conflict 160–61
    dealing with gender discrimination
      156–7
    early motivations 154–5
    mistakes, processing 157–8
    responding to social expectations
      159
    success attributions 155–6
    success factors 161–2
  study implications discussed 162–5
  study methods and sample 153
  see also entrepreneurial advantage;
    expectancy theory
advantage, *see* entrepreneurial
  advantage
age-related factors 39, 171, 180–82,
  208, 216, 218
agricultural enterprises 38–9

Ahl, H. 3, 9, 15, 226, 231
Alcalá Cortijo, P. 58, 59
Amit, R. 137
Analysis System of Iberian Balances
  (SABI) 210
Anna, A.L. 210, 211, 219
associations, membership of 164

Baines, S. 118
Ballinger, G. 233
Bandura, A. 152, 208
Bangladesh, *see* SME owners in
  Bangladesh
Bangladesh Business Award 50
Bangladesh Small and Cottage
  Industries Corporation (BSCIC)
  37
Bangladesh Women Chamber of
  Commerce and Industries
  (BWCCI) 38, 39–40, 45
Barbosa, S.D. 210–11
Barnett, F. 118, 129
Barnett, S. 118, 129
Baron, R.S. 207, 208
Board of Investment (BOI),
  Bangladesh 37
Bojica, Ana M. 56
Borden, R.J. 139
Bowen, D.D. 173
Boyd, N.G. 205
Bruni, A. 2, 58, 135, 206
Brush, Candida G. 24, 77, 162, 184,
  206, 227, 233

Calás, M. 3, 228, 236, 237
Canada 77, 140
Carter, N. 206
Center for Women's Business Research
  164
Chen, C.C. 210, 211
Chowdhury, N. 41

Cliff, J.E. 140, 206, 209
Cohen, B. 137
Coleman, Susan 75
competencies 195–6, 207, 231
conflict 160–61
Connell, R.W. 139
Cooper, Sarah Y. 56
copreneurial partnerships, *see* copreneurship
copreneurship 114–31
   definitions of 116
   earlier studies on 114–16
   family embeddedness perspective 116–17, 129–30
   outcomes, across business and family spheres 115, 120–21
      spillover effects of 121–2
   outcomes, contrasted with non-copreneurials 117–19
      business performance 118
      business satisfaction 118–19
      family performance 119
   outcomes, research results 124–8
      conclusions drawn 131
      contributions and limitations of 129–31
      research methods (questionnaires) 122–4
   sustainable family business model applied to 116–17, 120, 130
   see also roles and identities
country-specific factors 241
   economic systems 97
   employment choice research and 171–2, 175
      surveys applied to 177–8
   Esping-Andersen typology 99–102
   importance of 95–6, 108–9
      future research suggestions 242–3
   see also government support
Crowley, M. 138
cultural factors, *see* country specific factors; ethnicity; religion; socialization

Davidson, D.J. 139
Dawson, A. 59, 60
de Bruni, A. 2, 58, 135, 206
De Nobel, A. 210, 211

Denmark 176
Díaz García, Cristina 204
Drnovšek, M. 220
Duffy, J.A. 162

Eagly, A.H. 138
Economic Activities National Classification (CNAE) 209
economic negotiation, *see* financing
economic systems 96, 97, 101–2
economic value creation, *see* gender role theory
ecopreneurship, *see* gender role theory
education 164, 205, 208, 216, 217, 220
El-Ganainy, A. 59
employment choice and institutional equality
   institutional factors 171–2, 174–6, 182–5
      surveys applied to 177–8
   mainstream emphasis on the individual 173–4
   study aims and hypotheses 172–3
   study findings 177–8
      age-related factors 180–82
      descriptive statistics 178, 180
      GDP statistics 178, 180
      regression model 180–81
      self-employment gender ratios 180, 182
      variables used 179
   study methodology 177–8
   see also gender equality issues; institutional theory; nascent entrepreneurs
entrepreneurial advantage 226–37
   alternative research framework 229–32
      the optimal view 230
      tokenism, uniqueness and gender 230–32
   earlier research framework 227–9
      critical theory 227–8
      feminist theory 228
      foreshadowed problems 227
   moderated models: positive outcomes 232–5
      career paths 234
      contextual factors 234–5

parenthood, behavioural effect
        233–4
    sexuality considered 235–6
    see also accomplished entrepreneurs
entrepreneurial research
    central premises 227–9
    concept of gender 190
    contextual and perspective factors
        2–3
    future directions for 242–4
    multiple methodologies 3
    showing variability 1–2
entrepreneurial self-efficacy (ESE)
        204–21
    earlier studies 204–6, 211
    research framework hypotheses
        education and age variables 208
        gender and sector variables 206–8
        growth intentions 208–9
        multidimensional construct 205–6
    research methodology (survey)
        209–12
    research results
        decisional, relational and financial
            self-efficacy 214–18
        discussed 218–21
        sample characteristics 212–14
Esping-Andersen typology 99–101
Essers, Caroline 15, 23, 25, 27, 28
ethnicity 25–6, 27–9, 30, 109
European Labour Force Survey 16
Evald, Majbritt Rostgaard 171, 176
expectancy theory 79; *see also*
    accomplished entrepreneurs

Fairclough, Nicholas C. 95
family factors, *see* copreneurship;
    roles and identities; work–family
    balance; work–family conflict
family-embeddedness approach
    115–17, 129–30, 241–2
female advantages, *see* entrepreneurial
    advantage
Fielden, S.L. 204
financing
    experience of migrant entrepreneurs
        21, 23
    self-efficacy and 206–7
    SMEs, *see* SME owners in
        Bangladesh

supply- and demand-side issues 76–7
    see also motivation and financing
Fitzgerald, M. 118, 129, 195
Fletcher, C. 208
Foley, S. 121
Foucault, M. 236
France 104
Francis, J.L. 139
Frese, M. 205
Freudenberg, W.R. 139
Fuentes-Fuentes, M. Mar 56

Gartner, W.B. 172
Gatewood, E.J. 220
gender-based performance differences
    (US study) 75–89
    descriptive statistics, by gender
        initial capital structure 83
        motivations and goals 87
        performance outcomes 81–2
        revenues 81
    earlier studies on
        financing 76–7
        performance 77–8
        size, growth and survival 77
    number of women-owned firms 75
    performance outcomes
        descriptive statistics 81–3
        differences between men- and
            women-owned firms 85–7
    research hypotheses
        financing differences 79–80
            analysis results 83–5, 88
        growth expectations 80, 89
        motivational theory and
            performance 78–9, 88
        resource-based theory 78
    results from multivariate analysis
        83–7
        financing ratios of startup capital
            83–5
        firm outcome regressions 85–6
    study data 81
    study hypotheses
        foundational theories 78
        on financing through outside debt
            79–80
        on motivation and satisfaction 80
        on performance in early years 79,
            80

GDP statistics 37–8, 178, 180
gender as social construct 190, 199
gender equality issues
    equity within copreneurial businesses
        120–21
        spillover effects 121–2, 129–30
    ethnicity and 24, 28–9
    negative discrimination reports
        156–7
    welfare provision 109
    see also employment choice and
        institutional gender equality;
        socialization
gender role theory
    hypotheses drawn from
        female/environmental value
            construct 139
        female/social value construct 138
        male/economic value construct
            137–8
        subjects' activity 139–40
    study, theoretical framework 135–6
    study results 142–4
        findings discussed 144–7
    study testing methods 140–42
    see also roles and identities;
        socialization
Germany, as corporatist regime 100,
    101, 107
Gherardi, S. 196
Global Entrepreneurship Monitor
    (GEM) data 1, 36, 97, 135, 140
Global Entrepreneurship Monitor
    survey 177
Godwin, L. 220
government support
    Netherlands/UK and Turkish
        businesswomen 26–7
    policies, Bangladesh 41–4
        equality and egalitarianism 52
        improvement to loan facilities
            51–2
    see also country-specific factors;
        social welfare and support
Greene, Patricia G. 36
growth
    gender differences and 77, 87
    gender identity and 197
    self-efficacy and 163, 208–9, 216–17,
        219, 221

Hamilton, E. 189
Hechavarria, Diana M. 135
hegemonic masculinity, *see* gender role
    theory; roles and identities
Hisrich, R.D. 173
Hughes, Karen D. 1, 241
human capital 60, 213–14, 221
Humbert, Anne Laure 15

identity, *see* roles and identities
informal businesses 37–8
Inglehart, R. 138
Ingram, Amy 135
institutional theory 57–9, 96; *see*
    also employment choice and
        institutional gender equality
interpretist approach 192
Isaak, R. 139

James, Albert 226
Jennings, Jennifer E. 1, 7, 114, 130,
    241
Jennings, P. Devereaux 114
Justo, Rachida 135

Katz, J.A. 173
Kauffman Firm Survey (KFS) 79, 81–7
Kickul, J. 206, 210
Kirkwood, K. 207
Klyver, Kim 171, 176
knowledge transfer activities 70–71
knowledge-intensive industries 209–12
Kofman, E. 19
Korpi, W. 97, 98
Krueger, N. 210

Leitch, C. 192
Lévesque, M. 96, 171
Linstead, J. 191
Lucaccini, L.F. 192

macro- and meso-environments 58–9
Malinowski, B. 227
manufacturing enterprises, Bangladesh
    38
March, J. 96
Markman, G.D. 207, 208
Marlow, Susan 189
Marshack, K. 115, 116, 130
Marshall, T.H. 98

maternity 58–9, 65, 174
  and age-related factors 171, 180–82
  and parenthood 233
    childcare provision 62, 63, 107
    social welfare regimes 104–5
Mau, W.C. 220
McAdam, Maura 189
McDougald, D. 130
McGee, J.E. 204–5, 209
McGrath, R.G. 103
Medawar, P. 227
MEETS programme, University of
    Cambridge 71
Menzies, T.V. 77, 221
micro enterprises, *see* SME owners
micro-financing 24
migrant entrepreneurs (UK/
    Netherlands comparisons) 15–33
  study contexts
    key participating characteristics 22
    methodology 20–21
    opportunity and agency
        perspectives 17–18
    opportunity in migration history
        context 19–20
    opportunity in national context
        18–19
    subjects as different ('other') 15,
        23, 31
  study differentials discussed 30–32
    conclusions drawn 32–3
  study findings (interviews)
    coaching 26–7
    ethnic factors 25–6, 27–9, 30
    financing 21–4, 30
    networking 24–6, 29
Milkie, M.A. 106
Minniti, M. 96, 171
Morley, L. 59
motivation and entrepreneurship
    59–60, 66, 68–9, 154–5, 205–6
motivation and financing 75–6
  earlier theories on
    firm survival 77
    performance 77–8
    risk aversion 76–7
  study data and results
    expectation and satisfaction 88–9
    financing ratios of startup capital
        83–5, 88

initial capital structure, by gender
    81–3, 87–8
    performance, by gender 81–3, 88
  study hypotheses 78–80
    expectation and satisfaction 80
    gender and financing 79–80
    gender and performance 79
    gender and start-up capital 80
    theoretical basis of 78
  see also financing; performance
motivational theory 78–9
multivariate analysis of variance
    (MANOVA) 142, 145
Muscat, E.J. 192
Muske, G. 118, 129, 195

nascent entrepreneurs
  early motivation 154–5
  ethnic community support 25
  see also employment choice and
      institutional gender equality
National Action Plan (NAP) 42
necessity entrepreneurship 107–8
Netherlands, *see* migrant entrepreneurs
    (UK/Netherlands comparisons)
networking
  gender issues within academic
      entrepreneurship 59
  migrant entrepreneurs 24–6, 29
  restricted opportunity and
      Bangladeshi associations 46–7,
      50
New Zealand, copreneurial
    partnerships 193
Nielsen, Suna Løwe 171, 176
non-profit sector 138
Noordenbos, G. 59
Norris, P. 138

occupational segregation, *see* roles and
    identities
OLS regression 124–6
Olsen, J. 96
Olson, P.D. 116, 121, 129, 130, 188
opportunity entrepreneurship 107–8
opportunity structure approach 17,
    18–20, 31
Organisation for Economic
    Co-operation and Development
    (OECD) 108

Panayiotopoulos, P.I. 16
parenthood, *see* maternity
Peltola, P. 106
performance
    copreneurships 118
        equity outcomes and 120–21
        family embeddedness perspective
            115
        research findings 124–5, 127
        gender-based research, *see* gender-
            based performance differences
    and growth
        gender differences and 77–8,
            87
        gender identity and 197
        self-efficacy and 163, 208–9,
            216–17, 219, 221
        revenues for women-owned firms
            (US) 75
    see also motivation and financing
Pierson, P. 98
Poggio, B. 196
political science 176
Porter, L.W. 118, 120
Porter, M.E. 97
Powell, G. 121
Pullen, S. 191

Rabobank 23
Raihan, A. 41
Rauch, A. 205
reflexive approach, *see* entrepreneurial
    advantage
relationships/relational connections
    159, 164
    dealing with conflict 160–61
    effect of unexpected exchange
        outcomes 233
religion 20, 27–8
resource acquisition 233
resource-based theory 78
revenues for women-owned firms (US)
    75
Rhodes, E. 59
Riebe, Mary 152
Robb, Alicia 75, 77
Robinson, S. 230
Rockman, K. 233
roles and identities 183–200
    study contexts

        dimensions of copreneurial
            partnership 194
        methodology 192–3
    study findings
        ambition/growth and gender
            identity 197
        competences and gender identity
            195–6
        competences and gendered norms
            196
        decision-making 197
        femininity as subordinate 197–9
        market choices carrying gendered
            connotations 194–5
    theoretical framework
        gender as social construct 190,
            199
        subordination by gender
            ascription 191
        woman as leader 192
    see also copreneurship; gender role
        theory; socialization
Rosa, P. 59, 60
Ruef, M. 114, 130

Sappleton, N. 210
Sargent, P. 194
satisfaction, research into copreneurial
    businesses 118–19, 121–3, 125–6
Scandinavia 176
Schenkel, S. 152, 157
Scotland, *see* academic entrepreneurs
Scott, W.R. 96, 175
segregation, *see* roles and identities
self-efficacy, *see* entrepreneurial
    self-efficacy (ESE)
self-employment 118
serial entrepreneurs 229
sex role theory 233
sexuality 235–6
Shane, S. 95
Sharifian, Manely 114
Shaw, E. 206
SME owners in Bangladesh 36–53
    national/governmental plans
        41–4
        at banking level 51
        development policy 43–4
        industrial policy 43
        poverty reduction strategy 42

obtaining finance
  business characteristics and
    challenges 46–7
  complex loan processes 48–9
  costs and risk 47–8
  cultural expectations 45–6
  enhancing capabilities 52–3
  guarantors and repayments 49–50
  institutional conditions 41
  institutional recognition and
    training 50–52
  work–family balance 45
property law 42
recommendations for change 50–53
survey findings
  characteristics of enterprises 38–9,
    43–4
  demographics (age/education)
    39–40
  employee and GDP figures 37–8
  financing 40–41
  numbers 37
  sector distribution by gender 38–9
  training 40
SME owners in Bangladesh 36–53
social capital, *see* networking
social entrepreneurship, *see* gender role
  theory
social welfare and support 95–109
  earlier research 95–6
  effects on entrepreneurship 176
    and those with children 104–5,
      106–7
    and those with exogenous support
      105–6
    firm creation 102–4
    firm survival 104
  necessity entrepreneurship and
    107–8
  social change and 109
  study typology 96
    country-specific factors/economics
      97–9, 108–9
    Esping-Andersen's
      de-commodification 99–101
  varieties of capitalism 97
    country comparisons 101–2
  see also government support
socialization
  gender as social construct 190, 199

gendered roles 233
  beliefs and expectations 152–3
  individual factors 152–3
  individual responses to 159–60
  individual employment choice and
    173–4
  institutional theory and 58–9
  see also gender equality issues;
    gender role theory; roles and
    identities; work–family balance
Spain
  academic entrepreneurs, *see*
    academic entrepreneurs
  firm samples, self-efficacy study
    209–18
Stafford, K. 115, 116–17, 129
Stephan, P.E. 59
survival, firm size, growth and revenue
  77–8, 81, 104
sustainable family business (SFB)
  model 116–17, 120, 130
Sweden, as social-democratic regime
  100, 101–2, 107

taxation 98
Terjesen, Siri 135
tokenism 230–31
training, *see* education
Trevelyan, R. 208–9
Turkish women entrepreneurs, *see*
  migrant entrepreneurs (UK/
  Netherlands comparisons)

United Kingdom of Great Britain,
  see migrant entrepreneurs (UK/
  Netherlands comparisons)
United States of America
  accomplished entrepreneurs, *see*
    accomplished entrepreneurs
  gender equality, *see* gender-based
    performance differences
  revenues for women-owned firms
    75
  social welfare, comparisons 103–4
    Esping-Andersen typology 100,
      101

value creation, economic, social and
  environmental, *see* gender role
  theory

Vanawelst, I. 57
Venkataraman, S. 95
Vozikis, G.S. 205

Watson, J. 77
Weiner, B. 152
Women's Entrepreneurship Forum,
    Bangladesh 50
work–family balance 24, 45
    entrepreneurial partnerships, *see*
        copreneurship; roles and
        identities

maternity 58–9, 174
and parenthood 233
    childcare provision 62, 63, 107
    social welfare regimes 104–5
    see also socialization
work–family conflict 106–7
World Economic Forum 172
World Economic Forum's Global
    Gender Gap index 177

Zelezny, E. 139
Zohir, Salma C. 36, 41